An Adventure in Service-Learning

To Margaret, Sinéad, Cormac and Eoin

An Adventure in Service-Learning

Developing Knowledge, Values and Responsibility

ANTO T. KERINS

Routledge
Taylor & Francis Group

LONDON AND NEW YORK

First published in paperback 2024

First published 2010 by Gower Publishing

Published 2016 by Routledge
4 Park Square, Milton Park, Abingdon, Oxon OX14 4RN

and by Routledge
605 Third Avenue, New York, NY 10158

Routledge is an imprint of the Taylor & Francis Group, an informa business

Publisher's Note
The publisher has gone to great lengths to ensure the quality of this reprint but points out that some imperfections in the original copies may be apparent.

British Library Cataloguing in Publication Data
Kerins, Anto T.
 An adventure in service-learning : developing knowledge,
 values and responsibility.
 1. Service learning.
 I. Title
 378.1'03-dc22

Library of Congress Cataloging-in-Publication Data
Kerins, Anto T.
 An adventure in service-learning : developing knowledge, values and responsibility / by Anto T. Kerins.
  p. cm.
 Includes bibliographical references and index.
 ISBN 978-0-566-08894-0 (hardback) 1. Service learning. I. Title.
 LC220.5.K47 2010
 361.3'7--dc22

                                                                              2009036419

 ISBN 13: 978-0-566-08894-0 (hbk)
 ISBN 13: 978-1-03-283822-9 (pbk)
 ISBN 13: 978-1-315-56672-6 (ebk)

 DOI: 10.4324/9781315566726

Contents

List of Figures

List of Tables

Preface

This book is about an adventure in education. It is about how learning can be made more interesting, effective and relevant. It is about a teaching method called service-learning. And it all started for me in the corridor.

A friend of mine and I were walking down a corridor one day in the Dublin Institute of Technology when we started talking about how empty the college was when classes were over.[1]

> 'Have you noticed how students seem to vanish after class these days?'

> 'They come to college, go to class, sometimes they use the library, and if they are hungry they go to the cafeteria. After that they're gone.'

> 'There isn't as much life in the place as there used to be. Things seemed to have thinned down a lot.'

> 'Many of them have part-time work which may explain some of the change.'

> 'However, there still appears to be less life in the place than when I was a student. There seemed to be plenty going on then apart from just class and study. Some even did meals on wheels for the old folk.'

> 'It would be nice to put some life back into the place.'

> 'You know we should try and do something to liven things up.'

---

1   This discussion took place in the School of Hospitality Management and Tourism, Faculty of Tourism and Food, Dublin Institute of Technology (DIT), Ireland.

A lot of things were happening in the college at the time. What with course reviews, new course and subject development, and plenty of institute-wide developments the place was a hive of activity. But student life and activity seemed somewhat quieter than it used to be.

The conversation struck a chord and led, after much work, to the introduction of a new subject. This was provided as a pilot and a small number of third- and fourth-year students took it the following September.

The Pilot

This new subject required students to set up and manage a volunteering project to help the college or local community. Although the original conversation above was about putting life into the place, this subject required students to use their knowledge and skills to manage a project that helped others in some way. It was first run between September and December 2001 and resulted in a number of different projects, some of which are mentioned below.

One project helped a local primary school by putting on a children's Christmas drama. Three of the projects worked with different secondary schools. One of these organised study support for weak students, another ran a special careers evening for pupils and one ran a fundraising project for those who had to deal with the aftermath of the Bosnian war. Two students ran a 36-hour camping and activity event which included a mountain walk and a range of outdoor activities to help improve class morale. Finally, one student acted as chronicler and gathered stories from the different projects so she could record things. Each student then submitted an individual report which was assessed.

None of us had heard of the term service-learning. It was not until someone suggested we look at the US experience that we realised we were not alone in our endeavours.[2]

We then began to look at the service-learning literature and over time we made contact with some of the US specialists in the field. For example, we contacted Barbara Jacoby who wrote widely on the topic. In addition,

---

2   It was not unusual for people to be involved in service learning and not to be aware of it. Research indicates that a 'remarkable range of universities and colleges' internationally offer what might be considered the equivalent of service learning. See Annette (2002: 87).

Stephen Fisher, a specialist in service-learning, visited us and talked about his experience of service-learning. We also contacted Jeffrey Howard who edited the important *Michigan Journal of Community Service Learning*.

Developments

During this time our school was undergoing a review of its programmes.[3] As part of this process the pilot subject was evaluated and in 2002 it was substantially reworked and replaced by three optional modules which could be taken one after the other over a period of time. These were project management, leadership and consultancy management.[4]

Two things were now happening. First, the new modules were being run and developed and their operation and effectiveness was amended and improved over time. In addition, efforts were being made to find resources to investigate them so they could be improved and the details disseminated to others as good practice models. This proved a more challenging task.

In May 2002, after much work and preparation, a research funding proposal was submitted to the Royal Irish Academy. This was unsuccessful.

That October, however, a national report on volunteering submitted to the Irish government contained a suggestion that the modules be investigated so as to consider how they could be used in higher education.[5] Following this, the government set up a pilot project on service-learning.[6] This ran from September 2005 to September 2008 and led to US service-learning specialists Edward Zlotkowski and Andrew Furco visiting us.

Running alongside this was a five-year research project on service-learning. This investigated the modules and looked at their effectiveness and potential as best practice models for higher education. The investigation led to this book.

---

3   This refers to the School of Hospitality Management and Tourism, DIT as mentioned above.
4   My thanks to Katherine Kenny DIT's Web Administrator.
5   See National Committee on Volunteering (2002: 72).
6   See www.dit.ie/news/archive2005/fundingforditcommunitylearningprogramme and the related links.

Future

Clarity is everything. When we see things clearly we can understand better where we are and where we can go next. Much of the fear and hesitation that weaken our endeavours relate to a lack of clarity. This book discusses in clear and simple terms one of the more important educational developments in recent times.

A society that is concerned about how it does things pays careful attention to its education system and how it can be improved. Everyone who has gone to school or college knows what it does. However, not many know what it can really do. How it can change people; how it can improve people's knowledge, skills and values; how it can contribute better to their development and ultimately to their well-being.

This book talks about these things. It is the result of a long journey through education; one that required perseverance and determination. It is, therefore, no weekend read with short crisp comments that simply confirm or challenge what you may already know.

The book summarises the work and ideas of many different people and charts a passage through the detail. Although it covers a lot of topics, it focuses on the educational needs of students.

Whenever you sit back and wonder what else we can do to improve our education system you should know that I have asked myself this question many times. This book is my answer.

I hope you enjoy it.

Anto Kerins
Dublin Institute of Technology

Acknowledgements

An adventure is a singular experience. Even when we travel with others, our experiences are significantly our own. When a journey is one of understanding we are even more alone. Although we can learn things from other people and can discuss our findings with them, no one else can do our learning – we do it ourselves or not at all.

However, every journey needs provisions and resources, advisors, friends and supporters. The work has been supported by the Dublin Institute of Technology and in particular the School of Hospitality Management and Tourism, Staff Training and Development and the Directorate of Research and Enterprise. It has also been supported by the National Committee on Volunteering and the Department of Community Rural and Gaeltacht Affairs.

Sheila Flanagan and Michael Mulvey have provided significant support and encouragement over the years. So too have the following: Noel O'Connor, Joe Ruddy and Marlene Proctor; Phil Kenna and colleagues in Staff Training and Development; Sandra Fisher and Steve Jerrams in the Research and Enterprise Directorate; Frank McMahon, Brian Norton and others who set up the structures for encouraging research, writing and project work; Elizabeth Heffernan, Elaine O'Connor and Jean Cahill and their staff; Gerry Murphy, Farhad Shakeri, Michael Donaghy, Finbarr O'Leary, Martina McTigue, Patricia Mulligan, Gerard Dunne, Jennifer Lawlor and Therese Cadden, Jen Harvey, Anne Murphy and colleagues in the Learning and Teaching Centre and Tommy Cooke in Community Links. Katherine Kenny and Donal O'Malley in Public Affairs.

Every adventure needs property owners who let you wander through their lands. Here I would like to thank all my school colleagues for the infrastructure of courses they have developed and for the exciting ferment of teaching innovations of which I am but a small part – in particular Neil Andrews, Peter

Griffin, Alex Gibson, Louise Bellew, Lucy Horan, Colin O'Connor, Adrian Davis, Dominic Dillane, Daire MagCuill and the programme teams who originally included the service-learning modules in their programmes.

When you travel intellectually you need people to act as sounding boards for your ideas and findings. Here I am grateful to my friends in the School of Education in Trinity College Dublin: David Limond read every major draft of this work in its various stages over a six-year period – his advice, insight, and good humour were very helpful; Mona O'Moore read the original drafts and strongly encouraged me to start the study; Damian Murchan and Dwight Giles (from the University of Massachusetts Boston) read an earlier draft of the study; Michael Grenfell read one of the final drafts and Michael Shevlin facilitated me in retaining my happy and fruitful connection with Trinity so I could finish this book. Sean Byrne and Kevin Griffin, Dublin Institute of Technology, PJ Sexton, Mater Dei Institute of Education, Dublin City University and Sinéad Riordan, Royal Irish Academy made helpful comments at the final drafting stage as did others including Martin O'Neill, Jacqueline Potter, Helen O'Sullivan, Mary Bailey, Mary O'Rawe and Cathy Ball.

Noel Ahern, the government minister who set up the Community Learning Programme Project, became a passionate and important supporter of the possibilities of service-learning as soon as he heard about it; Kevin O'Kelly, David Brennan and their staff in the Department of Community, Rural and Gaeltacht Affairs, and Miriam Broderick and Farrah Kelly.

In the early years I was lucky to teach service-learning with Karen O'Sullivan and I benefited from her kindness and insight. I was also fortunate to have a number of service-learning specialists visit us to talk about their work. Our first visitor, Stephen Fischer, came from Emory and Henry College in Virginia; Edward Zlotkowski, from Bentley University in Massachusetts, came as a Fulbright Scholar; finally, Andrew Furco, now in the University of Minnesota, came to talk to us about his work in the University of California at Berkeley.

The students who took service-learning over the years and in particular those who were interviewed for the four studies mentioned here. Also Brian Gillespie, Irene Kealy and colleagues in DIT library; Robin Adams and colleagues in TCD library; the government-funded electronic research library (Irish Research eLibrary) which provided access to online research publications, in particular journals.

My publisher, and in particular my commissioning editor, Jonathan Norman, who heard about the idea over the phone one day and did not let go until the book arrived safely in the world and also his very efficient staff including Fiona Martin and Kevin Selmes, David Givens of Liffey Press and Alex Miller.

Everyone needs to be in good shape to survive the rigours of book writing. My family, Margaret, Sinéad, Cormac and Eoin, contributed greatly to the happy space around my work; Marcella for her constant care, encouragement and wise counsel; Tim, now gone, for sharing his wonder of the world and the belief that education is essential; Theresa who advised me on parts of the final draft of the book; Louie, John and also Frank in Crossakiel; Paul Nevin for organising my visit to see the Estonian banking and property sector at work.

Finally, to Mellifont Abbey: Laurence for his good humour and for egging me on to do the study in the first place; Thomas for introducing me to his love of philosophy and Patrick who showed me what a good and simple life can be without uttering a single word on the topic.

Thank you all.

List of Abbreviations

AAHE   American Association for Higher Education

CERI   Centre for Educational Research and Innovation, OECD

CERT   Council for Education and Restaurant Training (now part of Fáilte Ireland)

CLP   Community Learning Programme, DIT

CV   Coefficient of Variation

DIT   Dublin Institute of Technology

ERIC   Education Resources Information Center

EU   European Union

HEA   Higher Education Authority

HMSO   Her Majesty's Stationery Office

IBEC   Irish Business Employers Confederation

NGO   Non-Governmental Organisations

NSLC   National Service-Learning Clearinghouse

NSLE   National Service-Learning Exchange

NUI   National University of Ireland

OECD   Organisation for Economic Co-operation and Development

OJT   On-the-Job Training

RIA   Royal Irish Academy

SIP   Service Integration Project

SME   Small and Medium Sized Enterprise

SPICE   The Scottish Parliament: The Information Centre

S-L   Service-Learning

TASC   A Think Tank for Action on Social Change

TCD   Trinity College Dublin

UN   United Nations

UNESCO   United Nations Educational, Scientific and Cultural
            Organization

WCHE   United Nations World Conference on Higher Education

Introduction

Did you ever sit in class when you were a student and wonder how it could be different? How the teaching, note-taking and endless study requirements could somehow be changed? How learning could be made more interesting and engaging?

Did you ever consider how you could use your college learning usefully? How you could help others? So rather than just sit and swot for some test or other, you could help people with your knowledge and skills.

Many students find the standard classroom and study method challenging. Although some of them eventually get used to it, and a few may tell you they like it, the vast majority find it hard going.

However, things can be different. There is a teaching method called service-learning that can increase the level of interest, engagement and enjoyment in learning. Although hard work and effort are still needed, service-learning strengthens the quality of our learning because we become personally involved in the process and interested in the results.

Service-Learning

Service-learning is like any other teaching method, it facilitates subject learning. However, it differs in that it requires students to use their subject learning to help others. In this respect, students are given the opportunity to use their subject knowledge or skills to carry out an activity, project or task that benefits others.

Service-learning contains two parts – service and learning. The service part refers to the activity of helping others by, for example, working in an old people's home, fundraising for a charity, helping children with their homework or running a drugs or alcohol awareness campaign. Here students use their subject knowledge or skills to help them perform the service.

The learning that occurs in service-learning includes the normal subject or knowledge learning that occurs in any other teaching method. It also includes the development of skills and values that arise from the service activity.

The acquisition of knowledge, skills and values is enhanced by having the student reflect on the service activity and the subject theory. This reflection can occur by students, for example, writing a report, essay or analytical diary that helps to improve and connect the different types of learning.

In applying subject content to community needs, students can connect their classroom learning to real life. Service-learning is therefore like a bridge that helps to connect the academic to the outside world.

USE

This teaching method can be used in any subject. One source provides syllabi examples in a large number of different disciplines ranging from archaeology to management, from engineering to law and from politics to urban planning. There are also several studies showing how to use it in a wide variety of different subjects ranging from accounting to women's studies, from biology to philosophy, and from history to nursing.[1]

The method can be used to improve the quality of subject learning in a discipline and can thereby strengthen the learning of both theory and concepts. It can also improve the quality and range of skill learning. In addition, it can help to develop civic and social justice values and encourage social responsibility. The ability of service-learning to encourage subject, skill and values learning all in one package is rather unusual.

Service-learning empowers students in a way that is not possible in an ordinary class. This is because students are responsible for the service element of the activity as they go about helping others with their subject knowledge and skills. It responds to a need in students to be out in the world using their

---

1   See examples of syllabi at www.compact.org/syllabi/syllabi-index.php and the *Service-Learning in the Disciplines* 21-volume set at http://styluspub.com/Books/BookDetail.aspx?productID=117882.

education to help others. The altruistic dimension of the method provides them with a rich source of personal learning and development. Finally, the method can breathe new life and energy into the routine and sometimes tedious nature of university learning.

We discuss service-learning in Part 1. We introduce the topic in Chapter 1 and discuss the learning element in Chapter 2.

Learning

You can learn much in a service-learning class. As mentioned above you can acquire new knowledge, skills and values and on occasion you can develop new insight and meaning.

The range and variety of learning in service-learning is potentially broader than the standard teaching method because of its mix of classroom and experiential activity and also because of its altruistic nature. The learning locations are also varied and contain not just the formal classroom but also the situated learning locations of the charity, old people's home, local school, and so on. In these environments the students have to deal with more than just the symbols, concepts and theories of the classroom. They also have to learn on the run and under pressure working with and through other people, many of whom they may have never met before.

RESPONSIBILITY

When students are responsible for a charity fundraiser, an awareness campaign or people needing help, the buck stops with them. This is real life and if they fail they have to take the consequences. One student said that 'if you go into an exam and you bomb at it, there's no one there looking at you'. However, if you fail in the service activity there is no hiding place.

The nature of learning in service activity is different to classroom learning: ideas are grasped or apprehended rather than acquired or comprehended. The student has to deal with and manage the whole phenomenon rather than just the textbook and teacher talk element.

This is not the synthetic learning of the classroom where you are asked to imagine real phenomena through a particular subject lens. The learning here includes the reflected learning from the felt experience which is integrated with, and strengthened by, the subject learning of the classroom method.

CHALLENGING

The experiential element of service-learning can contain challenging and conflict-filled situations that need to be dealt with. Experiential learning can sometimes feel like white water rafting with unexpected difficulties and problems coming out of nowhere. Running charity fundraisers, school support projects, old people's parties and drug awareness campaigns can produce considerable and unexpected pressures. All of this is very different to doing supervised lab work, case study analysis, poetry essays or management reports.

Learning however, is never an automatic process even for the most gifted of students. Our universities can provide great teachers and attractive subjects. They can also provide interesting teaching methods such as service-learning. However, we still need willing, responsible and motivated learners to succeed. Students must be willing and capable of travelling the long hard road of college learning.

They must also be what we call 'personally centred' so they have the energy and capacity to face the challenges of learning. Although interest and excitement can encourage and support learning, they may not be there when most needed. College learning can be tough going and students need the capacity for the hard work involved.

SOLITARY ACTIVITY

Learning can be a solitary activity. Even though students sit in large classes or tackle team assignments, much of it involves many lonely hours sitting at a desk reading books, articles or notes. And while we may frequently read other people's ideas we rarely get to talk to any of them and cannot therefore benefit from the stimulation of one-to-one conversation.[2]

Much of what we really learn and deeply feel is socially experienced and happens with and through others. Service-learning is strong on the social aspect of learning and encourages students to work with and help others and this engagement improves the quality and depth of learning.

---

2   Despite this point it must be admitted that the world of books, articles, web sources and libraries is a very efficient information transmission system.

College life is generally a relatively sheltered environment. Demanding as it can sometimes be, we have to admit that studying in classrooms, libraries or work rooms is a comparatively safe and almost genteel activity. However, running a charity fundraiser, a high school support event or a drug awareness campaign can be a challenging, sometimes exhausting and at times even risky activity as we see later. Service-learning can bring some of the difficulties of the outside world into the college environment. We discuss service in Chapter 3.

Service

The service part of service-learning allows students to run activities or projects that help others. How can students help others as part of their course? Students taking a project management course, for example, can use their subject knowledge to help manage a fundraising project for children in need. Similarly, accountancy students can help with a charity's accounts, environmental science students can use their knowledge to help a community with environmental issues or chemistry students can help check such things as lead levels in house paint or river sediment. Finally, all students, from whatever discipline, can inform school pupils of their subject area. Therefore, service-learning students need to know their subject well so they can use it to carry out their service.

But what is service? How do we identify it and why would we want to encourage students to do it as part of their course?

CONTENTIOUS CONCEPT

Service is a contentious concept and has been much debated. Some feel that students should undertake service for the experiential learning benefit it brings. However, this does not tell us why students should undertake service activity rather than any other type of activity.

Some argue that students should do service because it can encourage them to be good citizens. Being a good citizen can mean obeying laws, paying taxes and supporting a charity. It can also mean participating in civic life by being an active member of a community or being a reforming citizen who works to change things.

However, using citizenship as the benchmark of service is not always useful. The good citizen in one country is not necessarily so in another; citizenship in one place can mean something different elsewhere. Important as it is as a service objective, citizenship is not an adequate measure of the possibilities of service. We should be looking at what drives real and enduring citizenship to ensure that what it stands for in any particular place is good.

Others feel service should be about social reform.[3] After all our graduates are meant to be our brightest and best and should we not prepare them for a more advanced role in society than simply helping others?

Social reformers are needed today. However, social reformers need not necessarily be good neighbours or kind colleagues. Indeed social reformers may sometimes introduce change that creates hardship. Reforms to reduce unemployment by cutting unemployment benefit may, for example, cause a lot of hardship. Service needs to be defined by something more compelling than social reform, otherwise it may face similar challenges to citizenship.

CHARITY

Service is best defined by relating it to kindness, love or care for others. It does not matter whether we do this in London or New York, Cairo or Beijing, caring for others and kindness means roughly the same thing everywhere. One relatively challenging benchmark of kindness, love or caring for others is the Christian concept of charity. This concept is used later as the benchmark for service so as to help us understand and evaluate the service component of service-learning.[4]

To help us to interpret the service in service-learning we introduce the concept of a service spectrum in Chapter 3. This allows us to gauge the service impulse by having a spectrum of intentions going from helping others because we deeply care about them to helping others because we are mainly concerned about ourselves and getting a good grade.

When students carry out service voluntarily they can be classed as volunteers. This type of volunteering can be categorised as formal volunteering since it is organised within the curriculum.

---

3   For example, Morton and Saltmarsh (1997: 138) state that Dewey's legacy includes 'an abiding faith that education leads to social reform' and articulates 'public and civic roles for ordinary people that would lead them to social and political activism'.

4   It is important to clarify that we are using this concept as a convenient standard or benchmark of service and nothing more. Other religions and beliefs have concepts and standards that are similar to charity and we discuss some of these similarities later.

Service is always a relational activity in that it is done for and often with others. It is frequently carried out in the college's external community. Here it can be carried out in the local neighbourhood or further afield. However, it can also be carried out in the college's internal community.

The community where students provide service can be defined territorially – for example, the Dominic Street community in Dublin or the Garfield Park community in Chicago. A community can also be defined relationally where people do not necessarily reside in the same area but are linked by a common factor; for example, the AIDS or homeless communities.

Sometimes, however, a community may be used by others as a device. For example, a homeless community close to a college might end up being used by students solely for grade purposes rather than for charitable reasons.

UNDER PRESSURE

Some students may first experience volunteering in service-learning. Volunteering is not a significant part of our modern culture. The service reflex is under pressure because of certain social trends. For example, the decline in social capital and the influence of the enterprise, market and entertainment culture all tend to discourage the service impulse.

The service reflex is also under pressure in the university. This is partly due to the fragmentation of the college community and the weak level of social interaction on campus. Many students today limit their college activities to study and related activities and do other things elsewhere.[5]

Despite this, community involvement is important for personal growth and development and being part of a caring community is an essential ingredient of normal development. Philosophers and others warn us that there is a great longing for community in people and we ignore this need at our peril.[6]

---

5 This is at least partly due to part-time work. A recent European study found that 'more than half the students in eleven countries work alongside their studies' and in some countries such as the Netherlands and Estonia more than two-thirds work. See Orr, Schnitzer and Frackmann (2008: 15).

6 See our discussion of community in Chapter 3.

Educational Role

Why bother with service-learning – why use it? To answer this we look at the role of higher education in Chapter 4 so as to provide service-learning with an overall context.

Our discussion here suggests that higher education has two distinct roles. First, it prepares students for the world of work. After all, if college does not help prepare them for the world of work why should they bother going? We refer to this as the dominant role of education.

Second, some regard it as having a role in preparing students for society and life after college. Many students travel non-stop through the education system from a very young age. When they graduate they often enter society beyond education for the first time. Therefore they need some preparation for this change. This is the ancillary role of education. Although preparation for the work world is dominant, preparation for participating in society is also important.

MARKET TURMOIL

The ancillary role has become more important in recent times with the turmoil in the market system. This turmoil has led to questions about our fixation on markets and individualism which, in turn, has led to concerns about the role of higher education.

Business schools, for example, have recently come under fire because of their strong commitment to market forces. Some feel they should cease selling education solely as a way to make more money and should address the 'corrosion of character' that is evident in certain management practices. They should avoid producing 'critters with lopsided brains, icy hearts, and shrunken souls' and a lack of 'moral muscle' by providing wise graduates who are 'true professionals with true character'. In short, they should have a moral mission.[7]

Adam Smith, the father of economics, says we have a moral responsibility to others and that the moral precedes the economic. Smith refers to the 'corruption of moral sentiments, which is occasioned by [the] disposition to admire the rich and great' in his *Theory of Moral Sentiments*, published shortly before he died

---

7   See Patriotta and Starkey (2008: 323–326) on the above points. Also see Fagan (2008: 34).

in 1790.[8] Smith would surely have been comfortable with the ancillary role of education as a counterbalance to the power of the dominant role.

Therefore service-learning has two roles – the dominant role of preparation for the workforce and society and the ancillary role which now becomes even more important with recent developments in the economy. Any evaluation of service-learning must therefore take account of both objectives.

Service-Learning in Action

How does service-learning operate on the ground? What does it look like in action? In Chapter 5 we look at an example of service-learning in action. This contains three integrated management modules: project management, leadership and management consultancy.[9] They are integrated in that the student must take project management before they can take leadership. In addition, the learning and teaching methods are similar.

MANAGEMENT EXAMPLES

Students study project and risk management along with networking and negotiation in the project management module. They learn the theory so as to enable them to manage a volunteering project of their choice over the period of the module. Having successfully completed this module they can opt to take the leadership one. Here students study leadership, management coaching, and business ethics and these subjects help prepare them to lead a volunteering project. Finally, the consultancy management module includes the theory of management consultancy which students use to carry out a consultancy project for a charity or similar organisation. Each module is assessed by a report.[10]

The modules usually start in the third week of September in any year. The first few weeks are used to introduce the relevant course theory. Students are also briefed on how to organise and manage a volunteering project and are given examples of possible projects. Finally, they are advised and helped with their project proposal.

---

8   See Patriotta and Starkey (2008: 325) for the above points.
9   The three modules operate within the School of Hospitality Management and Tourism, Faculty of Tourism and Food, Dublin Institute of Technology. See Chapter 5.
10 Service-learning has been running since 2001 in the School of Hospitality Management and Tourism, Faculty of Tourism and Food, Dublin Institute of Technology, Ireland.

The proposal is normally submitted and approved by the middle of October and the project runs from then to the last week in November – approximately seven weeks in total. So while they take their other five subjects they are running a project management, leadership or consultancy project over a seven-week period. This is generally a very busy time for them.

During class, students complete any outstanding theory or, where necessary, review material from an earlier service-learning module. Much of class time is used to monitor and support project progress. The project is completed by the end of November and they then have two weeks to prepare and submit their reports.

RESEARCH FINDINGS

How effective are these service-learning modules? To answer this question we discuss the results of an investigation into the modules in Part 2. These are dealt with in Chapters 6–9.

Here we find that students indicate that they acquire, for example, the following types of knowledge and skills: communication, teamwork, organisational, management, time management, event management, interpersonal skills, negotiation, project management and networking skills. On values and personal effectiveness they learn confidence, responsibility, understanding, and caring for others. Some students also develop insight or meaning.

One of the more unexpected findings is the number of students who find service-learning both challenging and enjoyable. Many also find its practical nature an interesting change from the standard teaching method. Finally, some find that their service experience has a significant impact on them.

The average service-learning grade was found to be higher than other grades. This finding may be due to the challenging but enjoyable nature of the modules leading to a strong determination to do a good job. Overall, we found that the service-learning modules met the needs of higher education by providing a mix of subject, skills and values learning that are relevant both to preparing for the world of work and society.

When we look closely at the evidence we also discover much about human nature and the real pressures of student learning and life in general. For some, the service-learning experience was nothing less than high adventure. For others, it was a significant challenge in a life already full of other responsibilities and activities. In all the study provides a valuable insight into student learning today with all its pressures, distractions and possibilities.

The Future

The final part of the book looks to the future. It indicates that service-learning can contribute to any higher education course. In particular, it discusses how our three service-learning modules can enhance business and management courses as well as a wide variety of other disciplines.

Service-learning changes the boundaries of learning. It does so by its capacity to enhance not just knowledge and skills learning but also values. It this context, it can generate new insight, meaning, and on rare occasions, metanoia.

In all of this it makes an important contribution to preparing students for the changed economic and social landscape that we inhabit. Now that the global economy has had its first significant experience of weakness in recent times it can help graduates better prepare not just for the economy but also for society whose well-being in many ways precedes and supports it.

Finally, doing service allows students to exploit a latent capacity to help others and may also fulfil a human need. Therefore, rather than just seeing service as a task or duty we may also see it as a way of becoming fully human and meeting our potential.

The Reader

This book will be read with interest by teachers, researchers, managers, and policy makers throughout education. It will particularly benefit those involved in the business and management, service-learning, community based learning and education areas. It will help policy makers, teaching and learning staff and those concerned with the citizenship role of education. Finally, it will benefit those in government, state bodies and elsewhere who are interested in education and how it can be improved.

READING THE BOOK

You will find the book varies somewhat in presentational style. Much of Part 2, for example, records in narrative form the views of students. By contrast, Parts 1 and 3 mainly use the normal presentation style in a book of this nature.

A professor of mine once admitted he had to read a new book as many as three times before he understood it. That is not to say readers will need to read this book more than once to be at ease with its content. However, this, like many other books, is a multi-layered phenomenon.

Readers may respond to the book in different ways. Some may find it interesting, challenging or just plain different. Others may find it helps clarify certain topics, concepts or theories. Then there are those who will read it to see how it might improve their teaching. Finally, some will look to see how it might clarify their perspectives on education so as to help with their administration, management or policy activities.

I wrote this book to talk about the things I learned so I could help others in their work and efforts. I did not write it to add to the theoretical body of knowledge that resides in any of the disciplines it impinges on. What I really wanted to do was get my experiences and findings out there so they could help others. Although I am interested in theoretical developments, I have relatively little interest in theory that does not help us either do things better, or improve our understanding of things that are important.

The book has been informed by my reading, teaching, and research activities. It has also been influenced, however, by my biography. My life experiences have facilitated the development of certain insights and perspectives that might otherwise have been different had I been someone else.

To take an example, the discussion later on the nature of service is a contentious one. In the end, having taken everything into account I came up with charity or love as the core of service. This for me passes all tests including biographical.[11] Those, for example, from the Islamic tradition may reach roughly the same point through the impact of Sufism or Islamic mysticism, which encourages selfless love. Others from an Eastern tradition may arrive at a similar point through Confucianism and the concept of 'ren'. Those with no

---

11   By this I am referring to my experiences and background which has had some influence on my understanding of things.

such beliefs may reach it through the principles of humanism or from a general belief in the decency of people and the importance of helping others.[12]

REVIEWING THE BOOK

Some of you may review or comment on the book. Well written reviews can help the development process that arises from any work. People may find weaknesses in this book. After all, some of the fun in reading something new is to catch up with it and at some stage move ahead.

Getting reviewed is like being graded. However, while reviews are important I sympathise with MacIntyre. He says that 'disagreement on fundamental issues is taken to be the permanent condition' of his discipline. Reviews, he says, can be based on the quality of 'analytic and argumentative skills, especially in their negative use to expose failures in the distinction-making of others or gaps in their arguments, together with an ability to summon up telling counter-examples'. This type of review is, in the end, incapable of providing a decisive resolution to any central issue under dispute.[13]

Therefore, although I might have been tempted in this study to try and 'knock down disagreeing thinkers by the sheer force' of my argument, Lewis tells me 'it cannot be done'. This, he says, is due to the fact that 'once the menu of well-worked-out theories is before us', one's position 'is a matter of opinion'.[14]

Despite agreeing with Lewis on the arguments between theories, I feel we can improve the lot of others by telling them about things we have discovered. Definitely, if we tout a particular philosophical theory, Lewis is probably correct. When we analyse from the perspective of a particular theory we may be limited in what we can do about our detractors.

However, if we are engaged in practice we need not feel as constrained by particular theories. Although they may snap at our ankles, the real test for ideas that wish to influence practice is whether they are aligned with our own views on things and whether or not they can work and how and under what conditions. We do not really need to win the theoretical argument – whatever particular one that happens to be.

---

12 See our brief discussion of these points in Chapters 3 and 10.
13 See Gillespie (2009). MacIntyre was speaking at 'MacIntyre at 80: A Conference on the Life and Work of Alasdair MacIntyre' hosted by the School of Philosophy, University College Dublin, 6–8 March 2009. See www.ucd.ie/philosophy/macintyre/programme.html.
14 See Lewis (1983: x–xi). Both Lewis and MacIntyre are philosophers.

However, some of you may ask 'what about theory'? This question reminds me of a meeting between academics and business people some time ago. The director welcomed everyone and encouraged us to work together. He then said that academics may inadvertently deal with problems by making them more complex whereas business people had no choice but to simplify them. Business people have to get to where they can act whereas academics have to try and explain things. Being on the academic side of the table I was a little put out by his comments but his advice has since kept me from getting too serious about theory.

ADVENTURE

Some who read this book may look to see if it is in harmony with their perspective on things. If so, they may continue reading, if not they may put it down. This book was not written from a particular perspective. Its preparation was originally based on a certain view of things but the discoveries made during the research and write up changed me considerably.

Writing this book was an adventure of the mind. I had to travel far and wide to learn new things about what was just beside me. This was not a journey to distant lands but an adventure in understanding.

I have been a student and teacher for years and knew it all. What hubris!

The endless reading, research and discussion, the watching, listening and learning that went into this study has in some ways turned me inside out. If I had read it ten years ago I would have been much changed. Clarity is everything.

Every book we read is eventually put aside while we move ahead renewed and reinvigorated and ready for something better. In the meantime enjoy where it takes you.

PART 1
Service-Learning

Part 1 is based on a review of the literature. It contains the following chapters.

1

What is Service-Learning?

What is service-learning? Where does it come from? Can we define it and are there service-learning principles to help us understand how it should work?

This chapter introduces service-learning by looking at some definitions and discussing it as a teaching method. We also look at some principles of good practice and consider its roots and background. We then look at the work of the American educationalist John Dewey to help develop a conceptual framework. Finally, we consider its popularity and summarise its main characteristics.

Service-Learning

Service-learning is for the most part a US development. Although it is to be found in the UK, Ireland, Europe, Australia, Asia and Africa, the extent of its use differs from place to place. Certain educational institutes have adopted it successfully in the UK. However, in Australia, Asia and Africa, it is a relatively new concept and there are only a select few using it.[1] Research indicates that a 'remarkable range of universities and colleges' internationally also offer the equivalent of service-learning but do not necessarily call it that.[2] However, despite its international spread, its most important location is still the US.

DEFINITIONS

There are a many definitions of service-learning. In fact there are so many that one particular writer grumbled about being forced marched 'through a decade's worth of service-learning definitions'.[3] Getting an agreed definition is no easy

---

1   See Shalini, S. (2008: v, Chapter 8 *passim*) on the above material.
2   See Annette (2002: 87).
3   See Cooper (2000: 6).

task. This is partly because any attempt to define service-learning requires us to link two different and relatively complex processes – service and learning.

This situation has led to both practitioners and writers on the topic failing to agree on a common meaning. The problem is compounded by the fact that even in studies where a very specific definition of service-learning is used some respondents have interpreted the definition differently.[4]

VARIATIONS

The definition of service-learning can vary depending on who uses it – teachers, students, college administrators, government agencies or others. This is because some groups see service-learning as mainly a type of learning. Others meanwhile see it as a teaching method and therefore part of the curriculum and others still as some combination of both.[5]

Those who see it as a type of learning, however informal, talk about the service or volunteering activity and the learning which arises from it. This could, for example, be volunteering to help out on a summer camp for young people. The volunteers providing the service have new experiences and learn new things but the learning is personal and unstructured and is not measured or assessed in any way as it would be if it was part of a formal course.

Those who see it as part of the curriculum view it as a teaching method. Here the service activity and course content are intentionally linked. For example, the learning from the service or volunteering activity is linked to the curriculum by requiring students to complete a report or essay on their service internship. This assessment is then marked.

Those who see it as some combination of both suggest that service-learning can have both curricular and co-curricular options. A co-curricular option might mean, for example, a summer internship programme where students help a charity and receive academic credit for their work. From a curricular point of view, however, this only works as service-learning when students complete an assignment or report on their summer internship. In other words, receiving credit for a summer internship is not enough. The credit must be for the academic learning which can be assessed through an assignment.

---

4   See Abes, Jackson and Jones (2002) and Litke (2002: 27).
5   See Crews (2002: vii).

To prevent any grumbling among readers I avoid discussing a list of competing definitions. Instead I put my cards on the table at the outset by stating that I see service-learning as a curricular activity and nothing more.

Teaching Method

Service-learning is first and foremost a teaching method and a component of the curriculum. Although it may have additional benefits beyond the specific needs of the curriculum, it does not operate outside it. From a learning perspective its purpose is to provide students with the opportunity to use experiences from helping others to strengthen their understanding of classroom material.[6] From a student development perspective however, its purpose is to provide students with the opportunity to use their classroom theory and knowledge to help others.

Since it connects classroom learning with real life experiences, it is a bridge that connects the academic with the outside world. It also provides a structure for grounding students' educational experiences in rigorous, text-based coursework while moving their learning beyond the classroom and out into the community.[7]

ALL SUBJECTS

Service-learning can enhance learning by breathing life into a subject and, therefore, can help students learn more about specific course content. Zlotkowski says there is probably no discipline – from architecture to zoology – where it cannot be used to strengthen a student's learning.[8] Even business subjects, with their general concern for the private sector, and accountancy, with its profit focus, can benefit. Indeed, some writers feel that it represents the most effective teaching tool available to business school teachers and others discuss how it can increase the student's understanding of accountancy.[9]

Although the service experience contributes to classroom learning, this does not happen automatically. The service experience must be purposefully reflected upon to ensure it contributes to learning. For this reason structured

---

6   See Cohen (1994: 101) and Chapman and Ferrari (1999: 1) on the above.
7   See Weatherford and Ownes (2000: 125) and Kenworthy-U'Ren (2000: 55) on the above points.
8   Zlotkowski is editor of the American Association of Higher Education's (AAHE) Series on Service-Learning in the Disciplines. His statement is made in Godfrey and Grasso (2000: vi).
9   See Papamarcos (2002: 31) and Gujarathi and McQuade (2002: 67) on the above.

time must be provided for student reflection so that the service experience gets connected to classroom learning. Service-learning can also empower students by making them responsible in a real world context.[10]

BEYOND THE CLASS

Service-learning takes students well beyond the class. It encourages them to apply their newly acquired academic skills and knowledge to real community needs. Here classroom learning can assist communities and this gives the pedagogy a different dimension to other forms of learning. It takes its purpose outside the students and their own needs. It also takes it beyond the needs of the educational institute and its knowledge requirements and incorporates an unusual, altruistic dimension into its configuration. No other pedagogy does this. This dimension provides students with a rich resource for personal learning and development.

Service-learning also responds to students' 'desire to be in the world, learning from experience as well as classes' and putting their education to use for the good of others.[11] This means that it taps into certain needs within the student.

In going beyond the classroom, service-learning can introduce students to different worlds outside the campus.[12] Students, however, do not travel through these different worlds as detached visitors or tourists. They go there to serve others. That is the core of their experience and differentiates this particular teaching method from other experiential methods. When they visit other worlds or communities it is to provide service.

Service-learning is not a new form of internship. Nor is it the same as simply helping others in the community. The experience of helping others is not necessarily synonymous with learning.[13]

---

10 See Abes, Jackson and Jones (2002) and Rosenberg (2000: 8) on the above.
11 See Campus Compact (2009). Campus Compact is an umbrella organisation of over 1,200 university and college presidents. It promotes public and community service that develops students' citizenship skills, helps campuses forge effective community partnerships, and provides resources and training for faculty seeking to integrate civic and community-based learning into the curriculum. See www.compact.org/about located on 12 March 2009.
12 See Crews (2002: viii).
13 See Howard (2001: 10).

EXPERIENTIAL

Service-learning is a particular example of experiential learning of which there are others such as internship, practical or lab work. Experiential learning can be described as 'emotionally engaged learning' where the learner experiences a visceral connection with the subject matter.[14] Experiential learning is not simply learning by doing. Good experiential learning combines meaningful student experience with guided reflection and analysis.

Experiential learning methods achieve a number of things.[15] First, they integrate the experience with classroom learning and help students to connect the concepts and theories of the classroom with the experience. They also use a more open-ended learning method where teachers take a less directive role and facilitate students to participate more fully in their own learning.

BALANCE

What should be the balance between the service and learning elements of service-learning? How much service, how much learning?

Sigmon helps us to summarise this issue.[16] First, he says there is '*service*-learning'. Here the service activity or volunteering work dominates and the theory or classroom element is secondary. Then we have 'service-*learning*' where the subject or theory element dominates and the service is a minor element. There are many service-learning courses that contain only a limited service dimension.[17]

Next there is 'service learning' where the absence of the hyphen indicates that the service and learning are separate and not integrated. The service activity may interest students but they are left to make the learning connections themselves.

Finally, there is 'service-learning' where the service and learning have the same approximate weight and are purposely integrated together in the curriculum. This is the preferred option of a variety of writers and practitioners.[18] We also take this approach to the meaning of service-learning.

---

14 See Campus Compact (2009) on experiential learning which it attributes to Bill Proudman.
15 See Crews (2002: viii).
16 This analysis was first developed by Sigmon. See Eyler and Giles (1999: 3–5).
17 See Jacoby (1996: 4).
18 For example, Sigmon (1996), Jacoby (1996) and Eyler and Giles (1999).

Many programmes may not fit this balanced category. In some cases the service dominates, whereas in others the academic does. In this regard, Eyler and Giles state that they are not interested in using definitions that may limit analysis. Thus they accept that any programme that attempts to integrate academic study with service can be defined as 'service-learning'.[19]

Nevertheless, we need to develop a firm understanding of service-learning. Therefore, I agree with those who state that grafting a service element (or option) onto an otherwise unchanged academic course does not constitute service-learning.[20]

KNOWLEDGE, SKILLS AND VALUES

Most, if not all, subjects and teaching methods encourage knowledge learning. Some subjects and methods facilitate skills learning by providing experiential opportunities.

However, service-learning is out on its own because it provides the opportunity to help others and thereby facilitates values learning. Helping others as part of college learning is a new experience for most people and can influence what is valuable to them.

Students can acquire knowledge and skills in service-learning. In Chapter 6 we see how it can help develop such knowledge and skills as communication, teamwork, organisation, management, time management, event management and interpersonal learning.

Students can also learn values in service-learning. In Chapter 7 we see how it can enhance or develop certain values. Here we find the experience of helping others in their service projects can encourage students to become more responsible, understanding and caring and also more confident.[21]

So, having considered the definitional issues, the balance between service and learning and the type of learning involved, let us consider some of the principles of service-learning.[22]

---

19 See Eyler and Giles (1999: 4).
20 See Howard (2001: 11).
21 Confidence is considered a value of efficacy as mentioned in Chapters 2 and 5.
22 A principle can be a source of action, code of conduct, procedural rule, or fundamental truth. See Oxford English Dictionary (2009). We focus on the first meaning by looking at principles of practice.

Principles of Practice

A good set of principles has universal application which, when internalised as habits, can help people to develop a variety of practices to deal with particular situations.[23] In this respect service-learning principles were developed to help practitioners to develop their practice and writers to clarify their thoughts. Let us consider two important sets of principles – those elaborated at the Wingspread conference and those developed by Howard.

WINGSPREAD PRINCIPLES

The Wingspread principles originated in a 1989 conference in Wingspread, Wisconsin. The conference was a response to the growing interest at the time in community service and service-learning programmes and to the belief that improvements do not happen automatically. Here a group of educators, researchers, service-learning practitioners, government officials, students, staff from national organisations and others gathered in the Johnson Foundation's Wingspread Centre.

The Wingspread principles state that an effective programme combining service and learning should:[24]

1. Engage people in responsible and challenging actions for the common good.

2. Provide structured opportunities for critical reflection on the service experience.

3. Articulate clear service and learning goals.

4. Allow those with needs to define those needs.

5. Clarify the responsibilities of all involved.

6. Match service providers and service needs.

7. Expect genuine, active, and sustained organisational commitment.

---

23 See Mintz and Hesser (1996: 27).
24 See Johnson Foundation (2009). The principles have been slightly edited.

8. Include training, supervision, monitoring, support, recognition, and evaluation to meet service and learning goals.

9. Ensure the time commitment for service and learning is flexible, appropriate, and in the best interests of all involved.

10. Be committed to programme participation by and with diverse populations.

These particular principles provide an important insight into the nature of service-learning. However, they are not limited to education but relate to programmes and policies in various settings – community organisations, corporations, government agencies, and research and policy organisations. They also refer to people of all ages and all walks of life.

Their benefit to practitioners and theorists, however, was more important in the early days when they helped to clarify the practice of the new method. Nowadays they provide an important part of the foundation rather than a continuously used reference point against which theory and practice are gauged.

HOWARD'S PRINCIPLES

Howard's principles are relevant to third level education in general and teaching staff in particular. These are quite frequently referred to in the literature. For example, Jacoby and Crews both refer to them in their works on service-learning in higher education.[25] Howard's principles are as follows:[26]

1. Academic credit is for learning, not for service.

2. Do not compromise academic rigour.

3. Set learning objectives.

4. Set criteria for the selection of service placements.

5. Provide educationally sound learning mechanisms to cultivate community learning and realise course learning objectives.

---

25 See Jacoby (1996: 33) and Crews (2002: 38).
26 See Howard (2001). The principles are slightly edited.

6. Prepare students for learning from the community.

7. Minimise the distinction between the student's community learning role and the classroom learning role.

8. Re-think the teaching staff's instructional role.

9. Be prepared for uncertainty and variation in student learning outcomes.

10. Maximise the community responsibility orientation of the course.

These principles outline some important considerations from an educational perspective. We do not elaborate on the principles here. However, we briefly discuss the first one because of its significance for higher education.

ASSESSMENT

Howard's first principle states that students get credit for learning, not for service. In traditional courses we assess students' learning from traditional course resources such as lectures, textbooks, student research, and class discussion. Although service-learning assesses the learning from such resources, it also assesses the learning from the service experience.

This has a number of implications. First, higher education students are traditionally assessed on what they learn, not on their efforts or intentions. They may do a host of other things but it is the learning and its evidence that counts. If they do wonderful and important service work, but do not exhibit learning, they get no marks.

Providing service to others is not an academic activity. In the grand scheme of things service may indeed be more important for personal development and society's well-being. However, this is not the issue here. We are dealing here with a teaching method that lies within the confines of tertiary education. This system educates and then assesses students' learning.

The teacher's ability to assess and the range of assessable phenomena became clearer with my increasing involvement in service-learning. Assessment became an issue when certain colleagues felt strongly that students who successfully completed important service projects should be marked more highly.[27]

Teaching management is not the same as teaching, for example, dance classes. The dance student should be able to dance better after the lessons. Therefore the dance teacher has to assess the student's dancing ability, not their understanding of dance theory. By contrast, the management teacher will find it very difficult to assess accurately the student's service activity. Doing service, as we will see later, is a complex process and developing a fair and reasonable objective methodology for grading it accurately can be very difficult.

On this point, Howard's ninth principle states that we should be prepared for uncertainty and variation in student learning outcomes. In traditional courses, the learning mechanisms – such as lectures or readings – are reasonably constant for different students. In service-learning, however, we can get greater variation in service experiences and this can affect student learning outcomes. Consequently, Howard warns teachers to be prepared for greater variety in learning outcomes and some loss of control over student learning stimuli.[28]

Regarding the objects of assessment, it can be argued that teachers assess most effectively and easily when dealing with such artefacts as reports, essays, articles, presentations and portfolios. Developing other indicators of service would be very difficult if not impossible. This fact becomes very evident when you have to deal with grade appeals.

Therefore the student's grade is for the objective illustration of learning and not for the quality or quantity of service provided. If the service done is inadequate and if the assessable artefact relies on a particular amount and quality of service, the assessable component will be weakened by inadequate service. In other words, although we cannot assess the service quality, the assessment process can be drawn up to help ensure that assessable artefacts have a critical mass of service activity to reflect and report on.[29]

---

27 Some colleagues, who had been impressed by the level of project work, felt students should be given some allowance for effort.
28 See Howard (2001: 18–19).
29 See the details of the service-learning modules in Chapter 5 and elsewhere. In particular see Appendix 1 which outlines how the modules are assessed. Although they are not micromanaged on the amount or quality of service activity the assessment tool clearly encourages an adequate level of service activity.

Roots of Service-Learning

Knowing the history of something helps us to understand it better. We need some understanding of the history of service-learning to prevent our analysis being flat and timeless.[30] Let us now discuss the background to service-learning and look at its early practitioners.

BACKGROUND

Service-learning is a relatively new teaching method or pedagogy. It developed in North America where the earliest definition goes back to 1966–67 when the phrase was used to describe a project in East Tennessee. This related to work done by Oak Ridge Associated Universities and it linked students and staff with a number of tributary area development organisations. Until the educational reforms of the 1980s in North America, its advocates were only a small, marginal group. However, with the boost provided to active learning pedagogies by these reforms along with the increased interest in volunteerism that was encouraged by certain public service initiatives, interest in it began to grow.[31]

Since the late 1980s/early 1990s therefore, interest in and use of this relatively innovative pedagogy has grown in North America as both teachers and educational institutions began to realise its potential for improving the quality of student learning.

EARLY PRACTITIONERS

The early practitioners of service-learning were a small, marginal group within higher education. They had an interest in experiential education and encouraging better learning by connecting student experience to reflection and the curriculum. They felt that a more complete education was only achieved by involving students with contemporary social problems and efforts to solve them. They also felt that academic excellence and community service were not competitive demands on student's time and energy but 'interdependent dimensions of good intellectual work'.[32]

---

30 See Wright Mills (1970: 167–168) on the importance of history in general.
31 See National Service-Learning Clearinghouse (2009), Berman (2006: xxii) and Stanton, Giles and Cruz (1999: 2, 5) on the above.
32 See Duley and Wagner in Stanton *et al.* (1999: 4) on the above.

Some of the early practitioners were interested in education issues, others in social justice and others still in preparing students for democratic engagement. One group came to discover service-learning from a motivation to make education serve social needs. Another was more interested in the relationship between service and social justice. Finally, a small group of practitioners entered the field through an interest in education as a way of encouraging a more engaged and civic society.

In spite of the differences among the early practitioners they had certain things in common. First, they shared a questioning stance towards life and society. Second, they were interested in encouraging the development of useful education and linking thought with action. Third, they shared a strong interest in service – either helping others in need or changing society.[33]

The third area of interest in service dovetails with the idea that education is not just for providing knowledge but is also laden with human and moral responsibilities. It must also help us acquire dispositions by which we can live life. Here education is seen as one of the most serious and accountable tasks of a society and confers not just intellectual obligations but also moral ones.[34]

While the early practitioners were working away, things were changing elsewhere. For example, there was a growing interest in active learning pedagogies. In addition, there was increased interest in, and support for, volunteerism by public service organisations. Alongside these developments the work and published output from the Wingspread conference helped stimulate and clarify the activity. What was once a marginal teaching method, now reached the 'front burner' of many higher education organisations.[35]

MODELS AND THINKERS

There were also several role models or writers whose work or activities helped the early practitioners as they grappled with this new pedagogy. Some needed to theorise their work and connect it to a broader framework to clarify their thinking. The most popular ones mentioned here were writers such as John Dewey, Paulo Friere, David Kolb, Margaret Mead, and William F. Whyte. Others mentioned political leaders and activists such as Gandhi, Ivan Illich, Saul Alinsky, the Kennedys and Martin Luther King.

---

33 See the above in Stanton *et al.* (1999: 19–32, 50–51).
34 See Banner and Cannon (1997: 5–6, 134 and *passim*) on the above points.
35 See Stanton *et al.* (1999: 6).

Finally, several referred to philosophical and spiritual mentors such as Dietrich Bonhoeffer. Spirituality helped by providing moral examples reflecting the strong moral dimension to some of the pioneers' work.

One of the pioneers, Stanton, said he had a gut sense of where he wanted to go at the outset, and looked for theories to help him get there. Another pioneer said that the more he read Dewey and the other philosophers who talked about the role of experiential learning, the more he became convinced that he was on the right road. [36]

SOCIAL MOVEMENT

However, in spite of these developments there was a niggling worry at the back of some people's minds. Had service-learning just become a social movement or, worse still, was it just 'fluff'? Some argued that it had come to suffer from a distinct lack of a conceptual framework.

Giles and Eyler stated that service-learning needed to become a field of study and analysis with its own conceptual framework. They argued that the introduction of the term service-learning in the 1960s was the first step towards developing conceptual clarity. However, they felt that in subsequent years, people concentrated more on developing principles of good practice and focused more on processes and programmes rather than on theory development.[37]

Some indicated that this was the safest route at the time. For example, Korowski states that progress is made through extensive work in the field, rather than through a proliferation of theoretical debate.[38] There was, therefore, a growing interest in the early 1990s in researching the area in order to analyse its progress and guide its development.

However, there was no parallel interest in developing a conceptual framework and according to Giles and Eyler the topic was absent from conferences in the field. As a result they argued for the development of an underpinning theory of service-learning and for this purpose they turned to the work of John Dewey.[39]

---

36 See Stanton *et al.* (1999: 192–194) on the above discussion.
37 See Giles and Eyler (1994: 77–78).
38 Quoted in Giles and Eyler (1994: 77).
39 See Giles and Eyler (1994: 77–78). Giles admits that when he read Dewey he gave voice to what he was thinking. See Stanton *et al.* (1999: 193).

Following their suggestion a number of others looked at how Dewey's work could be related to service-learning.[40] As a result of this interest, Deans was able to say that by 1999 Dewey had been cast, more than anyone else, as the founding father of the philosophy and theory of service-learning. He also said that Dewey, the uniquely American intellectual, had been incorporated for legitimising purposes. Because his work held sway in several disciplines, his imprimatur lent 'academic credibility to service-learning research and pedagogy'.[41]

Dewey's Influence

Although Dewey had a number of areas of interest, his main focus was philosophy and psychology where he largely concentrated on educational reform. In tune with his times, Dewey felt that the best approach to social and ethical problems was scientific investigation. He disagreed with the concept of a fixed moral law derived from a consideration of the nature of man.[42]

Dewey suggested that a well developed philosophy of education would provide a plan for conducting education. Like any plan it has to be framed, he said, with reference to what is to be done and how it is best done.[43] As service-learning is a way of educating others, it too can benefit from such a plan.

EDUCATION AND EXPERIENCE

All genuine education, according to Dewey, comes about through experience. Education is the 'emancipation and enlargement of experience' and 'is a development within, by, and for experience'.[44]

Since service-learning incorporates experience into the curriculum, this gives us an interest in Dewey's ideas on experience being educational. Although the material we discuss below relates mostly to children rather than tertiary level students, his analysis is useful.

---

40 See for example, Saltmarsh (1996), Hatcher (1997) and Morton and Saltmarsh (1997). In addition, the standard service-learning works of Jacoby (1996) and Eyler and Giles (1999) indicated his contribution to the pedagogy.

41 See Deans (1999: 15).

42 See Encyclopaedia Britannica Online (2009) on *John Dewey*.

43 See Dewey (1963: 28).

44 See Dewey (1933: 202) and (1963: 28) on the above.

The child's world, he argues, contains individuals and their personal interests, rather than facts and laws. Teachers, by contrast, are so familiar with the idea of logically ordered reality that they do not easily recognise the amount of separation and reformulation that the 'facts of direct experience have to undergo before they can appear as a ... branch of learning'.[45]

Here he refers to the difference between the child's world and the curriculum and compares the unity of the child's life with the specialisation and divisions of the curriculum. He also contrasts the abstract principles of the curriculum with the practical and emotional aspects of the child's life.

This contrast between the child's world and the curriculum has led, according to Dewey, to two fundamentally different educational approaches.[46] The first emphasises the importance of the curriculum. This argues that where the child's life is narrow, the curriculum shows a world that is full and complex. Where the child's life can be egotistical, impulsive and self-centred, the curriculum can expose a world of order, law and truth. Finally, where the child's experience can be confused, uncertain and capricious, the curriculum can show a world that is well-arranged, measured and defined. This approach proposes that we minimise and ignore the child's individual peculiarities, whims and experiences and focus on the curriculum and what it has to offer.

The alternative approach, according to Dewey, is a pupil-centred one where the child's world is the starting point, the centre and the end. Here all study is subservient to the growth and development of the child. Personality and character formation is more important than learning the formal curriculum. Subjects here cannot be imposed on the pupil's mind from outside. Study and lessons must not become a burden and a task. Learning should be active.

Both approaches contrast the child's experience with the formal curriculum. This is incorrect according to Dewey. There is no fundamental difference between them. The child and curriculum are not two different things but are two 'limits which define a single process'.[47] The process of moving from the child's present experience to that represented by the formal curriculum is one of continuous reconstruction. In order to be educative, experience must lead into

---

45 See Dewey (1990: 184).
46 Outlined in Dewey (1990: 185–186).
47 See Dewey (1990: 189).

the world of the curriculum through a process of continuously reconstructing experience.[48]

CURRICULUM AS EXPERIENCE

Then Dewey makes an interesting point. The curriculum and its subjects are themselves forms of experience. However, they present this experience in an organised and systematised way. This is because they embody the cumulative outcome of the efforts and successes of people. This type of experience is not a mere accumulation or 'miscellaneous heap of separate bits of experience' but an organised construct.[49]

Therefore the facts and detail of the child's own experience and those embedded in the curriculum are the initial and final terms of one reality. To oppose them is to 'oppose the infancy and maturity of the same growing life'.[50]

In order to elaborate his approach, Dewey classifies the child's experience as 'psychological' and the curriculum element of experience as 'logical'. The psychological identifies the actual growth of experience. Dewey says it is historical, uncertain and tortuous, along with being efficient and successful. By contrast, he says the logical or curriculum form of experience assumes that the development has reached a stage of positive fulfilment. It neglects the process and all its details and focuses on the outcome. It summarises and arranges things and therefore 'separates the achieved results from the actual steps' taken.[51]

Subjects

Each subject or discipline can be viewed from two angles. For scientists, it represents a body of knowledge to be used for research purposes. For teachers, the subject matter of a discipline is a stage in the development of experience. The teacher is interested in how the curriculum can be used to extend the development of the pupil's experience. Teachers, he says, are 'concerned with the subject matter as a related factor in a total and growing experience'.[52]

---

48 See Dewey (1963: 87).
49 See Dewey (1990: 190).
50 See Dewey (1990: 190).
51 See Dewey (1990: 197).
52 See Dewey (1990: 201).

Concepts

According to Dewey an educative class or subject should lead to conceptualisation. Without this, nothing is gained that can be carried over to the better understanding of new experiences. The moment a concept is understood it becomes a working tool for understanding other things. Concepts, he argues, begin with experiences, become more definite with use, and eventually acquire generality.[53]

Dewey contributes to our understanding of the relationship between experience and the curriculum. His fundamental statement that education occurs through experience is developed by clarifying that the formal curriculum is a type of distilled or reconstructed experience. The two worlds of subjects or concepts and experience do not exist as separate realms but are integrated under the one roof by Dewey's analysis. Dewey also refutes the 'dualism' which makes a dichotomy between the world of education and the outside world. His approach connects the school with the outside world.[54]

Reflection

He also provides us with a philosophical base for integrating classroom theory with experience. Here he says that experience should incorporate reflection in order to set us free from the limiting influence of sense, appetite, and tradition. He offers a number of examples of integrating education and experience. Although these are much less developed than what occurs in service-learning today, they are still of interest.[55]

His analysis so far provides a rationale for linking experience and the curriculum. This offers service-learning some encouragement for its experiential component. However, it shares this encouragement with other forms of experiential learning. To relate his ideas more directly to service-learning, however, let us consider his suggestion that the experience should be a service for others.

---

53 See Dewey (1933: 153–157).
54 See Saltmarsh (1996: 15–16).
55 See Dewey (1933: 202) and (1990: 18–23, 194–195) on the above.

EDUCATION AS SERVICE

A school where students simply absorb facts can lead to selfishness. This can be the case to such an extent that mutual assistance between pupils, instead of being the most natural thing in the world, can become a 'clandestine effort' to relieve students of their proper duty. Education by contrast should be a social process where students and teacher form a community group.[56]

These ideas point to the community aspect of the relationship within the school and between teacher and student. To identify more effectively his rationale for service to others, however, we have to consider other aspects of Dewey's social and political philosophy.

Dewey says that education has not led to a more humane and moral society. He argues that the machine age has destroyed the local community and replaced it with the 'great society' without counterbalancing this with what he calls the 'great community'.[57]

His philosophy of instrumentalism sees ideas as instruments for helping to improve society and proposes a connection between knowing and action. He believes that education must result in social action so people's skills can be used to improve society.[58] He says that schools that provide self-direction skills and become embryonic communities through saturating students with the spirit of service will provide the best guarantee of a larger society that is 'worthy, lovely, and harmonious'.[59]

Democracy

Education, he argues, needs a frame of reference without which it would be aimless and lack a unified purpose. This purpose is to contribute to democracy.[60] Dewey saw democracy not just as a mode of governance but as a way of being in the world. He saw it primarily as a 'mode of associated living'.[61] In this he considered its essence to be community life. In a parallel point, Dewey argued that the purpose of education is social and suggested that democratic education

---

56 See Dewey (1990: 6, 15–16) and (1963: 58).
57 See Giles and Eyler (1994: 81–82).
58 See Hatcher (1997: 24).
59 See Dewey (1990: 29).
60 See Saltmarsh (1996: 15).
61 Dewey quoted in Deans (1999: 17).

provides an opportunity to 'shift the centre of ethical gravity from an absorption which is selfish to a service which is social'.[62]

The role of education is to develop people to their fullest potential. But Dewey then goes on to clarify the meaning of an individual's development. This he explains as forming a society of individuals who, through their work, 'contribute to the ... enrichment of the lives of others'.[63] This he argues is the only environment in which an individual can fully develop.

Dewey's perspective on individual development and democracy provides a strong philosophical base to the service component of service-learning. Dewey does not suggest that classroom work should be supplemented by and integrated with service activity. That is the invention of service-learning. What he does say, however, is that education must be based on experience, supported by reflection and linked with social improvement. Education for democracy would lead to social change that would signify a society where every person is occupied in making 'the lives of others better worth living'.[64] Democracy for Dewey 'must begin at home and home is the neighbourly community'.[65] Under the democracy and education framework we can then see that providing service is also a means of contributing to a student's individual development.

CONCEPTUAL FRAMEWORK

Elements of Dewey's philosophy offer useful material for the development of a conceptual framework for service-learning. His idea that all genuine education comes through experience provides support for the experiential element of service-learning.

His idea that education should contribute to how we live and operate in the community provides support for the service element of service-learning. Here he remarks that teachers are interested in how the curriculum can be used to develop the student and feels that education should encourage people to move from self-absorption to unselfish service. Education must therefore help to develop people so they can contribute to the enrichment of the lives of others.

---

62 Dewey quoted in Deans (1999: 18).
63 Dewey quoted in Deans (1999: 18).
64 Dewey quoted in Morton and Saltmarsh (1997: 144).
65 Dewey quoted in Morton and Saltmarsh (1997: 144).

Popularity of Service-Learning

How popular is service-learning? It is difficult to say because of the lack of international data on the method. Most of the data comes from the US where its use is significantly greater than elsewhere.

In North America 12 per cent of teaching staff in Campus Compact's colleges and universities teach a service-learning course. In addition, the number of Compact's campuses that offer service-learning courses increased from 87 per cent to 91 per cent between 2001 and 2006.

At secondary level the figures are also relatively high. The US Department of Education found that 46 per cent of high schools and 32 per cent of public schools had service-learning on their curriculum.[66]

Why has service-learning grown? After all teaching can be a 'fiendishly difficult' task without having to encourage student service and the full development of the individual.[67]

However, the growth of service-learning has been encouraged by certain developments. First, its dissemination was encouraged by the writings and examples of the early practitioners, the related research, conferences, and principles, and the linkage of the pedagogy to various models, thinkers and philosophies. Second, it was encouraged by the growing support for active learning styles and the various forms of experiential education. Third, the increased interest in volunteerism played an important role in its spread. Fourth, it has been encouraged by a 'scholarship of engagement' and the growth of interest in the engaged university.[68] Finally, its spread has been encouraged by staff who found the pedagogy satisfying.[69]

Characteristics of Service-Learning

The main characteristics of service-learning can now be summarised. Service-learning:

---

66 See Campus Compact (2007) and National Centre for Education Statistics (1999: 6) on the above data.

67 See Banner and Cannon (1997: 136).

68 See Butin (2006: 473).

69 As a teacher I found the pedagogy rewarding.

- Is a teaching method that provides students with the opportunity to use experiences helping others to strengthen their understanding of a subject.

- Contains a balance of classroom work and service activities.

- Integrates the service activity with the classroom learning by structured reflection. This integration improves the understanding of theory and breathes life into academic work.

- Encourages the development of knowledge, skills, and values.

- Assesses the academic learning, not the service quality, by using academic artefacts such as reports, essays, and so on.

- Gives students the opportunity to apply academic knowledge and skills to real-life problems and responds to their need to be in the world, learning from both experience and class and putting their education to the good of others.

Conclusion

This chapter discusses the nature of service-learning. It considers its principles and historical roots and, through Dewey, the elements of an underlying framework or philosophy. It also refers to its level of use. Finally, it summarises its characteristics.

We now discuss the two elements of service-learning – service and learning. In Chapter 2 we consider learning and in Chapter 3 service.

2

The Learning Involved

Football, dancing, and rock climbing are visible activities. Learning is not. We cannot see it. We can only infer its activity and impact by seeing people do things they could not previously and by hearing what people tell us about their learning. People who can fly a helicopter or write an economics assignment for the first time demonstrate new learning.

This chapter discusses the meaning and nature of learning so we can better understand the learning in service-learning. First, we look at the different types of learning. Here we consider the basic, advanced and development types of learning and develop a learning framework. Then we consider topics such as classroom learning and learning locations.

Because of the experiential activity in service-learning, we discuss experiential learning. Then the issues of motivation, responsibility, and centring in learning are considered. Finally, we discuss the social process involved and consider the education sector as a relatively safe and supportive space for learning.

The early efforts of psychologists to understand learning concentrated on relatively simple units of learning and were often based on the study of animals.[1] Here laboratory techniques from biology and physics were used and the learner was treated as an empty organism who responded to external influences in a more or less automatic or even random way.

To some extent, the early behaviourists were reacting against the sophisticated explanations of learning based on religious and philosophical interpretations. In trying to disprove these approaches, attempts were made

---

1   The following benefits from Kidd (1973: 160).

to develop an explanation of behaviour based on the notion of the 'human animal'.[2] Today our understanding of learning is more sophisticated.

Basic Types of Learning

There is a wide variety of basic learning types. These include learning to discriminate and identify sets and oddities, learning to carry out a series of responses in a definite order (chaining), and learning through conditioning.[3]

The learning in service-learning can be considered under these basic types. We could for example, consider the conditioning or chaining that may occur among those who take service-learning more than once. However, our study is not concerned with basic types of learning.

Advanced Types of Learning

We are concerned with the more advanced types of learning. These include knowledge, behaviour and skill learning which we now consider.

KNOWLEDGE

Learning can lead to the acquisition of knowledge. In this respect, it can lead to changes in the stock of knowledge. It can also lead to changes in the nature of knowledge and the level of mastery by which we can act on knowledge.[4]

Knowledge is the accumulated stock of facts, truths, information or principles. It is the awareness and understanding of this stock gained from experience, introspection or reasoning. It is also the understanding of the interconnections between these facts, truths or pieces of information which in isolation are of less value. In educational terms knowledge is the confident understanding of a subject along with the ability to use this subject for a particular purpose.

Knowledge is also the set of beliefs we hold about causal phenomena. These beliefs are never certain. For example, football coaches will have plenty

---

2   See Kidd (1973: 160).
3   See Encyclopaedia Britannica Online (2009a).
4   See Banner and Cannon (1997: 7) and Sanchez and Heene (2000: 26) on the above.

of ideas about how to score goals and win games. However, their knowledge is never certain and good coaches will continually try to upgrade and improve their ideas.[5]

Understanding

Knowledge is similar to understanding.[6] Aristotle says that to know something is to understand it and to understand it is to grasp its causes or principles. In the technical arena, having knowledge means 'understanding the vast amount of specific information and techniques existing' in a particular field. In the inner world, self-knowledge has been seen as the ability to understand one's strengths and weaknesses.[7]

BEHAVIOUR

Learning can lead, as we saw above, to behavioural changes. Behaviour refers to how people act or control themselves under certain circumstances. It also refers to a person's pattern of actions. It can also be a new capacity that allows the person to perceive or change behaviour. Learning a new behaviour excludes changes caused by illness, fatigue, alcohol or drugs.

Many speak of behaviour and skill in the same breath.[8] However, if we use behaviour as referring to how people act generally, we can consider skills as a more specific classification of behaviour.

SKILL

Learning can lead to the development of skills. The word skill has, from time to time, been used by policy-makers and academics in a vague or amorphous way.[9] We, however, must be clear about its meaning.

---

5   See Sanchez and Heene (2000: 24–25) on the above.
6   Heller says 'knowledge means understanding' (1982: 103).
7   See Witt (1994: 15), Löwgren and Stolterman (2004: 44), and Piderit and Morey (2008: 67) on the above. We incorporate understanding with knowledge and classify insight and meaning below as forms of development learning. I found that understanding, knowledge, and skills are more frequently identified in the literature on learning than meaning and insight which are given separate consideration here.
8   See for example, Wolpawa (1998: 588), Emery and Flood (2003: 9) and Carr and Horner (2007: 5–6) on the above.
9   See Korczynski (2005).

A skill is not a reflex action. Recoiling from a hot surface is a reflex movement, not a skill. Being able to cook a meal, by contrast, is a skill.

We can distinguish between acquiring a skill and, say, memorising a poem. Some seem to find it easier to retain skill learning than verbal learning and are more likely, to remember say, driving skills than poetry.

A skill is a complex set of movements with a multitude of integrated components and requires at least a minimal amount of practice. Being skilled in a particular task involves the ability to perform the task in a reasonably consistent manner on different occasions.[10]

A skill is a competence or proficiency in carrying out a task and indicates an ability to do something well.[11] Skills can be viewed as hierarchical, starting with the simpler skills and ending with the most complex ones. This is based on a progression, from the mainly psychomotor skills to the predominantly cognitive skills.[12] Skills are also determined by the degree of complexity and discretion involved.

For example, skills can be classified into an ability to carry out either usual or unusual operations. Usual operations skills are routine, monotonous, and repetitive and are normally measured by the speed and exactness of the work. Unusual operations skills are the ability to deal with changes in work routine and problem solving. These, for example, require a worker to know the operation and structure of machinery and the flow and logic of the production process and demand greater ability than usual operations.[13] Skills can also be categorised as either 'generic' skills useable across a range of occupations or vocational skills relevant to a particular occupation.[14]

Personal skills

Increasingly, employers look for generic personal skills when considering new employees. These include communications, team working, decision

---

10 See 'Psychomotor Learning: The Range of Skills' and 'Phenomenon of Psychomotor Learning: Retention' in Encyclopaedia Britannica (1999).
11 See Felstead, Gallie and Green (2002: 20).
12 For example, motor skills, perceptual skills, simple cognitive skills (for example, procedural skills) and complex cognitive skills (for example, decision-making skills). See Seamster, Redding and Kaempf (1997: 3).
13 See Koike (1989: 6) on the above.
14 Vocational skills are relevant to a particular occupation whereas generic skills as we see below can be used more broadly. See Felstead *et al.* (2002: 9, 14).

making, negotiation and problem-solving skills along with the capacity to take responsibility and initiative. Although these skills are not new, they are now receiving greater attention as organisations face new competitive pressures.[15]

The increased emphasis on personal skills does not mean that occupational and technical skills are not important. These skills, although essential, are now seen as not enough and, in certain sectors and circumstances, are viewed as 'easily trained in'. Finally, personal skills become more important when job instability and mobility become greater since they 'help people to adjust to new demands and cope with change'.[16]

There is also evidence that employers look for strong communication skills, honesty, and integrity when evaluating college graduates as potential employees. They also value candidates who show experience in teamwork, interpersonal skills, initiative, and motivation.[17]

Although knowledge, behaviour and skills learning are important we concentrate later on just the knowledge and skills impact of service-learning. We now look at development learning.

Development Learning

Some make a distinction between learning and development. Here development is seen as a deep, fundamental, and irreversible change, whereas learning is seen as a superficial, simplistic and reversible change. Others disagree with this dichotomy and talk about 'developing learning' that contains development attributes. Although this type of learning can occur with the support of a teacher 'the learner has an active role in the process'.[18]

We distinguish learning from development although the distinction is not a fundamental dichotomy. For this reason, we see development as part of the same spectrum as learning and not something entirely different.[19] Here we talk

---

15 See Dench (1997: 190, 192) on the above.
16 See Dench (1997: 193) on the above two quotes.
17 See Hartman, Bentley, Richards and Krebs (2005: 348).
18 See Granott (1998: 17–18) on the above.
19 Others likewise see learning and development as a part of a spectrum. Kolb for example, places learning in a conceptual framework of performance, learning and development (1984: 34). We discuss his ideas under the section on experience below.

about people developing insight or meaning, learning values or undergoing a fundamental shift in perspective called metanoia. First, we consider insight.

INSIGHT

Learning can lead to insight. Insight occurs when we apprehend or realise something new. Insight provides us with new meaning or understanding that extends beyond a specific experience and can change our understanding of our self, others or the world in general.[20]

Lonergan refers to vulnerable and invulnerable insights. Vulnerable ones are open to further questions and each new insight complements the accuracy and 'covers over the deficiency of those that went before'.[21] He argues that the greater one's accumulation of insight, the broader one's base from which one can move forward. An invulnerable insight is when there are no further questions to ask.[22]

Teaching can help encourage the development of insight by providing the clues and hints that lead to it. In addition, it poses the questions that reveal the need for further insight to modify and complement the acquired store.[23]

MEANING

When we acquire new meaning we in fact learn something new. Meaning is the interpretation of experience and refers to the significance, the importance or the purpose of something. When something has meaning, it has a special significance for us. We develop meaning from experience and our experiences are examined and filtered for meaning in order to help guide our action.

Having lots of experience, however, does not necessarily lead to meaning. An experience leads to meaning when we are better able to understand and learn from that experience. Experiences must be significant if meaning is to occur.[24] For example, people may find it easier to learn a poem or a language

---

20 See McLean and Pratt (2006: 717).
21 See Lonergan (1958: 174).
22 See Morelli and Morelli (1997: 282, 520).
23 Lonergan states that 'learning is not without teaching' for 'teaching is the communication of insight'. See Lonergan (1958: 174).
24 See Heine, Proulx and Vohs (2006: 88), http://wordnet.princeton.edu/perl/webwn?s=meaning accessed on 15 April 2009 and Restine (1997: 255) on the above material.

when significance is attached to it.[25] For example, when an American boy falls in love with a French girl he may become more successful at learning French.

To develop meaning is to develop insight into something. Gaining insight is different to learning a lesson. Learning a lesson refers to learning something that can help direct future behaviour in a similar situation. By contrast, gaining insight refers to gaining meaning from an experience that can be applied to a broader area of life.

When we gain meaning, there is often a significant change in our understanding of our self or our relationship with others. Taking meaning from something is developmentally more advanced than lesson learning.

Take the boy caught throwing an egg at his mother. If he learns he should never throw anything at her again, he has learned a lesson. If, however, he realises he has an anger management problem, he has gained insight and learned something meaningful because the learning extends beyond the egg throwing incident.[26]

When we develop or 'make' meaning we construct an account of experience, so we can better understand it and better organise and structure our life. Meaning-making allows us to step back from experiences and reflect on their implications for our self-understanding, behaviour, goals, and values.[27]

Meaningful experiences

The impact of any particular experience on meaning is affected by the type of experience. Those dealing with relationships, autonomy, and mortality can have significant impact on meaning. By contrast, those dealing with achievements tend to have less impact.[28]

---

25 See Strang (1951: 371) on the impact of meaning on learning poetry.
26 See McLean and Thorne (2003: 636–638) on the above example and material.
27 See Cacioppo, Hawkley, Rickett, and Masi (2005: 144) and McLean and Thorne (2003: 636) on meaning-making.
28 Mortality experiences can be powerful and meaningful. These are often about the first time one is faced with personal, or a close other's, vulnerability. This can lead to an exploration of the meaning of life and death, one's place in the world, or a re-evaluation of one's values. Significant relationship and autonomy experiences can also be powerful and meaningful. Achievements however, seem to evoke relatively less meaning because they are often prepared for over time and may in the end be hoped for and anticipated. See McLean and Pratt (2006: 716–718, 720–721).

Experiences of vulnerability in others can also be meaningful. For example, experiencing one's parents in distress can encourage self-sufficiency and personal development.[29]

Meaning can also emerge in situations of conflict. This is because conflict can brutally force us to evaluate or reflect on things. It can also force us to reconstruct our experiences so we can reduce the dissonance and cope with these types of situations.[30]

Importance

Meaning is important in people's lives. In fact Lonergan argues that meaning is no less important than reality. This is because human reality 'is not merely meant but in large measure is constituted through acts of meaning'.[31]

Meaning for the very young is initially confined to the immediate world of the nursery. Here Lonergan says that reality comes first and meaning second. However, as children develop and their command and use of language grows, things change and the larger world, mediated through meaning, moves centre stage.

He feels it is the larger world mediated by meaning that we refer to when we speak of the real world. Lonergan also says the real world is 'insecure, because meaning is insecure, since beside truth there is error'.[32] We now consider values.

VALUE FREE LEARNING

Our discussion above of learning as a change in knowledge, behaviour, skill, or insight is a value free one. None of our material tells us the value of the knowledge, behavioural, skill or insight change.

---

29 See McLean and Thorne (2003: 641, 644). Because McLean and Thorne's study focussed on emerging adults, experiences of parental vulnerability may have been particularly significant for them. Emerging adulthood focuses on the period from the late teens through the twenties, 'with a focus on ages 18–25' (Arnett, 2000: 469). Arnett sees it as the age of identity explorations, instability, self-focus, feeling in-between, and possibilities (2007: xiv).

30 The redemptive sequence, where bad turns to good, is one way that difficult experiences are reconstructed to contain meaning. Those who have more redemptive experiences in life and who find the good in the bad have 'higher well-being' (McLean and Pratt, 2006: 716, 721).

31 See Morelli and Morelli (1997: 387–388).

32 See Morelli and Morelli (1997: 388–389).

Therefore to say we want students to learn is not adequate for an educator. This is because learning as a stand-alone objective does not, for example, rule out a science student learning how to make a dangerous device for criminal purposes.

This difficulty reminds us of the statement by the Director-General of UNESCO. He argues that education that provides only knowledge does not provide enough.[33] Terrorists as well as good citizens learn. What he implies here is that learning should not be value free.

VALUES

People learn values. The value of something originally referred mainly to its economic worth, as in the work of Adam Smith. Throughout the nineteenth century its meaning expanded until Perry's *General Theory of Value* in 1926 brought clarity to the area. He discussed eight areas of value: morality, religion, art, science, economics, politics, law, and custom.[34]

The value of something can refer to its efficacy or capacity. For example, this might refer to a person's efficacy in interpersonal relations due to being confident or independent.[35]

Values can also refer to the intrinsic or relative worth, importance or goodness of something. To learn a value is to learn that something is important, good and desirable. Values define what is 'important … and worth striving for'.[36] We develop, use, and are influenced by our values.

Values are important because they provide a measure or standard that helps us formulate opinions and judgements. They help assess the quality of things and the information we gather can become knowledge by using values to interpret it. Values can therefore provide a general guideline to action. By contrast, norms are specific guides to action and only define behaviour and inform conduct in particular situations.[37]

---

33 See UNESCO (2001: 5).
34 The above has benefited from the article on 'Axiology' in Encyclopædia Britannica Online (2009b).
35 See Microsoft (1999).
36 See Haralambos and Holborn (1995: 5).
37 See Microsoft (1999) and Haralambos and Holborn (1995: 5) on the above.

Lonergan states that, although a value judgement differs in content from a factual one, it does not differ structurally since both state what is or is not the case. However, a value apprehension is 'given in feeling'.[38] He also argues that, although factual knowledge is reached by experience, understanding and verification, value knowledge is reached through discernment and love. Lonergan talks of the apprehension of values such as social, cultural, and personal.[39]

Lonergan argues that the development of knowledge and values lead to the discovery of oneself as a moral person. This discovery comes from realising that when we make a value judgement we not only choose a particular action or intention but we also make ourselves 'authentic' or 'unauthentic' beings. In this process there emerges in our consciousness 'the significance of personal value and … responsibility'.[40] Lonergan takes this argument one step further by stating that our value judgements are revealed as the door to our fulfilment or loss.

We now consider metanoia.

METANOIA

Learning can also involve metanoia. This refers to a fundamental shift in mind, character or heart. It can also mean a change in one's way of life, or a spiritual conversion or repentance.[41] In addition, it can refer to a change of direction or a rethinking of where we are headed. This 'is possible only as a result of watching ourselves on the journey, of picturing our path on the moral map'.[42]

It has also been referred to as coming to one's senses or conversion where 'the conversion experience' is regarded as the 'high-water mark' of a person's spiritual capacity.[43] For the Greeks metanoia meant 'transcendence', whereas in the early Christian tradition it refers to an awakening or direct knowing of God.[44]

38　See Morelli and Morelli (1997: 456).
39　He also talks of transcendent values. See Morelli and Morelli (1997: 477).
40　See Morelli and Morelli (1997: 457–458).
41　See Microsoft (1999).
42　See Kracher (2006: 331). The watching self and journey are metaphors for biography and self-understanding or analysis.
43　See Calvert (2006: 146, 152). Calvert also says metanoia captures several qualities such as repentance, transcendence, inclusiveness, open-endedness, movement.
44　See Senge (1993: 13).

Regardless of the different perspectives on metanoia, we can refer to metanoia here as a powerful or fundamental change in the person. This is the high-water mark of learning.

Learning Framework

There are many different types of learning. This reminds us of the comment that the world is incorrigibly plural with 'more of it than we think'.[45] So, too, learning is plural with more of it than we think.

In spite of this, we must keep the whole field in focus. Some writers develop a learning framework to do this and we do likewise.[46]

Figure 2.1 places the three types of learning in a simple framework. It conceptualises learning as either basic, advanced or development and indicates a development process moving from left to right.

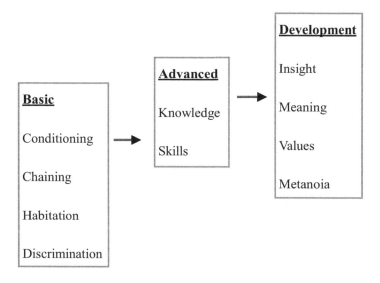

Figure 2.1   Learning framework: Types of learning

---

45 See Davis and Williams (2003: 269).
46 See Illeris (2003: 172).

It provides us with a device to consider the learning in service-learning. Our main focus is the advanced types of knowledge and skills learning.[47] We are also interested in values. Although insight or meaning may have some slight relevance, we do not anticipate any real indication of metanoia. Service-learning after all is not life. It is only a teaching method which has to compete for space on the curriculum with the more common methods.

BLOOM'S TAXONOMY

Bloom's taxonomy is a behaviourist framework for classifying higher order learning. It was originally published in 1956 and identifies three overlapping areas of learning: cognitive, affective, and psychomotor. These three learning domains represent the acquisition of knowledge, values, and skills.

The cognitive domain was discussed and detailed in the 1956 work. This framework contains six major levels – knowledge, comprehension, application, analysis, synthesis, and evaluation. In recent times it was revised to remember, understand, apply, analyse, evaluate and create.[48]

As the learner moves up the levels from remembering, to understanding, to application and so on, more is demanded. Each of the higher levels incorporates the previous level as a subset of it.

Some feel that the cognitive framework can help teachers organise course content so as to encourage students to learn more deeply and powerfully in a subject. Shannon, for example, argues that a short course can be configured to help students progress cognitively from the basic knowledge level to the comprehension one. A longer course can then be constructed to facilitate learning that helps the student to advance from the basic knowledge and comprehension level to the application, analysis, synthesis, and evaluation levels.[49]

The work on the values or affective domain was published in 1964. This domain consists of such behaviours as awareness, interest, attention, concern, and responsibility and relates to emotions, values, attitudes, and the like. Bloom and his colleagues did not develop a skill domain and excused themselves

---

47 We concentrate on skills rather than the more general behaviour area of learning.
48 See Bloom and Krathwohl (1956) and Krathwohl (2002) on the above.
49 See Shannon (2003).

for not doing so by stating that they had little experience of teaching manual skills.[50]

So, others were left to develop the psychomotor or skill domain. For example, Harrow's 1972 study proposed six psychomotor levels: reflex, fundamental movements, perceptual abilities, physical abilities, skilled movements, and non-discursive communication.[51]

CRITIQUE OF BLOOM

Bloom's taxonomy provides a useful framework to help us consider the learning outcomes in any educational programme. It has exerted a strong influence and is 'the most widely known classification of its kind'. However, it has been criticised for being too general, reliant on cognition, limited in scope and reductionist.[52]

The learning framework we developed above refers to knowledge, skills and values. However, it also mentions insight, meaning and metanoia and classifies learning into three groupings – basic, advanced and development learning. Although, as we said above, service-learning need not concern itself much beyond knowledge, skills and values, it may have some relevance to insight and meaning. We do not expect much relevance for metanoia. Our framework, although not at all as detailed as Bloom's, has the advantage that it incorporates a greater range of learning and is more useful for discussing service-learning.

Having discussed the various types of learning, we now look at learning in an educational context. Here we discuss the nature of classroom learning.

Classroom Learning

Service-learning has a classroom component. In our own case service-learning is used to teach project management, leadership and management consultancy. At the start of the semester, the students learn the relevant theory. For example, the project management students learn project management, risk management, networking and negotiation. This is delivered in class through a presentation

---

50 See Krathwohl, Bloom and Masia (1964) and Clark (1999) on the above material.
51 See Harrow (1972) and Kearsley (2009).
52 See Heinemann (2005: 287).

and discussion format and supported by relevant readings. We now discuss the strengths and weaknesses of classroom learning.

STRENGTHS

The classroom format has many advantages. For example, Shpancer says the classroom is a 'great place' to learn 'how to deal with knowledge and … people'. He refers to its 'unique value' and says it gives students 'direct, live access to trained minds as well as safe, face-to-face, and academically productive group interaction'.[53]

Learning maturity

Classroom learning can also help prepare students for learning through more developed formats. The concept of learning maturity suggests that learning occurs in steps, each stage building on the simpler material which went before.

The instructor's role in introductory classes is to build a strong level of conceptual understanding in the student. This helps students with limited material to relate to new learning. In addition, those with low learner maturity are more 'subject centred' and have a more dependent learning capacity. Therefore, these students may be somewhat less comfortable with self-directed learning. In contrast, those who gain learning maturity are better able to benefit from self-directed learning.[54]

WEAKNESSES

Nevertheless, there are significant weaknesses with the classroom format which we need to note when discussing service-learning. Some of these are mentioned below.

Content driven

The classroom can become a very content driven, one-way system. Teachers decide in advance what knowledge or skills will be transmitted and then arrange

---

53 See Shpancer (2004: 34).
54 The material above on learning maturity benefits from Nadkarni (2003: 337).

the content into logical parts. They also select the best method of transmitting the content and then present the content in some sort of sequence.[55]

To reduce some of the difficulties here, it has been suggested we improve the level of interactivity in the classroom.[56] In addition, Shpancer feels we should take our cue from the preschool playroom and organise each class as a safe place for intellectual exploration, rather than for a one-way knowledge transfer. He feels we should cultivate 'creative interaction and emergent properties' and view the process as 'open-ended ... rather than as a true/false item'. Finally, he says, we should invite students to bring their 'experience and stories into the classroom'.[57]

Others suggest the teacher become a facilitator, consultant, or change agent rather than a transmitter of knowledge. In addition, case studies, role playing, simulations, and self-evaluations, for example, could help.[58]

Concepts, symbols and instruments

In the real world a person's action is contextualised and mental activity makes sense in terms of its relevance to specific circumstances. People are continually engaged with situations and objects that make sense to them and they do not tend to fall into the trap of forgetting what their calculation or reasoning is about.

In class, however, concepts and symbols tend to become detached from real context and learning can become a matter of acquiring symbol manipulation rules. This focus on symbols that are detached from their real context can create difficulties for the learner.[59]

Class learning, by contrast, requires the learning of concepts and symbols and the ability to use and manipulate them. Since concept and symbol manipulation in class is detached from its referents in the real world it can create difficulties even for classroom learning.[60]

---

55 See for example, Knowles (1978: 108) and Mant, Wilson and Coates (2007: 1718).
56 See for example, Siau, Sheng, and Fui-Hoon Nah (2006: 398).
57 See Shpancer (2004: 34–35).
58 See Knowles (1978: 108) and Kearsley (2009a).
59 See Resnick (1987: 15). Resnick says workers in carpentry, street markets and construction often do virtually error-free calculations by applying mathematical principles flexibly. Yet in school, students regularly use calculation rules with slight errors in them that produce reliably wrong results.
60 See Resnick (1987: 15).

However, there have been efforts made to introduce contextualised learning into the traditional classroom. An example is the use of case study analysis in business courses. Even here the student's pressure point is not the best profit ratio but the best grading outcome. For this reason, class learning through its ultimate pressure point is at one remove from the outside world encouraging among students what Resnick refers to as the 'game' of symbol learning.[61]

Classroom learning also places greater emphasis on pure thought than elsewhere. Mental activity in class frequently occurs independently of tools and complex instruments. By contrast, mental activity outside class is often connected to tools and instruments and the quality of learning is thereby improved.[62] Although certain subjects incorporate tool manipulation, such as, IT, ophthalmology, medicine, dentistry, architecture and science, much classroom learning is still a relatively instrument free zone. In addition, where tool manipulation occurs, it mainly simulates the outside world and does not contain the pressures or dangers of real life.

General theory and skills

The classroom normally focuses on general and widely usable theory and skills. The main justification offered for this approach is its generality and transfer capacity.

Yet cognitive scientists suggest that students rarely transfer knowledge learned in class to real life. Students provided with classroom knowledge on problem solving, for example, often fail to apply the information when faced with real problems. Cognitive scientists refer to the difficulties of developing 'knowledge in use' in the 'de-contextualised' classroom and emphasise instead the importance of students learning in complex situations and actively constructing knowledge.[63]

---

61 See Resnick (1987: 15) where she refers to mathematics teaching and its real life referents.
62 See Resnick (1987: 13).
63 See Eyler and Giles (1999: 8). Resnick however, suggests that situation-specific competencies or contextual learning can have its own limitations. She says 'unschooled individuals' who have to deal with new situations can be at a considerable disadvantage to 'schooled people'. The latter do better although they rarely utilise the 'supposedly general algorithms taught in school'. Instead their schooling helps them to develop methods specific to new situations. See Resnick (1987: 15–16).

Individual learning

Individual learning still dominates the classroom. By contrast, much of life is social and people's ability to function effectively often depends on how they operate with others. There have of course been efforts made to increase the team element of class work, and teamwork is evident in the use of such mechanisms as group work, assessment and problem-based learning.[64]

The service part of service-learning can extend the nature and quality of learning and compensate for some of the weaknesses of the classroom format. We will develop a greater understanding of its potential contribution when we consider the issues of learning locations and experiential learning. We first consider learning locations.

Learning Locations

We discuss learning locations by considering institutional, formal and informal learning, situated learning, and the contextual learning to be had from community-in-practice.

INSTITUTIONAL LEARNING

Institutional learning has an 'in building' and embodied 'bricks and mortar' nature along with a particular philosophy and practice.[65] It occurs in colleges and universities, in work training and development, and in adult education. It has the following assumptions.

First, it is goal directed and depends on the learner's desire to achieve that goal. Second, it assumes the learner values the goal towards which the learning is directed. Third, the learning goal is assumed to be outside the learning process and is seen to be fixed.

Once the learner understands, accepts, and values its goals, the efficiency of the learning process becomes important. Learning speed now becomes an objective and the faster the learner can go the better. In addition, the greater the volume of material covered the more effective is the learning.

---

64 See Resnick (1987: 13) and Gordon (2000: 2) on the above.
65 The material below on institutional learning benefits significantly from Vaill (1996: 32, 34–37).

Vaill argues that institutional learning ill-prepares us for the 'messy learning world we inhabit'.[66] This system is primarily a control one where the learner's life can be a relatively private and lonely affair. This loneliness can be compounded by the significant internal competition it encourages.

Vaill suggests that institutional learning happens on very special terms. It is about learning predetermined material from someone who knows it all or most of it. It is also about being a member of a cohort where everyone learns 'pretty much the same thing'.[67] Finally, this type of learning is, for the most part, removed from those places where its fruits are to be used.

Institutional learning relates to the classroom element of service-learning. However, contrary to what Vaill says, some learning in service-learning classrooms can be both 'messy' and social. In addition, it may not always be about learning predetermined material with fixed learning goals.

The project management classes we talked about earlier are often used to discuss project progress, make decisions, and plan and iron out difficulties. In this context they can take a meeting, mentoring or discussion format. Having said that, however, the classroom activity can also take the ordinary presentation or tutorial format where it is goal directed.

Remaining with the location theme, we now discuss formal and informal learning.

FORMAL

Formal learning is located in a dedicated learning environment in contrast to informal learning which occurs outside one. Informal learning arises from people's interests and activities and may not be recognised as learning.[68]

Hager and Hyland provide a useful distinction between the two types.[69] They say teachers and trainers control formal learning, whereas the learner (if anyone) controls informal learning. Formal learning is prescribed by such things as curricula, standards and learning outcomes and learner is expected to be able to articulate what has been learned through exams or assessments.

---

66 On this quote and on the points below see Vaill (1996: xv, 39).
67 See Vaill (1996: 40).
68 See Cooke and Smith (2004: 2).
69 See Hager and Hyland (2003: 283–284).

Formal learning emphasises the teaching, content and structure of what is taught. By contrast informal learning emphasises the experiences of the learner.

Finally, they say that learning knowledge is generally regarded as more challenging than learning skills and that more teaching effort has been invested in knowledge learning than in skill learning. By contrast informal learning does not make a distinction between learning skills and knowledge.[70]

These concepts are rather limited for our purposes and do not add much to what we have already said on learning.[71] However, we can relate the formal learning to the classroom element of service-learning and the service part to informal learning. In addition, although the service activity, values and apprehension learning are regarded as important students are graded on an analytical report which is assessed on the quality of the knowledge analysis and evaluation.[72]

ON-THE-JOB TRAINING (OJT)

Our understanding of learning can be enhanced by considering OJT in the workplace.[73] Workplace learning can include both formal and informal OJT. Formal off-the-job training relates to seminars and workshops that sit apart from the workplace or work routine.

Informal OJT relates to learning that occurs during the actual work routine. Informal OJT might be as simple as 'sitting by Nellie' where the apprentice or novice learns from being beside the skilled worker or master. This could refer to an apprentice teacher doing an internship in a particular school and spending time as a class assistant with the regular teacher.

Alternatively it could be the more structured learning involved in planned OJT where for example, a worker is purposely rotated through a number

---

70 Hager and Hyland also discuss the shared and contextualised learning in informal learning which was discussed above.

71 In addition, there is some debate about the concepts. For example, Eshac (2007: 172–173) disagrees with those who see formal learning as in class and informal as out of class.

72 So much so that the external examiner when checking the lecturer's grading of the reports looks at these reports like any other assessment and takes no account of other factors such as quality of the service activity, values learning or apprehension.

73 For an outline or definition of OJT see Kerins (1993: 230–232) and Wang and Holton (2005: 98).

of posts for learning purposes. Here we can find induction rotation for new recruits or more long-term rotation for developing staff over time.[74]

OJT is not relevant to the classroom element of service-learning in that students are not on-the-job. Neither are they in work when they carry out their service activity. Even when their service engages them in volunteering work in a charity they are not doing an internship. According to Howard internships are not about civic learning. Rather, they develop and prepare students for a profession, and 'tend to be silent on student civic development'.[75]

However, an understanding of OJT helps to clarify the structuring of learning in the work place and provides a useful contrast with both the classroom and service parts of service-learning.

SITUATED LEARNING

The situated learning approach rejects classroom learning because it isolates knowledge from practice. This approach restores learning to the contexts where it has meaning. It sees class teaching as a transmission of abstract knowledge in a surrounding that excludes the complexities of practice and communities of practitioners.

In situated learning the learners construct knowledge out of a wide range of materials that include the ambient physical and social conditions. Learning is constructed from materials at hand and takes account of the structuring resources of the local conditions. What is learned here is 'profoundly connected to the conditions in which it is learned'.[76]

Situated learning involves becoming an 'insider'. Learners here do not receive or construct abstract or 'objective' knowledge. Instead they 'learn to function in a community' such as that of accountants, engineers, hoteliers or scientists.[77] In this way they acquire the particular community's subjective viewpoint and metaphorically 'learn to speak its language'. Learners are therefore socialised into their practitioner community.

---

74 See Dore and Sako (1989: 91).
75 See Howard (2001: 10).
76 The above quote and material on situated learning benefits from Brown and Duguid (2000: 153).
77 See Brown and Duguid (2000: 153).

Such learners acquire the embodied capacity to behave as community practitioners rather than the formal 'expert knowledge' provided by the trainer or teacher. Learning therefore means becoming a practitioner, not learning about practice.[78]

Learning happens by having access to and membership of the target community of practice. A community of practice comprises a group of people who 'share a concern, a set of problems, or a passion ... and who deepen their knowledge by interacting on an ongoing basis'.[79] Participants therefore are at the centre of the practice where they can pick up invaluable information, manner and technique.[80]

A weakness with the situated learning approach is that it sometimes seems to indicate that the relevant learning only takes place 'if a person is part of a community of practice'. This is because the assumptions or mechanisms about how people learn are not adequately explained or dealt with.[81]

In addition, it does not make it clear where a particular community of practice starts and ends.[82] Furthermore, are communities-in-practice substantial enough to provide situation learning? In comparison to schools, colleges and workplaces are they not rather fragile phenomena?

Service-learning students are not members of a professional community. However, they may in their service activity 'dip into' one or more communities of practices and some related learning may 'rub off' on them. However, the main benefit of our discussion of community of practice is the expanded understanding of learning it provides. In a sense community of practice is an extension of our earlier discussion of contextual learning.

Having considered learning under the above locations we now consider learning as experience. Here the learning *in* a particular setting is not the issue. What counts here is the learning *from* experience. Learning from experience, according to some, is treated in a purely de-contextualised way.[83]

---

78 See Brown and Duguid (2000: 154).
79 See Wenger, McDermott and Snyder (2002: 4). The term 'community of practice' is sometimes hyphenated.
80 See Brown and Duguid (2000: 155–156).
81 See Illeris (2003: 169) on the above material and quote.
82 See Lave and Wenger (2000: 172).
83 See Kayes (2002: 137, 141).

Experiential Learning

Service-learning provides the student with the opportunity to learn from experience by carrying out a volunteering activity. Thus service-learning researchers look to experiential learning theory to help them to better understand the service end of service-learning. Many find Kolb's experiential work helpful and use his model of the learning cycle because it is 'intuitive and easy to remember and apply' to teaching practice.[84]

KOLB

Kolb defines learning as an active, self-directed process involving transactions between individuals and their environment.[85] He says it is the central process of human adaptation to the social and physical environment. In defining learning as an adaptive process he views the learning as outcomes approach negatively in educational terms.

If the teacher transmits ideas then learning outcomes can be measured by how much of the fixed ideas the student has acquired. Kolb argues, however, that ideas are not fixed elements of thought but are formed and reformed through experience. In this way learning is an emergent process whose outcome represents an historical record, rather than some sort of knowledge of the future.

Kolb locates learning within a conceptual spectrum or framework. Here performance, learning, and development form a continuum of adaptive responses to the environment. Performance is a short term adaptive response to immediate circumstances. By contrast learning is a somewhat longer term adaptation to generic classes of situations. Finally, development is seen as a set of lifelong adaptations to a person's total life situations.

APPREHENSION

In explaining learning as adaptation Kolb makes a distinction between apprehension and comprehension and links this to research on the left and right side of the brain. This research indicates that left side functioning corresponds

---

84 See Eyler and Giles (1999: 194). Despite the model's simplicity some elements of his 1984 work suffers from a lack of simplicity. Even Bennis's preface admits it is 'no piece of cake' (Kolb, 1984: x).

85 See Kolb (2000: 34, 36 and 319–320) and (1984: 31, 34) on the material below.

to comprehension and is abstract, analytical, symbolic and verbal. By contrast right side functioning corresponds to apprehension which is concrete, holistic, and spatial. He then goes on to say that the view that the concrete apprehension process is co-equal with comprehension 'represents a dramatic change from that of 40 years ago'.[86] At that time concrete apprehension was seen as a deficit whereas nowadays both functions are equally favoured.

Levi-Strauss indicates that our primitive ancestors leaned towards apprehension and placed a strong reliance on immediate sensations and apprehension. By contrast the modern tendency emphasises the comprehension function and views 'with suspicion the intuitions of subjective experience'.[87] He concludes here that the proper approach to the creation of knowledge is to have knowledge of comprehension provisionally tested against apprehension, and vice versa.

HOLISM

Kolb favours holism in learning and is suspicious of the progress of specialisation which has taken the world apart and at no point put it together again. He suggests that an important function of the larger university is to provide the integrative structures and programmes that 'counterbalance the tendencies towards specialisation in student development and academic research'.[88]

He feels universities should provide experiential learning components that allow students to be more balanced in their learning. If this happens graduates will be better prepared to enter the workforce having 'already experienced multiple learning modes'.[89] The different learning modes in service-learning respond to Kolb's suggestion here.

CONFLICT

Kolb argues that learning from experience occurs in the interplay between expectation and experience. He quotes Hegel stating that 'any experience that does not violate expectations is not worthy of the name'.[90]

---

86   See Kolb (1984: 50).
87   See Levi-Strauss in Kolb (1984: 108).
88   See Kolb (1984: 204–205) on the material above.
89   See Kolb (1984: 205).
90   See Kolb (2000: 320).

He suggests that all learning is relearning and that one's job as a teacher is not only to implant new ideas but to modify or dispose of old ones. He feels that the difficulty with learning new theories of action relate to a tendency to hold on to the old theory-in-use. In this context he argues that learning by its nature is a 'tension- and conflict-filled process'.[91] As Aeschylus said to learn is to suffer.[92]

Illeris says we control our learning and non-learning in a way that can involve a massive defence of our 'already acquired understandings and, in the final analysis, our very identity'. Learning he says can become a question of what can or cannot penetrate a person's 'defence mechanisms and under what conditions'.[93]

LEARNING CAPACITIES

Kolb says effective learners have four different learning capacities and new learning is achieved by confrontation among these four modes of learning.[94]

First, they have the capacity to deal with concrete experiences. This means the ability to involve themselves fully, openly, and without bias in new experiences. Second, they have the capacity to reflectively observe. This means the ability to reflect on and observe experiences from many different perspectives. Thirdly, they have the capacity to abstractly conceptualise experiences. This means the ability to create concepts that integrate their experiences and observations into logically sound frameworks or theories. Finally, they can use these frameworks to make decisions and solve problems.

These four abilities are difficult to achieve at once. How can anyone, Kolb asks, act and reflect or conceptualise and decide at once? In learning we move from activity to observation and from specific involvement to analytical detachment. Here he argues that the way we use or do not use the four different abilities 'determines the level of learning'.[95] If we resolve the differences between the four modes the learning can then end up concentrating itself around one or other ability which then becomes dominant.

---

91 See Kolb (2000: 321–323).
92 See Banner and Cannon (1997: 8).
93 See Illeris (2003: 172) on both of the above quotes.
94 See Kolb (1984: 30).
95 See Kolb (1984: 31).

NEED TO LEARN

Kolb feels that learning is critical to civilisation and that civilisation is on the high wire, where one error can send us 'cascading into oblivion'.[96] He feels we cannot go back to a simpler society because the processes and technologies we have produced have developed their own momentum. We can only go forward. This is because the safety net of the natural order has been 'torn and weakened by our aggressive creativity'. Therefore he argues our civilisation has cast its lot with learning, and 'learning will pull us through'. Consequently this leaves us with an overwhelming need to learn just to survive and therefore learning is increasingly important to everyone.

VAILL

Vaill, in similar vein, discusses the social nature of the operating systems on which we rely.[97] He vividly describes the various operating systems that support an ordinary business trip. This includes such systems as transport, traffic control, parking, ticketing, security, passenger convenience, aeroplane, meeting, and infrastructure. We often take these for granted until one or more fail. He argues that these complex, interdependent, and unstable systems continually require creative responses by those working them. Vaill argues that our continually creative and imaginative responses to operating these systems are a process of continual learning.

Kolb's and Vaill's approaches to learning stem partially from their concerns for a world which has become increasingly complex and systematically interdependent on its myriad parts. They are concerned with what Vaill calls the world of permanent white water.

WHITE WATER

Vaill outlines the characteristics of permanent white water.[98] This world is full of surprises and unexpected problems. Our complex systems tend to produce novel problems which can be 'messy', ill-structured, costly, and can recur.

People can also create white water for themselves as they aim for more and more ambitious goals. In addition, the increased decentralisation, deregulation,

---

96 See Kolb (1984: 2) on this and the points below.
97 See Vaill (1996).
98 See Vaill (1996: 10–13) on this issue.

multiculturalism and service dominated world we live in tends to aggravate the situation. Service according to Vaill means a willingness to absorb the customer's white water and he suggests that the 'determination to be of service is an extraordinary commitment'.[99]

Vaill says people today *feel* the white water is intensifying. Since permanent white water puts people in the situation of continually having to do things they have little or no experience with, they have to become extremely effective learners.

Therefore he suggests learning should become a way of being – an ongoing set of attitudes and actions that we use to try and keep abreast of the 'surprising, novel, messy, obtrusive, recurring events' we must deal with.[100]

LEARNING BY DOING

Learning by doing is critical to experiential learning. In spite of this, learning by doing is often referred to as 'doing after learning' in institutional learning. Real learning by doing means doing real things and learning at the same time.[101] According to Vaill the institutional learning model subtly alters learning by doing to 'application' or 'demonstration' learning.

Institutional learning can incorporate learning by doing by using, for example, experimentation in a science lab. However, even here the science teacher anticipates the expected outcome of the experiment from the start. This then is not real learning by doing because it does not contain the unexpected.

The experiential learning approach normally puts the learner in various problem-solving situations, often with other students and normally with the lecturer in a facilitating rather than controlling role. The assumption here is that learning will occur through these experiences.

However, in spite of these efforts the experiential learning element is more an enrichment of the curriculum rather than a fundamental change in learning method. Institutional learning has succeeded in diverting the original energy

---

99 See Vaill (1996: 18, 19–20).
100 See Vaill (1996: 42).
101 See Vaill (1996: 65–69) for the material here.

of experiential learning and 'converted it into a harmless adjunct to the main business of imparting content'.[102]

LEARNING TO MANAGE AND LEAD

Two of the great hopes of institutional learning – management and leadership – have not achieved their expected success. These subjects have broken management and leadership activities into elements with various experiential exercises hoping that students can integrate everything. This integration does not happen because there is a learning leap from the parts to the whole that the learner has to make. Learners can really only make this leap when they directly do 'the thing that has been taught'.[103] In other words, they can only really learn to manage or lead when they are actually given the chance to do so.

Service-learning

The service in our project management and leadership modules allows students to manage or lead a real project and provides them with actual white water experiences. Students' projects can be very challenging and can fail. Apart from the starting and finishing dates nothing else is sure except that students are completely responsible for their projects. There is no safety net as in a science lab, restaurant class or internship where there is always a supervisor on hand.[104]

Having discussed the types of learning, classroom learning, learning locations and experiential learning we now consider some of the factors which encourage and support learning.

First, we look at the issue of motivation and responsibility in learning. We then look at how personal centring affects learning and consider the social process involved. Finally, we discuss the education sector as a relatively supportive and safe space within which learning takes place.

---

102 See Vaill (1996: 69).
103 See Vaill (1996: 70).
104 Nevertheless there are important safety mechanisms. For example, unnecessarily risky projects are not allowed at the proposal stage. Also students are mentored weekly on their project in class and if it becomes clear there are challenges to be dealt with they are given advice. However, many challenges have to be dealt with on the spot and cannot wait for class.

Motivation

Motivation is important for learning because of its positive influence on involvement, persistence, and willingness to undertake difficult tasks.[105] We discuss its impact on learning by looking at the concepts of interest, intrinsic and extrinsic motivation. We also look at how enjoyment affects learning.

INTEREST

An interest in something tends to encourage a positive and persistent approach that helps improve learning. It is also associated with a self-perceived ability for the topic in hand.[106] We distinguish between individual and situational interest.

Individual interest

This refers to a deep and enduring interest in something. For example, someone who loves football or pop music may spend time learning all about the topic. Individual interest develops slowly, tends to be long lasting and is associated with increased knowledge, value and positive feelings. Individual interest encourages learning because when people are interested in something they will persist at it longer.

Situational interest

This is an interest in the environment where the learning takes place. For example, some may like to learn project management through carrying out a real live project rather than through classroom learning. Situational interest can have two stages, first, where interest is triggered and then where interest is sustained. Situational interest may ultimately develop into individual interest.[107]

Ideally, we should cater more to students' individual interests in our courses. However, this may be expensive as it may require us to provide individually tailored programmes for different students. Some therefore suggest that

---

105 See Kinman and Kinman (2001: 135, 140) and Arnold (2007: 4).
106 See Ainley, Hidi and Berndorff (2002: 545) and Katz, Assor, Kanat-Maymon and Bereby-Myer (2006: 26–27) for the above.
107 See Hidi (2001: 193–194).

situational interest can compensate for a lack of individual interest in a topic.[108] This brings us back to the issue of the most appropriate teaching method.

INTRINSIC

Intrinsic motivation is similar to individual interest. It means carrying out an activity for the inherent satisfaction of the activity itself. It is the labour of love motivation which causes us to engage in something primarily for its own sake and because it is engaging, interesting, or satisfying in some way or other.[109]

Intrinsic motivation has both affective and cognitive elements. The cognitive element relates to the self-determination and drive for competence and mastery. The affective element by contrast relates to the interest, curiosity, excitement, fun, enjoyment and happiness gained from the task. Research indicates that intrinsically motivated students indicate explorative, self-regulated, and reflective behaviour patterns that contain deep learning.[110]

EXTRINSIC

By contrast, extrinsic motivation means learning as a means to an end. Here learning is performed not for its own sake, but for its consequences such as money or status. It can also be to avoid punishment or because of a desire to follow instructions from others.[111]

Some feel intrinsic motivation is necessary for developing the higher-level cognitive skills educationalists and employers prefer whereas extrinsic motivation tends 'to hinder the development of such abilities'. They also feel extrinsic motivation reduces the likelihood of learner autonomy and may indeed encourage 'learner helplessness'.[112] Others argue that organisations that try to build a learning environment on top of a culture that is traditional, hierarchical and competitive will fail.[113]

---

108 See Hidi (2001: 203).
109 See Hidi (2001: 203), Martens, Gulikers and Bastiaens (2004: 368), and Suh (2002: 137) on the above.
110 See Kinman and Kinman (2001: 134) and Martens *et al.* (2004: 368) on the above.
111 See Kinman and Kinman (2001: 134–135).
112 See Kinman and Kinman (2001: 136, 139) on the above quotes.
113 See Teare and Dealtry (1998: 54).

ENJOYMENT

Enjoyment enhances learning and is a type of intrinsic motivation.[114] The task of educators is to discover ways of teaching that stimulate student enjoyment, while at the same time fostering learning. Whether or not this can be achieved depends significantly on the extent to which enjoyment of a subject helps to improve learning. Here we want students to enjoy and learn subject matter. What we do not want however, is an entertaining experience that produces no learning or the standard teaching approach that achieves 'narrow educational goals, but turns students off further study'.[115]

MANAGEMENT STUDENTS

Although intrinsic and extrinsic learning are at opposite ends of a spectrum, some feel that many learners are 'located somewhere between the two extremes'.[116] In this respect students appear to pursue a mixture of learning motives. However, management students tend to give a higher priority to economic motives than other students such as those studying sociology or history.

Extrinsic motivation seems to be more prevalent today than in the past. This may be partly because students are picking up their cues from the environment within which they learn and from the emergence of a more dominant vocational discourse in higher education. It is also suggested that extrinsic learning may be related to instrumental teaching where staff see teaching as a 'necessary evil' which has to be survived so as to undertake research which is seen as far more rewarding.[117]

To resolve some of these difficulties teaching and learning should become more passionate and engaging and should encourage a sense of 'joyfulness, risk and even playfulness'.[118] This comment on playfulness reminds us that Vygotsky said that in play 'a child always behaves above his average age, above his daily behaviour'.[119]

---

114 See Yi and Hwang (2003: 435) and Sibbald (2004: 7). However, not everyone agrees – for example, Cheng and Hampson (2007: 4) and Ruona, Leimbach, Holton and Bates (2002: 219).
115 See Blunsdon, McEachern, McNeil and Reed (2003: 14) on the above quotations and points.
116 See Ottewill (2003: 190–191). Ottewill refers to extrinsic as instrumental learning and intrinsic as expressive learning.
117 See Ottewill (2003: 192) on the above points.
118 See Ottewill (2003: 194).
119 See Barab, Thomas, Dodge, Carteaux and Tuzun (2005: 89).

Responsibility

Responsibility is important for learning.[120] Being responsible for your learning means being answerable, accountable or able to fulfil the learning obligation or trust placed on you.[121]

Our response to the learning challenge is an important part of the learning process. Toynbee argues that a civilisation must respond to its challenges otherwise it will go into decline.[122] Similarly we must respond to our learning challenge.

Concepts such as motivation, agency and self-directed, active and autonomous learning have been used synonymously for responsibility.[123] These concepts however, miss the element of responsibility. In other words, they do not as readily help us to imagine students reaching with effort towards the challenging task of learning.

Learners must take personal responsibility for their learning. In many ways this is primary. If students do not bother to attend class or study nothing happens.

Teachers are responsible for the quality of the teaching, mentoring, or facilitation. If they do not meet their responsibilities even very determined students can fail to meet their potential. Finally, educational institutes and, where relevant, those who resource them have an important responsibility to provide a supportive and encouraging learning environment within which both the student and teacher can operate.[124]

Being responsible for our learning depends partly on how determined we are to learn. However, responsibility is not just a question of the students' raw determination to complete a learning task. This is because responsibility is not just an attitude but is also a capacity. How many times have people tried to learn something only to fail because they do not have the capacity or have not undertaken the necessary groundwork?

---

120 See Cantillon and MacDermott (2008: 254) and Linn, Lewis, Tsuchida and Butler Songer (2000: 12, 13) for example.
121 See 'responsible' in the *Oxford English Dictionary* (2009).
122 See Toynbee (1935).
123 See for example, Linn *et al.* (2000: 12, 13), Glennon (2008: 33–35, 39) and Cantillon and MacDermott (2008: 255).
124 See for example, Masella (2005: 1091) on some of the above points.

The 'gradual release of responsibility' model states that learning should shift slowly and purposefully from teacher-as-model, to guided instruction to collaborative learning and finally to independent experiences. The goal here is to help prepare students to eventually be capable to independently use knowledge and skills in particular situations. The model indicates in broad outline how we should facilitate independent learning. The idea is that students should not be expected to be responsible for doing tasks for which they have not yet been prepared. They first need to have the basic learning skills in place before they can move to the next learning task.[125]

The ability to take responsibility for one's learning can also depend on one's energy and vitality. A student's health and well-being are important here. So, too, are other factors. This takes us to the issue of personal centring.

Personal Centring Facilitates Learning

The capacity to learn can also be affected by the integrity and strength of our personality. We therefore consider the impact of an integrated and centred personality on learning. O'Shea's concept of centring helps us reflect on this issue. He discusses the importance of centring through telling us how he learned pottery.

POTTERY

When he first started pottery he spent a long time trying to prevent the clay flying all over the place. He struggled for hours on the potter's wheel until he began to notice how he sat at it. Slowly it dawned on him that the solution lay not in trying to centre the clay on the wheel but in centring himself. He found that as he spent more time working on the wheel the pottery began to draw him in – first, his hands, arms and shoulders, then his trunk and feet. When there was 'no more body to be drawn in' it drew in his mind by which time he had mastered the task. He can now do pottery 'as one force rather than as a cluster of contradictory ones'.[126]

Our energy and determination can be weakened by conflicting purposes within us. Our main challenge is seldom in the outside world. It is often within our self where we can often find a lack of clarity and integration. We need

---

125 See Fisher and Frey (2008: 2–3, 9, 12) on the above.
126 See O'Shea (1992: 10) on the above quotes.

personal centring. Centring is about learning who we are and what matters to us.[127]

Personal centring, for O'Shea, is also a spiritual thing. He feels that if we do not mature spiritually, virtue continues to mean 'what the world wants me to do' and vice 'what I want'.[128]

Regardless of what we think of O'Shea's enthusiasm for an integrated spirituality or value system, his general argument has important implications for learning. It suggests that our capacity to learn is to some extent affected by whether or not we have a clear and integrated centre. This provides us with a clear view of who we are and what matters to us and puts not just our learning tasks but all important tasks in a clear and purposeful context.

A centred person can more effectively interpret a troubled world in general and individual experiences and challenges in particular. Centring in this sense facilitates greater meaning and meaning in turn facilitates learning. Thus centring, and the meaning and interpretation it offers, facilitates and supports our learning. Students therefore who are not as centred and integrated as others may not be as effective at learning.

Learning also requires the energy necessary for continued hard work. We often presume young people have plenty of energy and good health even in the most difficult of circumstances. We should not, however, take this for granted.[129]

Mary, a character in the novel *Green Dolphin Street*, watches her kids play and wonders 'do strangers see them as just high-spirited kids' or do they know how 'provisional' they are and 'how gently they must therefore be treated?'[130] And it is not just children who are provisional. Even high energy and well centred individuals must recognise their need for centring, self-replenishment and work–life balance.

---

127 See Godsey (2005: vii).
128 See O'Shea (1992: 13).
129 See Ranson (1999: 55).
130 See Faulks (2002: 31).

Personal centring, a sense of purpose and self-worth, and energy are not educational objectives. Pedagogical discussions for the most part ignore these issues.[131] And yet they can be important for learning.

The above points indicate that motivation, responsibility, and centring are all relevant to learning. The social environment in which students learn is also important.

Learning is Social

Learning is a social process. George Mead's concept of the self as a social phenomenon is important here.

SOCIAL SELF

Mead argues that the development of the self is pre-eminently social.[132] Here the social process is prior to the processes and structures of individual experience. Communication for Mead is a social act since it requires at least two people to interact. He even suggests that there is no meaning without the interactive participation of two or more individuals.

Society, for Mead, is not a collection of pre-existing individuals, but a whole within which individuals define themselves through participating with others. The objects of the social world (clothes, shelter, food, and so on) are what they are because they are socially defined and utilised. For example, certain clothes or food are fashionable or nourishing because they are so defined. Mead says the mind and identity arise from social acts of communication and thereby emerge socially.

We need not fully accept Mead to agree with the point that much cognitive activity is socially shared. For example, the textbook explanation of recession cannot match the level of understanding that arises from a community's shared experience of recession. Therefore individual in-class cognition has limits in preparing students for a reality that strongly constructs cognition within a social process and framework.

---

131 However, counselling, medical, chaplaincy and sports facilities often provide an important resource for college students.
132 See Cronk (2005) on the material below and also Mead (1967).

PEERS AND TEACHERS

Mead's analysis is supported by the view that a student's most important teacher is often another student. Class mates, friends and reference groups can amplify, dampen, or distort the impact of the curriculum. In other words students' encounters can play an important role in learning and personal development.[133]

Learning can also be facilitated by a positive relationship between the student and teacher. Teaching is a sharing of knowledge and much of the learning is communicated within the 'context of relationship'.[134]

We sometimes find that people develop a passion for a subject from a favourite teacher. This happened to Sharon whose algebra teacher was so passionate about the subject that she saw it as a 'gift'.[135] Others refer to students enjoying school because of teachers who 'made us think we were good'.[136]

Learning, however, can be weakened where relationship is fragile or absent and this can lead to the student's encounter with school getting 'worse and worse'. The experience of being shamed by a teacher or of indifference can weaken a student's capacity to learn.[137]

Teachers with a passion for a subject can encourage learning. So, too, can teachers with compassion for their students. Compassion is the 'profound concern for students that springs from both the heart as well as the head' and indicates common experience. It also indicates 'suffering with' and teachers can sometimes feel its effects in the emotional and physical exhaustion that comes with teaching.[138]

Having discussed the social context of learning, the impact of peers, relationship and compassion we now reflect on the importance of a safe and secure space for learning.

---

133 See Chickering and Reisser (1993: 392–393).
134 See Davis and Williams (2003: 262).
135 See Davis and Williams (2003: 264). Teaching is the 'gift' not just of knowledge, but also of 'habits of mind and heart and powers of thought' (Banner and Cannon, 1997: 134).
136 See Davis and Williams (2003: 265).
137 See Davis and Williams (2003: 265).
138 See Banner and Cannon (1997: 81–83) for the above.

Safe Space

The institutional system provides a relatively safe space within which students can be temporarily shielded from, and better prepared for, the significant challenges of the outside world.

While experientialists can criticise the excessive reverence some have for institutional learning they should recognise its contribution. For example, some feel that although discovery through experience is necessary for 'real possession of knowledge' others suggest that experiential learning can be 'too time consuming to be used efficiently' in education.[139]

In addition, the capacity to learn from raw experience can vary significantly from person to person. For example, if students are required to help disadvantaged ten-year-olds with their homework, the student's task can vary depending on the particular ten-year-old in question. Similarly, if students are required to run charity events the actual task can vary considerably from event to event.

The institutional system can provide relatively safe and structured learning opportunities notwithstanding its drawbacks. Having reached this point in our discussion we return to service-learning where we summarise what researchers say about some of its learning outcomes.

Learning in Service-Learning

Service-learning can support the personal, interpersonal, social, academic and professional learning of students. It also encourages connected learning.[140]

PERSONAL, INTERPERSONAL AND SOCIAL

First, it improves tolerance, self-efficacy, confidence, leadership, communication, self-knowledge and interpersonal skills. In addition, it helps students question, evaluate and clarify their values and beliefs and encourages altruism and in

---

139 See Kidd (1973: 180–181).
140 See Toews and Cerny (2005: 264–267).

some cases, as we discuss later, Christian charity or its equivalent in other religions.[141]

It encourages social responsibility and most students who undertake service-learning feel more connected to their communities. It also encourages citizenship to the extent that it shows an increased willingness to participate in service. In this respect it provides the opportunity to learn about and practice being good citizens.[142]

CONNECTED LEARNING AND WORK

Service-learning also helps to connect the various dimensions of college life. Few, if any courses, involve such disparate activities as working with local communities, teaching staff, college societies, and so on in a way that service-learning does.[143]

Connectivity is a key factor in the efficiency of the work organisation. There has been a trend for some time now towards eradicating internal boundaries within organisations and moving towards cross-functional teams. Because of this we need 'boundary spanners' to work across the interfaces.[144] These people 'facilitate the sharing of expertise by linking two or more groups of people separated by hierarchy, location or function'.[145]

Professional development is also enhanced by the increased ability to speak in public and the improved confidence, communication and leadership skills referred to above that arises from service-learning.[146]

ACADEMIC

However, the evidence is weaker for its cognitive impact and 'many are dubious about its value' in college where the 'most important goal is learning subject matter'.[147] This weakness exists in spite of the fact that the 'intellectual

---

141 See Eyler and Giles (1999), Toews and Cerny (2005: 264–267) and Marchel (2003: 25). See also our discussion of Christian values or its equivalent in other religions in Chapter 3. Self-efficacy refers to a person's belief about his or her capacity to do certain things. See Linnenbrink and Pintrich (2003: 120–121).

142 See Toews and Cerny (2005: 266) and Eyler and Giles (1999: 156–157, 163) on the above.

143 See Eyler and Giles (1999: 10).

144 See Leonard-Barton (1995: 263).

145 See Gopal and Gosain (2009: 9).

146 See Toews and Cerny (2005: 265).

147 See Eyler and Giles (1999: 58).

outcomes – knowledge, cognitive development, problem-solving skills, and transfer of learning – are at the heart' of the educational mission.[148]

Some disagree and feel it contributes to academic performance. They feel it gives students a greater ability to apply classroom knowledge to real life situations. In addition, students are better prepared for class, are more interested and engaged in class and are more inclined to discuss course content outside class.[149]

Conclusion

This chapter has considered the learning part of service-learning. First, it developed a learning framework which classifies learning into three types – basic, advanced and development learning. Our main focus here is the advanced types of learning – knowledge and skills. Development learning is also relevant because values are an important concern of ours. Although insight or meaning has some slight relevance we anticipate very little indication of metanoia in our discussion later on.

We considered the strengths and weaknesses of the traditional classroom method and discussed how service-learning can compensate for some of the weaknesses of the classroom method by integrating classroom theory with service activity.

Learning can occur in different locations such as institutional, formal/ informal, OJT, and situated learning. The learning in service-learning incorporates the institutional or formal learning of the classroom with the informal learning of service. In addition, the service component has some similarity with OJT and situated learning.

Experientialists favour a holistic approach to education and support more integrative programmes such as service-learning. That experiential learning can involve tension and create distinct challenges for the learner has implications for the service element of the pedagogy.

---

148 See Eyler (2000: 11).
149 See Toews and Cerny (2005: 266). See also Hurd (2008: 47–48) for a useful summary of the research.

In discussing the factors that support learning we considered motivation, responsibility and personal centring. We also discussed the social process of learning and the fact that the institutional system can provide a relatively safe space for student learning. Although the transmission mode dominates, service-learning can enhance the experiential element of learning and help integrate some of the benefits of both approaches.

Finally, we discussed how service-learning provides a curriculum-based opportunity to learn personal, interpersonal, social, and academic learning, along with work related learning. We now move on to discuss the service part of service-learning.

3

The Service Involved

Getting the chance to help others as part of a college course is a totally new experience for most of us. Sitting in class and planning a service project is very unusual. What is this service activity and what does it mean?

Introduction

This chapter considers the nature of service in service-learning. First, we look at some definitions. Then we discuss what different writers have to say about the topic and, because of the amount of disagreement on the subject, we develop our own understanding of service.

Since students doing service are like volunteers in the community we also discuss the meaning of volunteering. We then consider how service can be carried out in either the college itself where there is plenty of good work to do or, more commonly, in its external community.

Service does not get a lot of encouragement from the prevailing culture and certain trends tend to discourage it. We discuss this point by considering such topics as social capital, enterprise culture, markets, and the entertainment economy. Finally, we look at how providing service can be good for people and can help them grow and develop.

DEFINITIONS

Service means doing good work and serving, helping, giving assistance or benefiting others.[1] In the business world it is seen as an activity or benefit

---

1   See *Oxford English Dictionary* (2009) and Microsoft Encarta World English Dictionary (2009b).

incorporating work or advice.[2] Here it is viewed as a heterogeneous and complex activity with the following characteristics.

It is intangible, experiential and perishable in nature and therefore cannot be stored. Because of this most services are provided geographically near to the recipient.[3]

The production and use of a service are often simultaneous and the recipient participates in its provision. Because the interaction between the service provider and recipient is a unique experience, the same service can be viewed differently by different recipients and by the same recipient on different occasions. Others not involved in the transaction may also affect the service experience – for example, by positive or negative commentary. Finally, its complex nature makes its planning, delivery and evaluation a relatively difficult activity.

Arguments

Different writers have different views of the exact nature and purpose of service and there has been much argument and debate on the topic.[4] Some see it as an act of citizenship, justice or reciprocity. Others feel that service should contribute to social change. Finally there are those who feel that service, at its limit, can be seen as an act of charity or an expression of human love.

Having discussed these viewpoints on service we develop our own understanding of service so as to help us clarify the nature and meaning of service-learning.

CITIZENSHIP

Some writers suggest we use service-learning to develop citizenship in our students.[5] Citizenship refers to one's status as a citizen of a particular country.

---

2 See Law (2006: 473, 475) for the material below.
3 Proximity is not always relevant – for example, retail services on the Internet or Robo-doc, a remote controlled robot that can move from bed to bed visiting patients (Ungar, 2007).
4 See Morton (1996: 280) and Pollock (1999: 18).
5 See Westheimer and Kahne (2004: 242).

This status has certain rights, privileges, duties and responsibilities. Citizenship can also refer to fostering solidarity within a particular country.[6]

Although there is much support for citizenship education, there is disagreement on its nature and the model of the good citizen to which we should aspire.[7] Our ability to agree on its meaning has also been weakened by the growth of globalisation and multiculturalism. This is because citizenship 'is almost always realised in a highly unequal – indeed, exclusionary – fashion' creating what is called a 'citizenship gap'.[8]

To bring some clarity to the concept, three types of citizenship have been proposed. These are the responsible, participating and reforming types of citizen.[9] Being a responsible citizen means acting responsibly in the community by working and paying taxes, obeying laws, volunteering in times of crisis or giving to a charity or blood bank.

Being a participating citizen means being an active member of a community organisation, helping to organise community efforts for those in need, promoting economic development, helping to clean the environment and so on. Being a reforming citizen can mean assessing social, political and economic structures to find the causes for social injustices and helping to address them.[10]

Despite these and other efforts to clarify citizenship many still feel the concept lacks clarity. Even some who support its use in service-learning find that 'students are no more in agreement on what good citizenship means than are teachers, policy makers, or politicians'.[11]

Citizenship is an inadequate benchmark for service not just because it lacks clarity but because being a good citizen in one country does not always mean the same thing elsewhere. Here it has been said that 'the character of citizenship varies systematically between different societies and over time'.[12]

---

6 See *Oxford English Dictionary* (2009), Microsoft Encarta World English Dictionary (2009b) and Dell'Olio (2007: 1).
7 See Dell'Olio (2007: 3) and Davies (1996: 120).
8 See Dell'Olio (2007: 3).
9 See Westheimer and Kahne (2004: 242) and Kahne, Westheimer and Rogers (2000: 44).
10 See Westheimer and Kahne (2004: 242).
11 See Westheimer and Kahne (2004: 241).
12 See Dell'Olio (2005: 27).

Citizenship is to be commended as a service objective. However, since it fails to provide a relatively clear and uniform benchmark for service we have to look elsewhere.

JUSTICE

Justice is a common objective of service and there is an 'emerging body of literature advocating ... an explicit social justice aim'.[13] People define justice in different ways.

Rawls defines it as fairness and says its central aim is constitutional democracy. He takes a 'political, not a general, conception of justice' and sees it as an alternative to utilitarianism which he says cannot provide a satisfactory account of the basic rights and liberties of citizens.[14] Everyone he says possesses an inviolability founded on justice 'that even the welfare of society as a whole cannot override' and argues that the loss of freedom for some is not made 'right by a greater good shared by others'.[15]

Mitchell sees social justice as the 'belief in, hope for, and imagination of a different kind of society'.[16] She says social justice education should encourage us to question inequality and prejudice and act as agents of change. She talks about social responsibility and community change where people are involved as active citizens. She feels that service-learning should redirect its focus 'from charity to social change' and advises that 'students must first come to believe and understand that the current community is somehow flawed'.[17]

Hartnett takes a broader approach to justice by referring to different paradigms. He mentions the liberal paradigm which focuses on human rights and the need for legislative reforms. He also mentions the socialist one which looks at the need for a 'radical transformation of the underlying structures' of society 'insofar as these engender poverty and exclusion'. He then refers to a pragmatic type of justice that identifies it with individual initiatives undertaken on behalf of those in need. Finally, he mentions relational justice which means 'fidelity to the claims of our relationships' and which encourages us to foster justice in all of our dealings with others.[18] Hartnett's paradigms of justice go

---

13 See Mitchell (2008: 50).
14 See Rawls (1999: xi) and Rawls and Kelly (2001: 11).
15 See Rawls (1999: xii, 3) on the above.
16 See Mitchell (2007: 102).
17 See Mitchell (2005: 2) and (2007: 102, 105) on the above.
18 See Hartnett (2000: 3) on the above quotes and material.

beyond Rawls's concept of political fairness and Mitchell's as social change in that he also allows for one-to-one justice.

Although justice is important and service-learning for justice is to be applauded it is too multidimensional a concept to act as a clear benchmark for service.

RECIPROCITY

Many writers refer to the importance of reciprocity in service-learning. For example, some argue that a 'distinguishing characteristic' of service-learning is the nature of the social exchange between the service learner and those being served.[19]

To reciprocate means to give and receive in return or mutually, to interchange.[20] The service in this context is a trade where the student can be seen for example, to provide service in return for being allowed to complete the experiential part of the course.

Some writers when queried about the trading nature of reciprocity refer to its mutuality element.[21] Reciprocity here is said to create 'a sense of mutual responsibility and respect between individuals' or a 'parity of esteem'. Mutuality has also being explained as the 'process by which two or more persons support and nourish each other for the enhancement of all'.[22] When we add mutuality to reciprocity however, we are still talking about mutually beneficial exchange or trade. This is an entirely praiseworthy service impulse.

However, if students help for example, in a retirement home for entirely selfless reasons there need be no trade or mutuality. Although they may feel better about themselves after helping out, the satisfaction they get need not be a trading outcome but an unplanned effect and the service need not therefore be a trading activity.

---

19 See Giles and Freed in Stanton (1990: 67). Stanton also refers to the 'social and educational exchange' not just between students and those served but also between education programmes and the community organisations with which they work (1990: 67).
20 See *Oxford English Dictionary* (2009).
21 For example, Dwight Giles said we must consider the mutuality element of reciprocity when it was suggested that Christian charity might be a more suitable benchmark for service rather than the trading involved in reciprocity. This arose in a discussion between the author and Giles on 24 June 2008 in Trinity College Dublin (TCD).
22 See Kendall (1990: 22) and Barak (2005: 141) on the above points.

Therefore although reciprocity is a significant service objective we must still allow the human spirit at its furthest point the capacity to provide service that requires no trade or mutual support – that is in the end entirely selfless.

SERVICE DEVELOPMENT SEQUENCE

Some argue that doing a particular mix of service activities over time can help us mature. They suggest there is a range of service experiences that students can go through which can help to develop them.

This idea was first raised in 1994 when it was asked if there is a development sequence in doing service.[23] This question stirred up a significant debate and was followed in quick succession by a variety of important articles on the topic. We consider some of these below.

Morton was first off the block. He suggests there is a service development sequence that starts out with charity work, moves on to project activity and at the top carries out social change type service. To clarify his development sequence we use the concept of a service ladder.[24] This runs from charity at the bottom to social change at the top.

This approach is supported by those who argue that the social justice aspect of service is more important than the charitable one.[25] It is also supported by those who favour service programmes that emphasise reciprocity and 'doing with' others rather than the lower level charity model of 'servant leader' and 'servee'.[26]

Social change

When students do charity work they may begin to feel compassion for those they help. Following this they may become curious about why people need help. This may then lead some to try and change the circumstances that cause problems for those they have come to care about. Therefore students may be attracted to social change service because they are upset by others' problems and become interested in trying to help resolve them.

---

23 See Giles and Eyler (1994: 82). They used the term continuum rather than sequence.
24 See Morton (1995: 22). Morton uses the term service continuum rather than development sequence. We use the ladder concept because it is simple and clear. Some regard Morton's paper as 'groundbreaking' (Moely and Miron, 2005: 62).
25 See Foos (1998:14).
26 See Varlotta (1996: 26).

The sequence here goes from personal concern, to education, to analysis and problem identification and then on to a cycle of reflection and action. Morton admits that this particular development sequence has helped to inform his own work.[27]

Social change is viewed here as a more mature form of service than charity. It focuses on building links with different groups and encourages a learning environment that helps clarify the causes and solutions to problems. It sees power as a key issue and focuses on empowering those who have been disenfranchised. At a macro level it contributes to the larger strategy of change by helping the redistribution process in society.

Morton feels the empowerment element indicates the superiority of social change over charity and project service. He feels that charity and project service only help people in the context of the world as it is and not as we would wish it to be. In this context therefore the ladder goes from the personal to the political and from individual acts of charity to collective ones.[28] We could also suggest that social change could be regarded as more technically and intellectually challenging than charity and therefore more suitable for higher level conceptual learning.

About turn

Morton, however, did an about turn at the end of the 1995 article when he discarded the notion of a ladder going from charity to social change. Here he admits that charity and social change each has their own significance, ranging from 'thin', with low integrity, to 'thick' with high integrity. He talks about 'thick charity' being deeply grounded in one's faith or personal view of responsibility. This he feels can therefore lead to personal and systemic transformation.[29]

Therefore charity, rather than being left at the bottom of the ladder, is now on a par with social change. In the end he conceptualises service as a set of three distinct but related paradigms – charity, project and social change.[30] We refer to this as Morton's spectrum of service activity.[31]

---

27 See Morton (1995: 20).
28 See Morton (1995: 20–22) on the above.
29 See Morton (1995: 28) and (1996: 281) on the above material.
30 See Morton (1995: 21).
31 Others support Morton's here and argue that charity and social change are equally important. They say that caring for others and justice are mutually supportive. See Foos (1998: 18).

Project

Morton's concept of project service is weak. In project service the student defines problems and their solutions and introduces plans for solving them.[32] An example of a service project might be the planning, delivery and organisation of a fundraising event for a charity. The project approach determines the problem, identifies the solution and then plans the implementation of the activities to deliver this solution.

However, Morton is confused in identifying project activity as a type of service. His project model is not a type of service. It is a service delivery mechanism.

Morton's project model can be more easily understood by using the discipline of project management. This provides a conceptualisation and methodology for providing any type of project – from a rocket launch to a product launch, from a charity fundraiser to supporting a homeless shelter. Indeed, a well run briefing on project management could, in certain circumstances, help students to carry out any type of service activity. Therefore he is talking about service delivery when he refers to the project model, nothing else.

Now that the project model is excluded from our service categories the service spectrum contains only two elements, charity and social change. Here charity and change are of equal importance.

However, social change of itself is unsuitable to use as a service benchmark because it is unclear what it means as it does not explain the nature of the social change. We need to have a service benchmark which provides some indication of what we are about.

This, if correct, leaves us with charity. However, we have a twist to our story with Morton again part of the drama. Now charity comes under fire and is replaced by a call to service.

---

32 See Morton (1995: 21).

CHARITY REPLACED BY SERVICE

In 1997 Morton and Saltmarsh analysed the nature of charity using the ideas of Addams, Day and Dewey. These three had to redefine the 'charitable relation' in a particular phase of history.[33] Charity at that time was felt to be a process of character regimentation rather than social reform and involved successful middle class people helping the charity dependant. Here charity was seen to lead to a division of society into philanthropists and recipients creating two different classes. In fact some went so far as to say that charity can distort people's ability to know others and can endanger community.[34]

Morton and Saltmarsh conclude their piece by referring to the politics of language. They argue that as the concept and language of charity was challenged in the early part of the twentieth century, a new language of 'service' replaced it. The concept of service, they argue, is a phenomenon of the cultural history of the US and is 'defined by an educated, middle-class seeking ways to live lives of integrity'. They conclude by proposing that community service in fact contains an 'antidote to the crisis of community'.[35]

Morton and Saltmarsh now take charity out and replace it with a call for service. Here students are encouraged to do service, not charity.

CHARITY RECONSIDERED

This negative outcome for charity is, however, built on an interpretation of the practice of charity at a certain phase in history. This interpretation reflects how some people viewed the charitable efforts of others at the time.

This interpretation is interesting. However, it is incorrect. What actually happens at the individual level is not easily aggregated, nor are peoples' intentions. People involved in charity are on their own personal journey. Because they do not always get very far does not mean their individual efforts do not have some integrity. The fact that their efforts do not meet the full requirements of charity does not mean charity should be discarded.

---

33 The 'charitable relation' was shaped by the Charity Organisation Movement of the 1880s according to Morton and Saltmarsh (1997: 139).
34 See Morton and Saltmarsh (1997: 139–140, 142) on the above material.
35 See Morton and Saltmarsh (1997: 146–148) for the above quotes.

Morton and Saltmarsh's decision, however, is to dispense with charity and replace it with the modern concept of service. Is it not strange that academics have, in this instance, dispensed with an ideal construct because of reality's inability to match it?

We now need to clear out the undergrowth of argument and bring clarity to our understanding of service. For this purpose we discuss the meaning of charity.

Charity

Charity means helping others or giving to those in need. It also means love, kindness, affection or leniency and tolerance in judging others. According to some charity in its fullest context is the highest form of love. Here charity is a translation of the Greek word *agape*, meaning love, and this form of charity is most eloquently shown in the life, teachings, and death of Christ. In Christianity, charity means love and is the foundation or root virtue for all other ones.[36]

BENCHMARK

If we take the Christian view of charity as our service benchmark we do not need to encourage students to progress from charity to social change. Indeed the advice, if any, may be in the opposite direction. Some may find social change activity less demanding than person to person charity. Loving your enemy, a difficult neighbour, cousin or boss may be a lot more trying than working for Amnesty International or a homeless agency.

Some argue that charity can also have a social change dimension in that it can also address 'the social and political dimensions of ... poverty'.[37] This talks about social and political charity and argues that 'social charity makes us ... seek the good of all people' where 'the neighbour to be loved is found "in society"'.[38] This says it is an 'act of love to strive to organise and structure society so that one's neighbour will not find himself in poverty'.[39]

---

36 The classical Christian description of charity is neatly summarised in the New Testament (see 1 Cor. 13). See also Encyclopaedia Britannica Online (2009c) and *Oxford English Dictionary* (2009) on charity.
37 See Libreria Editrice Vaticana (2005: 72). The page numbers here are based on the downloaded document as saved in Microsoft Word.
38 See Libreria Editrice Vaticana (2005: 81).
39 See Libreria Editrice Vaticana (2005: 72).

Service-learning

Bowes feels service-learning is often promoted in secular institutions as an activity that fosters good citizenship. He states however, that service-learning is much more than an exercise in good citizenship and proposes that it is a mandate for Christian living. He finds that colleges with Christian affiliations find it easier to attract students to service and enjoy a wider support among staff than other places. He suggests it is impossible to engage with Christianity without talking about the call to service.[40]

VARYING VIEWPOINTS

Our understanding of service varied significantly. We first considered citizenship, justice, and reciprocity. We then discussed the service development sequence. Here we go from three components (charity, project and social change) to just two (charity and change). The relative importance of these two then varied from social change being the best to their being of equal importance, to charity finally being discarded.

We then refreshed our understanding of charity and having redefined and clarified its meaning we chose it as the benchmark for service.

We could spend all day debating the nature of service without getting everyone on board. Despite the quality of the argument, people with different personal experiences may come to different conclusions on the same issue.[41]

Service Core

We take the Christian concept of charity as the core of service (see Figure 3.1). This supports and encourages service as citizenship, justice, reciprocity and social change. These are very important endeavours and add significantly to people's well-being.

However, as the ultimate benchmark they are surpassed by the reality of human love and charity. There is no greater service that we can do for others than love or charity. It is the most demanding, difficult, unselfish and trying activity there is.

---

40 See Bowes (1998: 26, 28) on the above material.
41 Words and their meaning tend to stand on the stilts of experience.

Figure 3.1   Charity at the centre of service

One can get the impression that in the real and difficult world out there we cannot realistically get beyond reciprocity and that we are stuck talking about Christian love as some sort of rare and extreme ideal of human behaviour.

However, Donati says charity or love 'after first having been placed on the margins of society in the modern period is now emerging increasingly as an indispensable element'.[42] He argues that charity has been seen as an 'irrational fact for a long time' and has been mistakenly viewed as an 'enigma' when in fact it should have been regarded as 'nothing other than life itself'.[43]

SERVICE BENCHMARK

Charity provides us with a standard to interpret student service. Students involved in one-to-one charity or one-to-many social change are both providing service as long as the charity impulse drives or partly drives their activities.

Take the homeless. Students can be defined here as providing charitable service when they do so because they care about people who are homeless. Similarly when they work to change the circumstances that affect the homeless because they care about them they can again be defined as providing charitable service.

By contrast those helping others for purely grade or career motives are not involved in charitable service. There is nothing at all wrong with this. In fact

---

42 Although Donati means Christian charity he uses the term 'free gift' instead. He does so because it has 'undergone many different mutations over the last 2000 years'. See Donati (2003: 243–244).

43 See Donati (2003: 268).

their motives in educational terms are entirely praiseworthy. However, their intentions define them as being involved in grade enhancement and career development not charitable service.

This does not mean that those helping others for purely self-improvement reasons could not start to care and feel for them. They could indeed and this may be one of the more important effects of service-learning. Likewise, those doing it for weak charity reasons may find that their concern for others expands during their service activity. Here, their service experience helps to improve their personal development and encourages them to become better people with better values.

This is where the potential for values enhancement in the service aspect of service-learning can occur. The student given an opportunity to experience service may become a somewhat better person, one more likely to help others in the future.

Therefore, students who do service for a mixture of self-improvement and charity reasons have what we can call mixed intentions. This is very often where the real world hangs out – the service and self-improvement impulses intermixed. People vary in their personal capacity to help others. Therefore, finding students who do service because they care deeply for others may be a rather uncommon occurrence. It may be more common for students to have mixed motives driving their service.

SERVICE IMPULSE SPECTRUM

The service impulse can be discussed as a spectrum ranging from underdeveloped at one end, to developed at the other. At the underdeveloped end there is a large self-improvement motive. By contrast, at the developed end there is a large charity element. The service impulse spectrum therefore calibrates things on the basis of student intentions and efforts.

These points are summarised using the service spectrum shown in Figure 3.2. Here service activity can initially contain a significant component of self-concern and progress ultimately to a deep concern for others. In between, we have mixed intentions varying from a large self-concern and low caring impulse to a low self-concern and a high caring impulse.

Service Impulse

Figure 3.2   Service impulse spectrum

This spectrum implies that the student's service values develop as they progress from self-concern as their sole motive to a mixture of self and other concern. This progress is complete when their sole service intention is concern for others.

Student service efforts may often fall short of the ideal. This is not a problem for our conception of service as we can applaud all genuine efforts towards charity. In addition, service-learning does not grade the service only the learning.

Christianity calls on people to keep their good work private.[44] However, service-learning requires students to analyse and often broadcast their good work. This is however an educational requirement rather than a vanity issue.

Some may disagree with a service standard based on student intentions. For example, Comte, the sociologist, argues that researchers should confine themselves to studying phenomena which can be observed. He feels we should not be concerned about people's meanings, intentions and the like. He argues that since these mental states exist only in a person's mind they cannot be observed and measured in any objective way.

Durkheim disagrees. He argues that researchers should confine themselves to studying social facts. However, these can include such things as meanings and intentions. For Durkheim social facts do not have to contain only things which can be observed.[45] Therefore our analysis of student intentions and charitable impulse is for Durkheim a legitimate area of analysis.

---

44 See Dingle with Sokolowski, Saxon-Harrold, Smith and Leigh (2001: 12).
45 See Haralambos and Holborn (1995: 809) on the above.

EVALUATION

Service has been conceptualised in a variety of ways by different writers, some of which we considered. Having considered these, we decided to use the Christian concept of charity or love to help us interpret service. Some may not be familiar with this approach and others may not agree with it. We, however, use the concept for the following reasons.

First, we use it because of its relevance and robustness as a measure or benchmark of service. We also use it because of its relative clarity and uniformity in comparison to some other measures and because of its relatively long tradition.

Second, the concept should be familiar to at least some people around the world where 33 per cent in total describes themselves as Christian. In particular it should be familiar in Latin America (93 per cent), North America (81 per cent), Oceania (80 per cent), Europe (78 per cent), and Africa (47 per cent).[46]

Third, using the concept does not imply we accept Christian thought. We are simply borrowing it from Christian thinking to help us analyse student service. However, people from other religious traditions will not find charity or love and the ethic of helping others strange or unknown.[47] We briefly summarise its equivalents in other religions and none below to place this point in context.

Islam

Islam for example, encourages a sense of brotherhood and has a strong interest in service. It teaches people not to be selfish and to use one's possessions to help others. Religious acts are considered a façade unless people actively assist the needy. Islam encourages the development of a close-knit community of the faithful who view each other as brothers.

---

46 Asia comes in at 9 per cent. The figures relate to those describing themselves as Christians or followers of Jesus Christ (either affiliated or not). Non-affiliated Christians are about 2 per cent overall. See Encyclopaedia Britannica Online (2009d) for the data.

47 There are statistically four great religions – Christianity (33 per cent), Islam (20 per cent), Hinduism (13 per cent) and Buddhism (6 per cent). Chinese folk religionists have slightly more numbers than Buddhism. Since however, the latter is a relatively more uniform religion we mention it here. See Encyclopaedia Britannica Online (2009d).

The Koran is its chief text. Under the section on alms this states 'have you thought of him that denies the last judgement? It is he who turns away the orphan and does not urge others to feed the poor'.[48]

Hinduism

Hinduism is not really a religion but a congregation of religions and contains a variety of doctrines, cults, and ways of life. Therefore efforts to define it have proved unsatisfactory. Although Hindus therefore are not in full agreement on how to be saved one of their most influential religious texts suggests three ways to reach salvation. One of these proposes the way of action. Here people are advised to carry out fully their religious and ethical duties and discharge their ritual and social obligations. This reference to social obligations may be seen to have some links to our concept of service to others.[49]

Buddhism

Buddhists achieve nirvana by cultivating four virtuous attitudes: loving-kindness, compassion, sympathetic joy, and equanimity. In order to have a better rebirth, they must focus on fulfilling moral duties as members of a family or society. This involves acts of charity, along with observing the five principles that constitute the basic moral code of Buddhism. These prohibit killing, stealing, telling lies, sexual misbehaviour, and the use of intoxicants. Such principles can be seen to encourage a concern for others.[50]

Judaism

Although Judaism holds only 0.2 per cent of world populations it has an interesting approach to charity and caring for others. The Hebrew word for charity is based on anger at injustice which in turn provokes one to remedy

---

48 Some feel we cannot make many general statements on Islam. Although some ideas are so widely accepted that they can be seen as distinguishing features yet there may be some Muslims who might disagree. In spite of this we make the above general points. See Gerald Hawthing on 'Islam' in Microsoft Corporation (1999a) and Fazlur Rahman on the 'Doctrine of the Qur`an: Social Service' in Encyclopaedia Britannica (1999). See also the Koran sura 107 on Alms. Muslims account for 21 per cent of the world's population. See Encyclopaedia Britannica Online (2009d).

49 See 'Hinduism' and the 'General Nature and Characteristic Features of Hinduism' in Encyclopaedia Britannica (1999) and the 'Song of the Lord' (*circa* 200 BC) on the above. Hindus account for 13 per cent of the world's population. See Encyclopaedia Britannica Online (2009d).

50 See the material on Nirvana in the section on Buddhism in Microsoft (1999a). Buddhists account for 6 per cent of the world's population. See Encyclopaedia Britannica Online (2009d).

the injustice. It encourages people to walk in the ways of God. Here God is described as nursing the sick, clothing the naked, comforting the bereaved and burying the dead, so that people may recognize their own obligations.[51]

Humanism

Those with no religion may still find service attractive as long as they share a belief in helping others. For example, humanists emphasise the dignity and worth of the individual. One of its basic principles is that people possess a capacity for truth and goodness. The emphasis on virtuous action as the goal of learning was a founding principle of humanism.[52]

Utilitarianism

One might well assume that utilitarianisms would not support charitable behaviour. The utilitarian philosopher Bentham argues that moral actions are measured by how much they achieve pleasure and avoid pain. This philosophy would seem, on first impressions, to recommend a selfish approach to life. However, nothing is further from the truth. Bentham himself once said that giving money to a beggar gave the beggar pleasure to receive the money but also gave him pleasure to give it.[53] Thus charity can even garner some support from utilitarianism.

Confucianism

Confucius was a Chinese thinker and social philosopher, whose teachings and philosophy deeply influenced Chinese, Japanese, Korean, Taiwanese and Vietnamese thought and life.[54] Confucius says that the goal in life is to be human. His all-embracing notion of humanity, called 'ren', refers to the ideal state of being human. He says that if we set our heart on 'ren' we 'will be without evil' and once explained it as 'to love one's fellow men'. He describes people of humanity as follows: 'if one wishes to establish one's moral character,

---

51 See Morton (1995: 25) and the article on the 'Ethical Emphasis of Judaism' in Encyclopaedia Britannica (1999). See also Encyclopaedia Britannica Online (2009d) for the datum on Judaism. In addition, Fromm a well known Jewish philosopher for example, talks about love as having the common elements of care, responsibility, and respect. See Fromm (1956).
52 See 'Humanism' and 'Basic Principles and Attitudes: Active Virtue' in Encyclopaedia Britannica (1999).
53 David Limond provided this particular vignette on Bentham.
54 See http://en.wikipedia.org/wiki/Confucius located on 12 March 2009.

one also establishes others, if one wishes to obtain one's goals, one also helps others obtain their goals'.[55]

Therefore, this study is addressed at the service end to readers who at least share a belief in the benefits and ethic of helping others. Whether the reader goes for the service spectrum based on charity, citizenship, justice, reciprocity or social change will be influenced by personal preference. For the moment however, we can do no better than mention what Kendal says about arguments on meaning and definition. She feels that, despite the diversity of language and meaning and the related disagreement that arises, there is broad agreement that there is something 'uniquely powerful about the combination of service and learning'.[56]

We continue our clarification of service by considering the meaning of volunteering.

Volunteering

To volunteer according to one source is to perform, or offer to perform, a service of our own free will and provide assistance or assume the obligation voluntarily. In doing so, we help those other than our immediate family.[57] Volunteering has also been described as 'a form of sustained helping'. Here people 'actively seek out opportunities' to help others in need and commit themselves 'without any bonds of prior obligation'.[58]

Therefore service-learning students volunteer to the extent that they actively seek out an opportunity to help others and do so of their own free will. If however, they are forced to take service-learning because it is a compulsory part of a course they are not volunteering. If on the other hand, the course is known to use service-learning and it forms a significant and visible part of the curriculum then when they choose the course they are, in effect, choosing service-learning. If however, it is a relatively small but unknown and compulsory part of a course we have problems. Here they have chosen the course but not necessarily the service in service-learning. The service is now a compulsory rather than a voluntary activity.

---

55 See Liu (2006: 57–58).
56 Quoted in Varlotta (1996: 26).
57 See Microsoft Encarta World English Dictionary (2009b) and the Department of Social, Community and Family Affairs (2000: 37).
58 See MacNeela (2008: 127).

PAY

Volunteering is done for the benefit of others and is without payment other than expenses, honorarium or token payment.[59] Students doing service in service-learning should not therefore incur any costs other than those they would expect from any other subject. If service puts students out of pocket beyond the bounds of ordinary subject expenses it might be best to have the beneficiary, voluntary organisation or college help cover the cost.

Volunteering is therefore not done for financial gain, nor is it done for career purposes. If, for example, students provide free nursing services in order to strengthen their career prospects their motive is not service or volunteering but job positioning. However, nothing is cut and dried. It depends on motive. For example, a student nurse may volunteer to help a poorly resourced hospital rather than a rich and well resourced one because of a combination of volunteering and career motives.

FORMAL OR INFORMAL

Volunteering can be either formal or informal. Informal means volunteering on your initiative and unrelated to an organisation and is not carried out for a family member or relative. This can also be called unmanaged volunteering and tends to be sporadic and spontaneous in nature.[60]

Formal or managed volunteering means voluntary work done with or through an organisation. A voluntary organisation operates for purposes other than making profits and is independent of government. A variety of terms refer to the voluntary sector including third sector, independent sector, charities, non-profit sector, and non-governmental organisations (NGOs). Mixed economies contain a public and private sector and a third sector that is neither government agency nor private company.[61] Students can, therefore, volunteer in a school, college, voluntary, community or public body. People of course can also volunteer to help a group without a particular physical location such as a virtual network.

The service in service-learning can be classed as managed or formal volunteering since it is part of a formal course rather than spontaneous good

---

59 See Larragy (2001).
60 See Dingle with Sokolowski, *et al.* (2001: 9).
61 See European Commission (1997: 1–2) and Pérotin (2001: 329) on the above.

work, unless of course it is compulsory and not a free choice by the student. In this latter case the concept of volunteerism is not relevant to our analysis of service-learning.

RELATIONAL

Volunteering is a relational activity since it creates and sustains a relationship between the volunteer and the 'other'.[62] The other can be a person, group, organisation, community or indeed society. It can also be a cause or ideal as in the case of doing something for the environment, world peace or animal welfare.[63]

The volunteering in service-learning should be healthy and safe. This is a primary concern for everyone. Where the service is being provided with or for a voluntary organisation they also share some of this responsibility.

Because students provide service in or for the community we consider the meaning and significance of community.

Community

The concept of community can be confusing and at one stage there were over ninety different definitions counted with the only common element being that they were all 'about people'. Things got so bad at one stage that some concluded that the term had become obsolete and meaningless.[64] We therefore need to clarify its meaning.

TERRITORY

Community has a variety of meanings. First, we have community as territory, which can be located on a map. In this sense community is spatially defined, whether it be Calcutta, Chicago or Cambridge in England. Here it would make little difference if the word community was replaced by the city's name.

---

62   This is not socialising. If students volunteer purely to socialise they are not engaged in service as we understand the term. When their activities contain elements of caring for others, however small, they are providing service as we define it. In addition, if their caring impulse strengthens during their course the quality of their service improves.
63   See National Committee on Volunteering (2002: 7).
64   See Charon (1992: 122), Worsley (1987: 239) and Peck (1994: 4) on the above.

RELATIONAL

Second, community refers to a relational phenomenon where it can be understood as a web of connections, friendship or mutual support. This type of community has shared experiences and meanings, ways of thinking and acting, beliefs and cultural objects. The relationships within such a community are informal and multidimensional rather than the formal and one-dimensional ones of a work organisation.

This type of community depends on people having considerable knowledge about each other's lives. It also depends on its members being able to take for granted that the attitudes, beliefs and experiences of others are probably very like their own. A relational community is small enough both for people to know something about each other and for the community to be a source of identity.[65]

A group has been defined as a collection of people who see themselves as belonging to the same entity.[66] They have a sense of 'we' or 'us'. Likewise a relational community has a sense of identity although the sense may not be as palpable as in a small well-knit group.

DEVICE

Community has also been regarded as a tool or device. For example, it has been used as a mobilising device to strengthen the nation since it implies unity, wholeness and belonging. Here community-based organisations were seen as a way of expanding state support in areas where its presence was weak such as housing, social welfare or policing.[67]

The community sector has also been discussed in the context of weak public finances and privatisation. Here it is suggested that community organisations can play a role in providing social and community services. This refers to an increasing delegation of public service provision to community organisations.[68]

---

65 See Griswold (1994: 139) and Tovey and Share (2000: 337).
66 See Handy (1999: 150–151).
67 See Collins (2002: 13–15, 17, 100).
68 See Pérotin, (2001: 327, 357–358) and European Commission (1997: 16) on the above.

IMPLICATIONS

Community can be conceptualised in three ways – as territory, relational, or device. The service in service-learning can therefore be carried out in a particular territory or for a relational community. Community as a device, however, is not a definition of community but rather a purpose or function. Nevertheless, exploring community as function enriches our understanding of the term.

We now consider some of the implications for service-learning of the meaning of community.

Territory and relational

Students who provide service in a territorial community with a weak relational component may find their work made difficult by the absence of a relational network. In addition, those who provide service to a relational community that lacks a clear geographical locus may come up against contact and linkage problems. They may also experience comprehension difficulties unless they are familiar with the community's culture and systems of meaning and are prepared for the engagement. This issue may become even more difficult if the community identity is built around principles of exclusion, homogeneity and the reduction of difference.[69]

Device

Community as a device is also relevant to service-learning. Where service-learning treats the community as purely a learning resource or device it views it as an object rather than a partner. In so doing it may weaken community.

Some say the needs of the community agency can conflict with the university. When this happens the relationship between the agency and college can 'often break and then heal only to break again' as they deal with new demands.[70]

Others feel that service-learning can emphasise student learning outcomes and teaching issues and pay inadequate attention to the needs of the community.

---

69 See Meade and O'Donovan (2002: 7).
70 See Cuban and Anderson (2007: 152).

Finally, some have found that certain communities have being 'partnered' to exhaustion.[71]

Next we consider the location of service and reflect on the issue of the internal and external community.

Location of Service

Where do students do their service? Must it be outside the campus walls, in the nearby town, or somewhere else? Can the service be done within the university walls? Alternatively, are not universities elite organisations and should not their students be encouraged to help others?

Most service-learning takes place in the external community as we see below. However, students can also find plenty of good work to do in the college's internal community.

EXTERNAL COMMUNITY

One of Howard's good-practice principles discusses the criteria for selecting service placements. He says that the service must comply with what both the community and faculty member define as important and refers to the need for knowing the community, the agency and its staff.[72]

Many others likewise refer to the external community. For example, some refer to 'sending students out' to do service and to community partners and service placement sites. Others refer to the scholarship of engagement and pilot sites for service.[73]

Finally, Jacoby states that the term community in service-learning refers to local neighbourhood, state, nation and global community.[74] There is nothing here about the internal community – it's all out there.

---

71 See Vernon and Ward (1999: 30) and Ramaley (2000: 3) on the above. There has been much discussion of how effective partnership works. See for example, Sandy and Holland (2006).

72 See Howard (2001: 17, 23–24).

73 See Battistoni (2001: 7, 12) and Applegate and Moreale (2001: 2, 3).

74 See Jacoby (2003: 4).

ADOPTING SERVICE-LEARNING

Engagement with the external community has been discussed by considering the stages of adoption of service-learning using the pyramid in Figure 3.3.[75] This refers to the development of service-learning by looking at the existence or otherwise of a service support centre.

In the introductory stage the college has no service centre. At the intermediate stage a centre exists. This helps staff and students link with community partners but only has an ad hoc involvement with the community. Its role is mainly to help support and administer the channelling of students and resources into the community. In the advanced stage the college has developed a strong volunteering centre which has built up significant strategic partnerships with various community organisations.

This approach indicates that the service provided is aimed at the external community. Therefore it would need to be modified to take account of circumstances where a college focuses some of its service projects on the internal community.

Service-learning supports the external community because it provides plenty of scope for student service activities. However, the internal community can be an important service location.

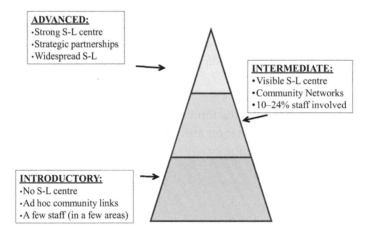

Figure 3.3   Adopting service-learning: The stages

---

75 This pyramid and the related discussion is based on Campus Compact (2002).

INTERNAL COMMUNITY

The potential of the internal college community for service projects becomes somewhat clearer when we consider some of the difficulties within its boundary. The college community is not always the happy place outsiders might think for either students or staff.

Staff can face work pressure and other difficulties in their job. Students can have difficulties learning, getting adequate grades and staying the pace along with other difficulties. Students' low performance, failure and drop-out are also an international concern. Although non-completion rates vary widely across the OECD, over 30 per cent of all higher education entrants on average leave without graduating.[76]

There are also concerns about aspects of student socialising. Here there is evidence that many students are socialised in college to heavy drinking. In addition, there is evidence that students are more likely to 'exhibit pathological and problem gambling' than others.[77]

The increased concern with student experience of college life has encouraged a greater interest in the topic. For this reason the internal college community offers plenty of scope for service projects.

Having considered service in terms of volunteering and the community we continue our discussion by considering some of the trends in society which impact on the service reflex.

Trends in Society

Here we discuss the concepts of social capital and the culture of enterprise, entertainment and celebrity.

---

76 See OECD (1998: 69–70), OECD (2008: 98), Skilbeck (2001: 73, 75) and Morgan, Flanagan and Kellaghan (2001: 16) on the above material.
77 See Newman (2000: 5). Student drinking, gambling and drug taking however, is also part of an overall problem in society.

SOCIAL CAPITAL

Social capital refers to the quality and nature of social networks and civic values in society. Some distinguish between bonding social capital within particular groups and bridging capital across groups (for example, ecumenical organisations or civil rights movements).[78]

Putnam argues that there has been a decline of social capital in a variety of spheres. For example, civic and political participation has declined in spite of the rapid increase in education that has given more people the skills and resources that once fostered it. In politics the decline in fact is greatest among the better educated.[79]

Work

There has been a decline in social capital in the workplace. This is surprising in view of the increased emphasis on teamwork and internal communications in employment. However, the weakening of the worker's ties to the firm and the increased contingency of work counterbalances this. In addition, the most common reaction to this situation is for people to put their head down and focus on their own job. Even staff whose jobs were spared after lay-offs often experienced what is called 'survivor shock'.[80]

Social

There is also evidence that we spend less time visiting and in conversation with people and less on leisure activities involving others. By contrast, we spend more time observing and watching things happen. Putnam refers to this as the silent withdrawal from social interaction. In addition, he finds that people go less frequently to church and the churches they still go to are less engaged with the wider community.[81]

Home

The decline in social capital has also been reflected in the home. Here there has been a weakening in the traditional family unit and a significant fall in the

---

78 See Putnam (2000: 22) and the *Oxford English Dictionary* (2009) on the above.
79 See Putnam (2000: 46, 63–64).
80 See Putnam (2000: 88, 90).
81 See Putnam (2000: 79, 115).

proportion married. This is related to the increase in divorce and single-parent families and the growth of one-person households.[82]

Criticism

Not everyone agrees that social capital has declined. Some deny there is a social capital crisis and argue that society has never been as participative, interactive, or charitable. This argument suggests that while many of the old ties and connections are weakened new ties replace them. Old social capital has been replaced by new forms is the message here.[83]

For example, the Internet now supports 'virtual communities' and the level and growth of network sites are considerable.[84] Some argue that such networking sites contribute to social capital where others feel it may not always improve the quality of interaction.[85]

It is difficult to adjudicate between these contrasting viewpoints except to say that Putnam agrees that new forms of social capital can appear but feels they do not compensate for the decline of the old ones. In addition, recent evidence indicates there is no strong improvement in social capital and in some areas it is falling.[86]

Therefore social capital remains a concern in society and to this extent does not strengthen the service reflex. Other things however, also affect the service impulse. One of these has been the rise of the enterprise culture with its emphasis on individualism.

---

82 See Putnam (2000: 276).

83 See Willis (2000: 13, 15). See also Saffer (2008: 1059–1060) who says that 'not all social interactions have declined in the past 30 years'. He says 'when memberships are aggregated there [was] very little change between 1974 and 2004. Individuals may have changed the organizations that they belong to but in the aggregate there is little decline in memberships.' He says there are less bowling leagues but 'there may also be more soccer parents'. He then says however, that visiting relatives has been declining since the mid-1980s and visiting friends has been declining for the past 30 years.

84 See *The Economist* (2005: 5).

85 See for example, Becker (2008) and Ellison, Steinfield and Lampe (2007: 1164).

86 This shows that the difference in social activity between countries is getting wider. For example, voluntary activity and membership of voluntary organisations is high and growing in Nordic and certain other European countries, stable or fluctuating in others, and falling in places like the United Kingdom, certain Central Eastern European countries, Portugal and Turkey. Engagement on this evidence is growing where it is already high but falling in some places where it is already low. In addition, the evidence on social trust in society indicates 'that the quality of social relations needs attention and is declining in some countries'. See OECD (2008a: 72–73) on the above.

ENTERPRISE CULTURE

Enterprise culture has invaded many areas of activity - personal, private, public and business. The individual at the centre of this culture is the entrepreneur. Being an entrepreneur has become socially legitimate and entrepreneurship has become an important human and cultural phenomenon. In fact some feel the entrepreneur has become a cultural hero as the Western world seems to be in the middle of a love affair with the idea.[87]

Enterprise culture applies market forces and entrepreneurial principles to all areas of life. It emphasises self-reliance, personal responsibility and risk taking and suggests we live our lives as an 'enterprise of the self'.[88] It suggests that the 'enterprising self' calculates things and works upon itself in order to self-improve. It also encourages people to self-steer and self-actualise. Enterprising individuals are, among other things, self-reliant and independent and are significantly driven by material reward.[89]

Enterprise culture places the private sector and its language and methods in a privileged position in society. Consequently, public sector and voluntary organisations have been encouraged to reconstruct themselves as enterprises and have seen the language of enterprise integrated into their vocabulary. Such phrases as 'the customer and client', 'customer care', 'market forces', 'operating in a competitive world', 'labour market forces', and so on have become part of their vocabulary.[90]

A business-style philosophy has also gained ground in the administration and management of education. In addition, efficiency-related pay and fast-tracking of high performers has become more common in teaching. It has also entered the classroom where enterprise education and course components have become more common. This philosophy has also been connected to the search for management excellence which exhorts individuals to reconstruct themselves as winners and champions.[91]

---

87 See Carr (2000: 68) and Morrison (1998: xiii, 4) on the above.
88 See Du Gay and Salaman (1992: 619) and Carr (2000: 68, 71).
89 See Du Gay and Salaman (1992: 628–630) and Carr (2000: 14).
90 Rather than using patient, student, applicant and so on they use customer and client.
91 See Du Gay and Salaman (1992: 616) and Carr (2000: 9, 13, 17, 49).

MARKETS AND EXCHANGE

The market is the central institution of enterprise culture and relationship here is based on exchange. It is, according to some, a co-ordinating device where strangers come and go and engage in limited relationships. Economic transactions here do not entail social obligation and the important thing is rational calculation and individual gain. This perspective denies the existence of community and favours individuality.[92] The market and enterprise culture is a contrast to community and a source of some fragmentation in society.

The arrival of reciprocity as a 'distinguishing characteristic' of service-learning seems to reflect the impact of the enterprise culture on the pedagogy. It is very difficult for our imagination to survive the intensity of the notion that relations are built mainly or solely on exchange. Even writers who argue for the extension of relationship beyond exchange and reciprocity have to use such terms as 'free gift', 'free giving', 'pure gift', and 'pure giving' to make their point in our enterprise dominated culture.[93]

Bhatnagar for example, sees 'pure gifts' as transfers between people that 'do not imply any exchange, reciprocity, or compensation' and 'pure giving' as something which occurs 'without the expectations of direct social exchange'. However, he indicates some discomfort with the concept of the pure gift when he says that 'the lack of social return does not mean that the giver receives no rewards' and refers to a 'psychic return' without providing any explanation for the term.[94] One can only assume that the enterprise culture got the better of his analytical imagination on this.

CRITIQUE OF MARKET

Some disagree with the above argument and feel that economic behaviour is more socially embedded and social relations are more responsible for bringing order and trust to economic life than this approach allows. In addition, such things as honesty or dishonesty have more to do with the quality of relationships rather than with the nature of the market.[95]

---

92 See Carr (2000: 177).
93 Donati as we saw earlier uses the term 'free gift' rather than charity. I used charity in the body of the text with Donati's permission (received by phone and email on 3 October 2008).
94 See Bhatnagar (1970: 210–211) on the above material.
95 See Granovetter (1985: 483, 491, 501–503).

Notwithstanding these points, we have to accept that markets do not, *per se*, support communal life or social integration. The British conservative politician and businessman Lord Young spoke wisely when he referred to enterprise culture as the 'restoration of the age of the individual'. He said that enterprise is built on the 'liberation of the enterprise of the individual'.[96] Therefore, even where there is some gain from cooperating in the market, the starting and finishing point is individual material need. The growth therefore of individualism through the markets and the culture of enterprise has noticeably affected the type of society today's student operates within.

We now look at the entertainment economy and the culture of celebrity.

ENTERTAINMENT ECONOMY

Some argue that consumers are changing from coveting 'real' goods to demanding 'feel goods'. They now want their purchases to make them feel better, less stressed, and so on. Experience is becoming a commodity.

Some years ago the service sector emerged as the dominant part of the economy. At first critics found it difficult to get to grips with the intangible nature of output. Now businesses have, for the main part, successfully turned services into well-structured commodities that are relatively easy to produce, market and buy.

The service economy is now going to be superseded by the experience economy.[97] Businesses that rely on producing just goods and services will be exposed to more effective competitors. To avoid this they must learn to incorporate rich, compelling experiences into the provision of their product or service. Coffee can for example, exist under four different guises – a commodity, a good or a service.[98] However, if you buy it in a trendy restaurant the high price you pay is for the additional experience of sitting in a nice atmosphere with a pleasant view. This gives us our fourth guise.[99]

The entertainment economy has for some become part of the economy. Although the quality and price of the product is still important, some expect to be amused or entertained by their purchases. For example, some consumer

---

96 See Arnason (2001: 303).
97 See Pine and Gilmore (1999).
98 For example, it can exist as a truck load of the commodity, a jar of supermarket coffee, or a cup of coffee in a fast food restaurant.
99 See Pine and Gilmore (1999: 1).

brands are trendy because they are linked to well known celebrities.[100] This view suggests that businesses should consider the possibility that they can more effectively market their products or services by associating entertainment with their purchase and use.[101]

Some also suggest that the culture of celebrity and the need for entertainment has become an important ingredient, not just of our economy, but of our culture.[102] They feel that our rich and privileged economies face the risk of consumer fatigue that may well lead to stagnant or falling demand.[103] Since affluence is the normal condition for many in rich countries, continued economic growth requires the creation of new consumer needs, ones that go beyond being satisfied with material goods.

Gray suggests that an increasing number of people work in order to keep others amused. Ordinary items such as cars, originally sold to get us from A to B comfortably and safely, are now sold partly for the new experiences they promise. He also suggests that celebrities have become significant social indicators of personal fulfilment.[104]

The focus on enterprise, entertainment and celebrity in our society carries a narcissistic core that is quite at odds with the service impulse. Enterprise culture's focus on individuality and self-advancement is at odds with helping others. The interest in celebrity has a voyeuristic element that encourages people to watch and be entertained by others. Even if celebrities are famous for their good deeds, they are packaged, sold and watched more for their spectator benefit than for anything else.

What is the situation in higher education?

HIGHER EDUCATION

Higher education has increasingly become 'market driven' and the university is now being referred to as 'a big, complex ... business'.[105] In addition, its

---

100 Gale and Kaur (2004: 79–80) say the endorsement or association of products with or by celebrities can appeal to consumers. They mention the examples of Elton John and Versace, Sharon Stone and Gap and Lady Diana and her Dior handbag.
101 See Wolf (1999).
102 See Gray (2002).
103 Keynes was worried as far back as the 1930s about this possibility (1936: 373).
104 Gray's exact words here are 'in this carnival of illusions, celebrities are at once alluring ciphers of personal fulfilment and the most fungible of commodities ...'. See Gray (2002).
105 See OECD (2007: 5).

students are now 'demanding customers' and its academics are 'expected to be active in commercial activity' which 'can be valuable' among other things 'for remuneration'.[106]

There are also indications that there has been an increasing fragmentation of community within the sector in that its underpinning principles now instil individualism, materialism and competition as controlling values. This suggests that the staff community and, in particular, the community of scholars is giving way to the 'service station' or 'cafeteria model' of higher education.[107]

If society in general has become more fragmented and the paradigms that interpret it more based on individualism and ease rather than effort and community what then are we to do? What does this mean for our students?

STUDENTS

Students today operate within a more fragmented college community which in turn operates within an enterprise culture that offers support and encouragement to winners and champions rather than to groups and community. The balance, therefore, has moved towards encouraging individual capacity rather than connectivity and integration. Added to this is the weakness of traditional integrating mechanisms such as the family and religion. This helps to explain the increasing indifference and individualism among some young people.[108]

SUMMARY

The above developments offer little or no encouragement to service, and students today live in a world where the service motive has a weak support base. Even service-learning, with its key role for reciprocity as service, has not escaped the enterprise culture and the concept of free giving has to incorporate the word free to counterbalance the cultural disbelief in the possibilities of love and charity. Indeed it may be the case that the overweening emphasis on enterprise culture, individuality, trade, exchange (and reciprocity as our furthest ambition) may so lower the bar of human expectation that our human capacities have become stunted.

---

106 See OECD (2007: 13).
107 See UNESCO (1996: 5–6, 34).
108 See European Commission (2002: 6, 41) on the above material.

Growth and Development

We now consider some of the benefits of being involved in community and helping others. We do so by reviewing the ideas of Vanier and others. This view suggests that student service and involvement in community can enhance personal growth and development and act as a counterpoise to social trends that encourage fragmentation and excessive individualism.

VANIER

Jean Vanier is a writer and founder of L'Arche. This is an international organisation that creates communities where people with developmental disabilities and those who assist them live together.

Vanier states that people today are nourished on independence and individualism and the desire to win and climb the social ladder.[109] Community, he feels, is no longer found in the marketplace, neighbourhood or village. The lack of community, he argues, pushes people into individualism. This increases the loneliness that is offered only slight relief in hard work, money and success. He suggests that people who lack community can suffer deep insecurity and proposes that children nourished on TV and the mass media can lack a sense of values and become rootless.[110] His points echo those above on the fragmentation of society and the decline of social capital.

Vanier's community is a place for people and their growth. Here people join to be happy but stay when they find that happiness comes in helping others. This type of community leads to openness and acceptance of others and is a place of belonging, caring, acceptance and growth in love. A group of friends can become a community when little by little its members begin to become responsible for one another.

Vanier argues that those who enter community to acquire something (for example, to learn) are in fact not joining a community. A community is not for getting something or producing things, although this may happen. Joining a community means being in a place where people care for and are cared for by others and where people can be vulnerable but safe.[111]

---

109 Vanier set up L'Arche in 1964 in France to help disabled people. It has now spread to 35 countries where it has 130 faith communities. See www.larche.org/l-arche-since-its-beginnings.en-gb.22.10.content.htm located on 12 March 2009 and Vanier (1989: 74).

110 See Vanier (1989: 1–4).

111 See Vanier (1989: 20).

VULNERABILITY

Being vulnerable from time to time is normal. For example, students can be vulnerable when it comes to exams and staff when it comes to renewing contracts or assessing progress. Vulnerability however, is not part of the language of the street and can be an awkward term to use in today's workplace or school and college.

When vulnerability is eventually noticed it has often reached its more difficult forms by which time it may be an issue for the counselling, chaplaincy, medical or other support systems in a college. Therefore, rather than being a normal, if awkward, part of everyday consciousness, it often becomes an issue only when it becomes severe. Although colleges provide counselling and other supports for such vulnerability, they have not widely incorporated it into the normal language of daily life. In Vanier's community, vulnerability and dealing with it becomes a normal part of a fuller life and this prevents us having to over 'psychiatrise' people and their problems.[112]

CELEBRATION

Celebration is important for community. Vanier says celebration is the communal experience of joy and thanksgiving and it nourishes, restores and gives us strength.

He makes a distinction here between going to a party, a film or a play with a celebration. In the former we are often spectators but in a celebration we are with family, friends or colleagues and are strengthened and renewed.[113]

Celebration can contribute to service-learning where it can be used to recognise students for their contribution and let them know their service is valued. Some refer to the importance of celebrating the accomplishments of service-learning and even go so far as suggesting that celebration is a characteristic of an effective learning organisation.[114]

However, while one may note the linkage between celebration in Vanier and service-learning, there are some differences. The celebration in service-

---

112 See Vanier (1989: 54).
113 See Vanier (1989: 312).
114 See Payne (2000: 11), Laroder, Tippins, Handa and Morano (2007: 32), Bucco and Busch (1996: 243) and Rubin (1996: 313) on the above.

learning is normally linked to achievement and recognition whereas Vanier's conception of celebration is imbued with a rather specific view of individual worth.

COMMUNITY AS PERSONAL GROWTH

Our earlier understanding of community as territory, relational or device is now broadened by Vanier's insight that community can support personal growth and development. This extends our relational description of community. By providing service in the community, the student can grow and develop.

This understanding of community also parallels our earlier definition of service as charity. Offering students the opportunity to provide and be involved in charitable service can provide an opportunity for personal growth and development.

Vanier is optimistic about our ability to develop community. He is, however, aware of the limits of human energy, the forces of individualism and the levels of fear, aggression and self-assertion that create barriers between people.

In addition, he realises that although people want community they may still refuse its demands and may also want the freedom to do what they wish. In this context he says community requires co-operation and a clear organisation and discipline.[115]

BENEFITS OF COMMUNITY

Others apart from Vanier talk about the need for community. For example, Buber says there is a great longing for community in Western culture. Like Vanier, but coming from a different faith tradition, he feels community is essential for the individual and society at large. He states that an individual's growth is enlivened, deepened and fulfilled by engaging in relationships. Interestingly he also suggests that the main function of education is nurturing relational capacities.[116]

---

115 See Vanier (1989: 133, 24–25, 35, 41, 111).

116 Martin Buber (1878–1965) was a German Jewish philosopher whose ideas centred on the dialogue of man with others. Although he did not live to witness the most recent manifestations of Western culture, he lived through two World Wars and all that went with them. See Friedman (1976: 43, 46) and Murphy (1988: 92) on the above points.

Durkheim, the sociologist, also refers to the need for community. Because of this need, he argues, community is something that constantly reappears, although not always in immediately recognisable forms.[117]

Finally, there is research indicating that helping others increases people's well-being. In addition, there is evidence that those helping others are less prone to depression, have more life satisfaction, have better health as they grow older and have a lower risk of early mortality.[118]

Conclusion

This chapter considered the service part of service-learning. First, it discussed its meaning. Service we found is a relatively complex phenomenon. It consists of work or advice and is intangible, experiential, heterogeneous, complex and interactive in nature.

It is also a highly contested concept among service-learning writers and there has been much argument and debate on the topic. We discussed service by considering citizenship, justice, and reciprocity. We also consider the idea of a service development sequence that includes charity and social change.

In the end we used the Christian view of charity as the standard or benchmark for service activity. The defining ingredient of service here is the impulse or intentions which drive it. Here, service can be evaluated using a service impulse spectrum going from a large self-concern and relatively small caring impulse, to a mixed motive impulse and on then to a deep caring impulse.

Students doing service in service-learning often do so voluntarily. Volunteering is a sustained helping activity which is done freely and for no pay. It is formal or managed rather than informal and is relational in nature and can be carried out in the internal or external community.

We define community as either territorial or relational in nature and look at its functional nature under the concept of device.

---

117 See Tovey and Share (2000: 337).
118 See Meier and Stutzer (2008: 42, 55).

We then considered some of the trends in society which affect the service reflex. Here we found that social capital and connectivity in general has declined in society. In addition, we saw how enterprise culture and market behaviour encourages people to reconstruct themselves as competitors rather than members of society with communal values and responsibilities. In discussing the entertainment economy we found that the demand for goods or services is increasingly being stimulated by encouraging narcissistic tendencies among consumers.

Such trends encourage students to view themselves as customers rather than members of a community. They promote an economic approach where identity is increasingly being directed towards an enterprise of the self. They also discourage social obligation and for the most part ignore community life. Finally, we looked at the benefit of community for personal growth and development and refer to how helping others can be beneficial to people.

Having now considered service-learning and its two components, learning and service, we are ready to look at the purpose of service-learning. We do this in our next chapter by reflecting on the role of third level education and applying our findings to service-learning.

4

The Role of Higher Education

What is the purpose of higher education? What should we expect from it in today's world? What in particular should we expect of service-learning?

This chapter discusses and clarifies the role of higher education. Having done this it applies the findings to service-learning.

Introduction

The traditional role of the university was critical intellectualism. Reason, evidence, proof and unfettered inquiry were emphasised. This role required a measure of distance and separation from society and the relevance and application of knowledge was only of secondary importance.[1]

Society's aspirations for higher education have now changed. To clarify this we look at what some of the key international organisations say on the topic. Here we consider the opinions of the Organisation for Economic Cooperation and Development (OECD), the European Commission and the World Bank. We also look at the views of the United Nations Educational, Scientific and Cultural Organization (UNESCO).

Although there are differences of opinions and sometimes outright disagreement on the topic, we formulate a clear purpose for higher education in general and service-learning in particular.

---

1   There was also a tradition of professional standards among certain courses. Here knowledge, competence, ethics and service to society were embodied in such courses as medicine, law, engineering, and theology. These students were preparing to become responsible professionals performing essential roles in society. See OECD (1998a: 43, 45) on these points.

Higher education has two roles – what we call the dominant and ancillary roles. The dominant role is economic and is aimed at helping students prepare for the work world and the economy. The ancillary role is social and focuses on the wider needs of society.

Having discussed both roles we develop a composite role for higher education. We then apply this to service-learning.

Dominant Role

The dominant role concerns itself with the needs of the economy and the economic needs of the individual and is most clearly seen in the reports of certain international bodies and government agencies.

THE OECD

The OECD has written widely on the topic and has long concentrated on the economic role.[2] One of its more interesting reports states that there is a crisis of purpose within the sector. It criticises those who embrace a nostalgic image of society where economic considerations take second place to other issues and says that international competition between countries has increasingly influenced the educational agenda.

Governments, it feels, are now more inclined to tell educators that universities must live in the real world and cannot be 'all praises and hallelujahs, and perpetually in the vision of things above'. It also mentions that the increased emphasis on knowledge and skills in society has served to 'domesticate' the university.[3]

Although it admits that higher education 'is not a pure market activity' it says 'market forces are of increasing importance' to the sector. Today the university is 'no longer a quiet place to teach and do scholarly work at a measured pace'. Now it has become 'a big, complex, demanding, competitive business', one which has become 'increasingly autonomous and market-driven'. Governments now require higher education to contribute to such things as

---

2   See OECD (2007a: 3).
3   See OECD (1987: 7, 12, 15, 16) on the above points.

economic development, up-skilling and life-long learning, knowledge-based developments, regional policy, and the like.[4]

National reviews

OECD reviews of national policies in higher education are an important part of the educational landscape and can make a significant contribution to national debates. The Irish review is worth mentioning because Ireland has been regarded as a 'miracle' economy up to recent times.[5] The OECD review says that Ireland was 'one of the first European countries to grasp the economic importance of education' and recognise that tertiary education is a 'key driver for the economy'.[6]

What sort of advice does it offer this successful economy? It provides 52 recommendations in all. However, not a single one supports the ancillary role of higher education. This review sticks to economic concerns and its various recommendations either directly or indirectly support the economy.[7]

In fairness it does state that the dominant role 'should not obscure' the artistic, intellectual, citizenship and civil society role of tertiary education. However, having made this point it then 'obscures precisely this role by ignoring it'.[8] Thus its advice to the higher education sector of what was a very high performing economy was to continue to meet the needs of the economy so as to encourage even further growth and expansion.

Supporting the economy

The OECD has sometimes argued for a non-economic role. Here it talks about how growth slowdown and ecological issues can provide a role for education,

---

4   See OECD (2007: 5, 10, 12, 18) on the above points.
5   This relates to the early 1990s and the mid 2000s period. See Baccaro and Simoni (2007: 426, 427, 429), Clancy (2008: 21) and Cooney (2008: 65) on the performance of the Irish economy and education's contribution to that performance.
6   See OECD (2006: 22, 94, 96) on the above points.
7   For example, it recommends that a new national council should determine a strategic agenda for tertiary education for 'innovation, skilled labour force and the economy'. It also suggests institutes of technology should concentrate on applied research which should be 'targeted against clear ... economic priorities'. Even when it refers to the need to recruit and retain students from disadvantaged backgrounds its rationale is economic. Here it states the time is ripe for a further attack on this problem because 'there is a risk of a national shortfall of qualified new entrants to the labour market'. See OECD (2006: 53, 64, 84) on the above material.
8   See OECD (2006: 24) and the Royal Irish Academy (RIA) (2004: 8) on the above. The RIA is referring to the earlier OECD examiner's 2004 edition of the report.

It also refers to drug taking and extremist activities that threaten peace and harmony and links these to materialistic values which lead some young people to 'lose sight of existential landmarks'.[9]

It also discusses the implications of unemployment for education and argues that we should reorganise our curricula to enable students in danger of social exclusion to 'situate their learning experiences in positive visions of the future'.[10] Therefore, if the university does not always succeed in enabling its graduates to enjoy gainful activity it should ensure that they are supportive members of society rather than negative malingerers.

In addition, it suggests that education should help students take more control of the construction of their own society and should foster their personal qualities along with transmitting traditional bodies of knowledge.[11]

In all of this however, the educator's primary role remains focused on preparing the student for the work world and, where unemployment, drug taking, extremism or ecological problems threaten this, the education system should help out.

THE WORLD BANK

The World Bank says higher education has the 'main responsibility for equipping individuals with the advanced knowledge and skills' required for jobs in 'government, business and the professions'.[12] It says that higher education contributes to economic growth by increasing productivity and income and encouraging external benefits such as long term returns to research and technological developments and transfer.

Higher education has both private and public benefits. The private benefits include better employment prospects and living standards. They also include better health, quality of life, and life expectancy which, in turn, can allow people to work more productively over a longer period further boosting lifetime income.

---

9   See OECD (1998: 8). This report focuses mainly on secondary level.
10 See OECD (1998: 52).
11 See OECD (1998: 52).
12 See World Bank (1994: 3).

Public benefits occur when tax revenues or technology expand from higher income or more technology-savvy graduates. Public benefit can also occur when the increased confidence and know-how from education strengthen entrepreneurship.[13]

Higher education can, however, also have a social role in that it can help to forge 'the national identity' and offers a 'forum for pluralistic debate'.[14] This role can also arise from improvements in equality of participation which in turn can enhance economic efficiency, social justice and social stability.[15]

Notwithstanding the above benefits it says higher education may have lower rates of social return than primary and secondary investments since basic education can have a greater impact on poverty and literacy.[16]

THE EUROPEAN COMMISSION

The European Commission states that Europe needs 'excellence' in higher education so as to 'optimise the processes which underpin the knowledge society' so that Europe becomes 'the most competitive and dynamic knowledge-based economy in the world'.[17]

The Commission discusses what it calls economic and social cohesion. Its interest here is to improve competitiveness and reduce economic inequality. Economic and social cohesion is an instrument for reducing regional disparities through competitiveness and sustainable development.[18] In one particular publication it discusses social cohesion in terms of unemployment and poverty and says high unemployment is often accompanied by poverty and other forms of social exclusion.[19]

It says here that education is the 'most important medium' for imparting and demonstrating the principles of 'equity, inclusion and cohesion' and in

---

13 See World Bank (2006: 15) for the above material.
14 See World Bank (1994: 3).
15 See World Bank (1994: 11–12).
16 It has since contradicted itself on this point by stating it is 'misleading' to suggest that higher education brings 'meagre returns compared to investment in primary and secondary schools'. See World Bank (1994: 12) and (2000: 10) on the above.
17 See European Commission (2003: 2). The Commission uses the term university to refer to all higher education institutions.
18 See European Commission (2008: 3, 6).
19 See European Commission (2008: 7, 34).

this context 'social inclusion and active citizenship feature prominently' in the European goals for education and training systems.[20]

However, the Commission also says we should develop knowledge and skills to meet the needs, not just of the economy, but also social and political life. The Knowledge Age, it says, has implications, not just for economic life, but also for cultural and social life. In this context it argues we should encourage the development of knowledge, skills and competence for improving both employability and citizenship.[21]

The move to what it calls lifelong learning is urgent because of the need to strengthen competitiveness and improve the employability and adaptability of the workforce. This, however, is also urgent because we 'live in a complex social and political world' where we 'are expected to contribute actively to society, and … live positively with cultural, ethnic and linguistic diversity'. Its dual approach to lifelong learning therefore focuses on promoting employability for the economy and citizenship for resolving issues of social exclusion.[22]

IMPLICATIONS

The implications of the above are that education need not unduly concern itself with how graduates behave. It does a good job when it helps them build a capacity to handle, understand and develop useful knowledge and skills for the work world.

Therefore, course content and teaching methods should concentrate on preparing them to operate effectively in the knowledge economy. The dominant role does not centrally concern itself with what graduates eventually use their knowledge for, as long as they are gainfully employed and contribute to the economy. The OECD states here that the goal of personal development has become the 'acceptable face of individual ambition … even at the expense of others'.[23]

Therefore when we teach our courses we normally cross our fingers and hope our graduates never embezzle. Is this wise?

---

20 See Eurydice (2005: 8).
21 See European Commission (2000: 3–5) on the above.
22 See European Commission (2000: 5–6) on the above.
23 See OECD (1998a: 47).

Research on graduate values indicates there is plenty of work to do. This reveals that graduates on average have less respect for the law than those with secondary or primary education. It tells us they display relatively greater tolerance for tax evasion, drug taking, speeding, drinking and driving, making false insurance claims and buying stolen goods than others. With only one exception (falsely claiming benefits) graduates are 'significantly more ambivalent towards the law' than those with lower levels of education.[24]

Corporate scandals also lead us to question what some well educated people have done with their highly sought qualifications. There have been significant concerns expressed about activities such as price fixing, insider trading, theft, fraudulent accounting, bribery, the misuse of confidential information, and environmental misdemeanours.[25] There have also been lies by tobacco companies, criminal neglect of the dangerous nature of asbestos, and the suppression of adverse findings of deaths caused by certain drugs.[26]

The Director-General of UNESCO made an interesting point following the September 2001 terrorist attack. He said education that provides only knowledge does not provide enough – some terrorists, after all, have benefited from higher education. Therefore, he suggests our education system should help to cultivate values that support tolerance, respect and openness.[27]

Ethically challenged

Events such as weak values, corporate scandals, crime and terrorism indicate that we may live, not just in a knowledge society, but also in an ethically challenged one. Ours is a sometimes dangerous and often uncertain world where graduates have on occasion done dreadful deeds. These misdemeanours and events tell us a lot about the nature of our society.

This is because such events are not just one-off incidents. They can also reflect a systemic insight into the condition of our society. No event or misdemeanour – small or large – begins on the day it hits the headlines or gets noticed. It builds up over time and develops slowly out of view.

---

24 See Clancy, Hughes and Brannick (2005: 5, 17).
25 See Khan and McCleary (1996: 7) and Kaptein (2008: 1).
26 See Taverne (2008: 857). Although those involved in corporate scandals need not be graduates such misdemeanours often require people in positions of responsibility which in turn can often require a third level qualification.
27 See UNESCO (2001: 5).

When a big event occurs our communicators have a tendency to ignore or underestimate the real change. This is that a slow but systemic development has taken place. This development is reflected in a long string of small but telling incidents that are symptomatic of an underlying problem that should have been dealt with long before it became serious.[28]

Change

How do we change things? Aristotle said bad character is not likely to be changed by lectures. Therefore providing more ethics classes is not likely to help much.[29] We must distinguish between knowing and doing. Knowing something is one thing but doing is entirely different and is an act of the free will. Consequently people can fail to fulfil their known obligations.[30] Knowledge must therefore be supported by sound values and the will to carry out one's obligations.

Some feel we can improve our ethics courses by providing more engaging case examples and by getting students to do relevant experiential activities.[31] This is something which may be relevant to the service in service-learning.

We are indeed a knowledge society but we are also a society with issues which go well beyond knowledge. In the wider context we are a society which is challenged by misdemeanours, theft, corporate scandals, and, in extreme cases, terrorism.

Therefore, if we limit our conceptual apparatus to the knowledge role of third level, we ignore an important opportunity. We now consider another role for tertiary education – the ancillary one.

Ancillary Role

This role is subordinate to the dominant one and concerns itself with the wider needs of society and the individual in society. Indications of this role can be seen in some of the ideas of UNESCO.[32]

---

28   See Bernadette Bayada *et al.* quoted in UNESCO (2000: 24).
29   See Vallen and Casado (2000: 44), Donaldson (2007: 299) and Payne (2006: 177).
30   The free will is the capacity to make decisions. It has a habitual element reflecting the fact that people tend to have a certain way of doing things. See Lonergan (1958: 598, 612–614).
31   See Payne (2006: 177–178).
32   UNESCO is the only UN body with a higher education mandate. It helps governments and institutions develop strategies and formulate policies for higher education.

There are four areas of learning according to UNESCO.[33] First, there is *learning to live together*. This provides us with the ability to understand others and recognise our interdependence and our common challenges and risks. It encourages us to understand and respect others, implement common projects and, when necessary, manage conflict in an intelligent and peaceful way. UNESCO argues that this is the foundation of education in that the other three provide the basis of learning to live together.

Then there is *learning to know*. Here people need to know about economic, social, scientific and technological phenomena and be able to keep abreast of developments. This emphasises the need for a general education to provide us with a broad knowledge of things. This type of knowledge provides us with a foundation for lifelong education. General learning is complemented by in-depth knowledge of a selected range of topics or subjects in which the learner specialises.

Next, there is *learning to do* where people learn to do things by developing skills and competencies. UNESCO says skills and competencies are more readily acquired where students have the opportunity to try out and develop their abilities through work placement or social work experience.

Finally, students must *learn to be*. Here they should be helped to develop their personalities so they can act with greater independence, judgement and personal responsibility. This type of learning helps students develop important talents such as memory, reasoning, imagination, and aesthetic sense along with physical, communication, and leadership capacities.

Learning to know, do and be can be applied to both the dominant and ancillary roles of education while learning to live together relates to the ancillary one.

Elsewhere, UNESCO advises education to encourage both the 'intellectual and emotional development of the individual' and a sense of social responsibility. It also says education should be 'infused' with the aims and purposes of the UN Charter and the Universal Declaration of Human Rights.[34]

---

33 The points below are taken from UNESCO (1996a: 20–21, 37). UNESCO uses the term pillar rather than areas of learning.

34 See UNESCO (2000: 78) on the above material. The Declaration of Human Rights in fact states that education should promote understanding, tolerance and friendship among people.

Overall UNESCO's argument is that higher education should enhance ethical and moral values in society. In this respect it proposes the development of an 'active, participatory civic spirit among future graduates' and emphasises the personal development of students 'alongside preparation for professional life'.[35]

WORLD CONFERENCE ON HIGHER EDUCATION

UNESCO's most important contribution to the sector is the World Conference on Higher Education (WCHE). The first conference was held in October 1998 and the most recent one in July 2009.[36] The 1998 conference concluded with a Declaration on Higher Education.[37] Some of its points are important here.

Higher education should educate highly qualified graduates and responsible citizens by providing knowledge, skills and societal values to help them prepare for the economy and society.

In this respect it should cooperate effectively with the world of work and systematically take account of trends in the scientific, technological and economic sectors. It should also develop entrepreneurial skills in order to facilitate the employability of graduates and the creation of jobs. In addition, it should encourage the development of social responsibility, so graduates can participate in democracy and promote changes that foster equity and justice.

It should educate students to become well informed and deeply motivated citizens who can think critically and analytically, seek and apply solutions and accept social responsibilities. To achieve these goals we may have to 'recast' the curriculum and use different teaching methods.

In general the higher education sector should be scientifically, intellectually and ethically rigorous and be able to speak on ethical, cultural and social problems with authority so as to help society better reflect, understand and act on problems. It should also disseminate and, where necessary, defend the values of peace, justice, freedom, equality and solidarity.

It should have ethical standards, political impartiality, and a better articulation with the world of work and the problems of society. In addition,

---

35 See UNESCO (1995: 25–26) on the above material.
36 See www.unesco.org for the details on both conferences.
37 See UNESCO (1998) on the material below.

it should serve society and support the elimination of poverty, intolerance, violence, illiteracy, hunger, environmental degradation and disease mainly through its analysis of issues and problems.[38]

UNESCO has voiced its concern about wealthy young people who have a prolonged period of adolescence. These are full of energy but cannot always turn it to good use because of their long term dependency. Consequently they tend to have an 'existential anguish' and a 'desire to progress' so they can be fulfilled.[39] In this context UNESCO says that higher education must offer the young a set of values 'where the universal "We" takes precedence over the "I"' and where 'solidarity comes before competition'.[40]

UNESCO in a follow-up to the WCHE says the twenty-first century is the 'century of knowledge' where the 'university's main mission' is to 'help in knowledge production and dissemination'.[41] Therefore, when push comes to shove and a salient summary of WCHE is required, the knowledge goal survives the crush of detail.

Economy and Society

Higher education contributes to both the economy and society. What do these mean?

We use sociology to clarify our understanding of both concepts. Sociology is the study of society. It is also the study of human behaviour and social relationships and the social systems such behaviour creates.[42]

SOCIETY

Society is the largest group of people inhabiting a specific territory and sharing a common way of life. They share a common way of life because they interact

---

38 The above points are taken from Articles 1, 2, 6, 7 and 9 in UNESCO (1998: 21–24).

39 This description of prolonged adolescence reminds me of seeing a clutch of Kestrel chicks being refused food by their parents until they were forced to leave their nest. The parents spent all day calling them until they had no choice but jump from their nest. UNESCO also expresses great concern for those deprived of adolescence who are forced to accept poor working conditions, and are tempted to try the impossible in order to escape their situation. See UNESCO (1998a: 17).

40 See UNESCO (1998a: 24).

41 See UNESCO (2005: 16).

42 See Perry and Perry (1988: 9).

on a regular basis. In addition, they acquire behavioural patterns on which its members more or less agree. A society tends to be self-sufficient and to have had a substantial period of existence.[43]

All societies are united by their members being organised in structured social relationships and according to a particular culture. No culture exists without society and similarly no society could exist without culture. Without culture and the society within which it operates we would 'not be human at all'. We would have no language to express ourselves, no sense of self-consciousness, and 'our ability to think and reason would be severely limited'.[44]

Society contains five institutions or components – the economy, family, education, government and religion. These five are behavioural patterns that have developed around fundamental human needs. These needs must be fulfilled in order for the individual to survive and society to prosper.[45]

ECONOMY DOMINATES

The economy arises out of the fundamental need to provide food, shelter, and clothing. It entails production and exchange and is a key component of society because of how it can influence other areas.[46]

Why does the economy dominate the higher education debate? First, many go to college hoping to get a good job out of it. Its job preparation role has in fact expanded over time.[47]

Second, the identification of the link between knowledge and competitiveness underlines the economic importance of the sector.[48] The service sector now accounts for 'almost all new jobs' and since many services are knowledge intensive, knowledge has come to be seen as increasingly important for growth and prosperity. Consequently, education has been drawn into the growth

---

43 See Perry and Perry (1988: 60), Stark (1989: 40) and Baali (1988: 30) on the above.
44 See Giddens (2001: 22) on the above quotes.
45 See Stark (1989: 98–99) and Perry and Perry (1988: 50, 84) on the above points. Although religion has become less important over the years it remains a significant institution. Giddens argues that in spite of secularisation it still provides many with insights into questions on life and meaning that cannot be answered satisfactorily with rationalist approaches (2001: 552).
46 See Perry and Perry (1988: 84) and Giddens (2001: 688).
47 Those who receive their principal occupational qualification in higher education now include not only doctors, engineers and lawyers but also nurses, computer programmers, teachers, pharmacists, speech therapists, business managers, and so on. See OECD (2008b: 13).
48 See OECD (2007: 10).

agenda and much of the debate is now about how far the education system can go to 'respond to the demands of the knowledge economy'.[49]

Third, competition for public funding has increased as claims on the public purse intensify.[50] This has led to an increased urgency for higher education to establish its credentials and secure its support base in the public mind. In addition, all sectors, including education, have had to become more accountable and cost-effective. Therefore, the educational debate has of necessity become more focussed on economic and financial factors.[51]

Fourth, where education contributes to social or non-economic outcomes it may do so inefficiently. This may be because it is not as organised as it should be for this type of work. It may also be because education cannot solve such problems on its own and needs to develop better links or synergies with others. In addition, other sectors may be better at dealing with these issues.[52]

Service-learning

This latter point is important to bear in mind when arguing for service-learning. Where service-learning is argued for because it contributes to social outcomes it needs to do so effectively. It may also need to reconfigure itself so it can complement or at least not weaken the work of other sectors. There may also be better ways of dealing with societal concerns. For example, service-learning's interest in encouraging social change type service should not generate unnecessary expectations either within higher education or society.

Combining Both Roles

The dominant role argues that higher education should prepare students to operate within and support the economy. It does this by enabling students to learn knowledge. This knowledge should be economically useful, advanced and marketable and should allow them to become knowledge workers. Here

---

49 This argument is linked to the one which says we need to innovate to remain competitive. Here education is again drawn into the growth agenda by being asked to contribute to nurturing innovation and creativity. See OECD (2008a: 35, 36) on the above material.

50 For example, the public bailout of the banking sector in 2008 and 2009 and the continuing pressures from such areas as ageing, health, the environment, primary and secondary education.

51 See OECD (2007a: 21–22) on the above points.

52 See OECD (2007a: 22, 120) on the above material.

students are seen as customers who want marketable skills with minimum time, effort and cost. Graduates here hope to be able to develop attractive careers or a capacity to successfully run their own businesses. Such graduates are expected to earn a suitable living standard and be productive and adaptable.

Finally, they are expected to develop a capacity to support the cohesion of the economy. Here they are expected to have developed supportive attitudes towards the economy and positive visions of the future.[53] Figure 4.1 helps summarise the dominant role.

Figure 4.1   Dominant role of higher education

The ancillary role suggests that higher education has some responsibility for contributing to the student's values and ethical development.[54] The ancillary view arises from a concern for certain difficulties in society. Here misdemeanours, theft, corporate scandals, security problems and terrorism indicate weaknesses in society that the dominant paradigm does not consider.

This role, for the most part, shares the underlying philosophy of the dominant one in that it holds that the nature and main concerns of the person are economic and materialistic. It argues, however, that certain difficulties in the wider society may be ameliorated through a values role for education. However, these values are not called for because of a different philosophy or view of humanity than the dominant view. This is also why this role is called ancillary.

---

53 Here they develop a capacity to operate supportively within work and the broader economy. At a minimum this requires us to enable students to do no damage to the economy.

54 Providing students with ethical knowledge and attitudes to support the economy under the dominant view is not the same as encouraging graduate values to strengthen the wider society.

The ancillary role calls on third level education to make at least some contribution to strengthening society by encouraging students to develop values that help them live more effectively with others. The student can be helped to develop these values through encouraging, what UNESCO calls, the capacity to live together. Figure 4.2 helps summarise this role.

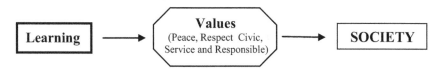

Figure 4.2   Ancillary role of higher education

This role however, does not call for a significant improvement in the ethical socialisation and values development of our students. This is not part of our remit. Nor is there any indication that we have the capacity to become involved in such socialisation.

Under this role however, we now have some responsibility for contributing to the development of a more ethical and moral person. However, building an operation that aims to 'form the person' is not on the tertiary agenda. From the staff's perspective the most we get here is a concern for the values and moral basis of academic professionalism. Here, for example, there has been a discussion of academic values such as truthfulness, respect, authenticity and magnanimity.[55] The ancillary role extends the values for our students to such things as peace, mutual respect, service, citizenship and individual responsibility. These, however, are only a subset of the values or morality of overall individual behaviour.

We now consider a composite role for higher education.

COMPOSITE ROLE

The composite role requires higher education to enable learning that generates and enhances student knowledge and values. Students should first be provided with a knowledge capacity that contributes to both their individual career needs and that of the broader economy. This role has both a cognitive and skill component.

---

55   See Nixon (2008) in particular Chapter 1, 4–7.

The ancillary role argues for graduates to be provided with a values capacity that helps contribute to the strengthening and well-being of the economy and also the society. The ancillary role has a values component in that it provides support for some third level contribution to the development of a more ethical and moral graduate.

In the composite role, although the knowledge objective (including both cognitive and skill elements) is primary, the values content cannot be ignored. Therefore higher education should concern itself with developing both a knowledge and values capacity in the student. Figure 4.3 summarises the composite role.

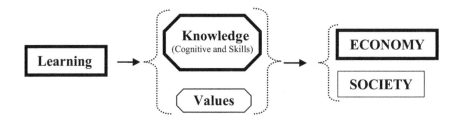

Figure 4.3   Composite role of higher education

Higher education should enable students to learn useful knowledge and values that enhance the economy in particular but also the society. This statement has implications for service-learning. This means that service-learning should be judged by how well it enables learning that generates and enhances student knowledge and values.

Conclusion

Earlier in Chapter 2 we identified the advanced and development forms of learning. These can be linked to our discussion in this chapter of the composite role of higher education.

This role requires higher education in general, and service-learning in particular, to encourage and support knowledge learning for working life and the economy. The knowledge capacity here has both a cognitive and skills elements in that the student must know things about the work world and be able to do things in or for it. In addition, the student must have knowledge of ethical values for economic cohesion.

The composite role however, also requires us to encourage and support the development of values that enable us to live harmoniously with others. This role is value laden.

This chapter provides us with a context and purpose for service-learning. In doing so it provides us with a standard with which to measure the usefulness or otherwise of any particular service-learning course.

We now come to the core of our book and look at service-learning in action. In doing so we move to ground level and look at a particular example of service-learning and how it operates in practice.

Service-Learning in Action: The Case Study

Elaine and I left the service-learning class.

> 'What a dreadful racket! Everyone is talking and arguing. How do you put up with it?'

> 'I'm sorry. What do you mean?' I replied.

> 'All that phone calling and texting; and what was happening over in the corner? One of those guys seemed to be getting a bit of stick. What was that about?'

> 'Actually he hadn't got the charity posters ready. His group was a little cranky', I said.

> 'How do you keep a handle on it? How could the rest concentrate with that racket?'

> 'Mmmh! I'm not sure. Maybe ...'

> 'What was all that stuff about up at the board when I walked in? There were three of them with you. They seemed to be telling you how to do the project. Aren't you the boss? I mean it's your class isn't it?'

> 'Well look. It's not ...'

> 'And the two women talking on the phone – how do they get away with that in class? Those two are final years aren't they?'

'*Look maybe it was a little noisy but they're doing really important* ...'

'*There was some buzz in there wasn't there?*' said Elaine. '*And did you hear those two talking about their visit to the homeless shelter?*'

'*I wouldn't mind that sort of activity in my class*'. '*My God, how boring can it be!*' she said.

'*Look it isn't always like this. Some classes are probably just as boring as yours, and anyway* ...' said I.

'*OK let's get some coffee. I need something strong after that*', and off she went.

Service-Learning in Action

Elaine had just walked in on a service-learning class in action. It is not easy to imagine how different service-learning can be and how busy it sometimes is; nor how much students can learn from it.

We can learn a great deal through service-learning. This is because it encourages not just subject learning but also skills and values learning. This is due to its mix of classroom and experiential activity and its altruistic nature. It is also due to its different learning locations where we have not just the classroom but also the situated learning locations of the charity, local school, home for old people, and so on. Here students have to learn on the run and under pressure working with and through others, many of whom are different from them and whom they have never met before.

Service-learning can also empower students. This happens where students are given complete responsibility for their service activity.

QUESTION

Can service-learning be this good? Can it really lead to knowledge, skills and values learning? We need some way to answer this important question. To do this we investigate the three service-learning modules mentioned at the start to see if they improve student's knowledge, skills and values.

CASE

The three modules provide us with our test pad for service-learning – our investigative case.

A case is a bounded object or a complex functioning system with working parts. It can be regarded as purposive and having a 'self'. In addition, it can have patterns, coherence and sequence.[1] In short a case is an object of research interest and something that with proper investigation can tell us a lot about a topic.

Although the three modules provide us with our case, not everything about them is relevant to our study. Clarifying our case unit is very important. This is because only certain aspects of the three modules are relevant. This is the situation with all case studies.

For example, if we are studying yellow fever, our case could be a male patient who survived the disease. Although we may identify him as the research case he is not in fact our case unit. The case unit or focus of the study needs to be much more closely defined. This can be done by looking at what the study is trying to find out. If we are asking why the patient developed yellow fever we should only focus on those aspects of the patient that can answer the question. The research question and some understanding of the average patient will help us narrow down and clarify the case unit.

This may seem a moot point. However, the individual is very broad and for analytical purposes hopelessly cumbersome. Some researchers make this mistake.[2] Similarly our investigation of the three service-learning modules needs to define not just the overall case (which is quite broad) but those aspects of it which form our case unit or focus. We must in other words bound and clearly define our case unit.

Therefore before we investigate the three modules we must clarify their nature and identify those aspects that need consideration. Elaine's one-off visit to the class gave her some insight into its operation. However, this one-off visit did not give her much insight into the knowledge, skills or values learning

---

1   See Stake (2000: 436).
2   For example, Yin makes this mistake when talking about a patient being a case. See Yin (2003: 24).

taking place. We therefore need to clarify the broad nature of our case and identify within that our particular case unit.

To do this we consider the three modules using what we call depth analysis. This analytical device can be used to help us understand any social structure.[3] Depth analysis operates by grouping the various characteristics of something into different vertical levels.

Depth Analysis

Each level groups different characteristics of the service-learning modules so we can get a clearer view of the nature and operation of our case (see Figure 5.1).

First, we have the physical level dealing with the physical attributes of the three modules. Then we consider the organisational structure and the various activity patterns. Next we consider meaningful objects. Then we consider emotional and knowledge characteristics followed by meaning and values. Finally, we reach the level of identity.

In travelling from the physical outer characteristics to the inner layers of knowledge, meaning, values and identity we go from the more visible level of the modules to the invisible. This is why we call the method depth analysis.

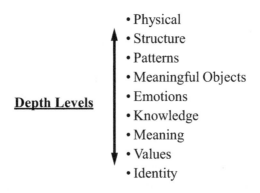

Depth Levels

- Physical
- Structure
- Patterns
- Meaningful Objects
- Emotions
- Knowledge
- Meaning
- Values
- Identity

Figure 5.1   Depth analysis: Service-learning modules

---

3   The depth analysis here is a development of the one used to analyse company organisation in Kerins (1999: Chapter 12).

We consider all levels in our depth analysis because they each help to clarify the nature of the modules. However, we focus on knowledge, values and patterns. This is because higher education in general and service-learning in particular should encourage the acquisition of knowledge and values as we discussed in Chapter 4. We also look at the patterns because they help provide the service-learning modules with their shape and form.

Physical

This refers to the physical characteristics of the modules such as students, teachers, classrooms, and other locations such as meeting, mentoring, and reading areas along with the volunteering sites.

Our three service-learning modules have particular physical characteristics. Service-learning was first piloted in September 2001 as a single elective. Following its success it was introduced the following September as three integrated modules. The student numbers are shown in Table 5.1.

Table 5.1   Service-learning numbers

2001/2	2002/3	2003/4	2004/5	2005/6	2006/7	2007/8	2008/9	Av.	Total
12	20	21	65	45	37	40	42	35	282

Service-learning classrooms are normally flat with loose tables and chairs to facilitate class interaction and discussion.[4] The modules are available in semester 1 of the academic year which runs from September to December. From 2001 to 2003 the modules were provided by two lecturers working together. Each had two teaching hours per week allocated to service-learning. This amounted to four hours in total and is equivalent to 25 per cent of a single lecturer's teaching load for any semester.[5] Since then one lecturer teaches the modules for 12 hours a week or 75 per cent of the standard teaching load.

Regarding student load, each student normally takes six full modules, one of which is service-learning. On average each full module is considered to

---

4   Rather than tiered for lecture type delivery.
5   Each lecturer has a standard weekly teaching load of 16 hours except where research, administrative, or other duties reduce this figure.

require 125 to 150 hours of work per semester. However, our research findings later indicate that some students feel they worked harder in service-learning than in other modules.[6]

Since the numbers of students who take service-learning are relatively small this may improve slightly the quality of the learning.[7] In addition, some classrooms may be more suitable learning locations than others. Therefore although the physical characteristics provide important background information it does not tell us whether or not the modules lead to knowledge, skills and values learning.

Structure

The structure level deals with the organisational framework within which the modules operate. This deals with the various positions and roles of those involved. The structure can be described by the standard organisational chart of management theory.[8]

The three modules operate within the School of Hospitality Management and Tourism, Faculty of Tourism and Food, Dublin Institute of Technology.[9] They therefore operate within a particular school, faculty and third level institute.

The School decides on the range of courses it offers. It then decides the core and optional subjects on each course. The three service-learning modules are offered as optional subjects from second or third year onwards on a number of full-time courses.[10] The students in all cases do their project for a particular beneficiary – a charity, school, home for old people, homework club, and so on. See Figure 5.2.

---

6   Each full module is worth five ECTS credits. The European Credit Transfer and Accumulation System (ECTS) is a standard for comparing the study attainment and performance of higher education students in the European Union (EU) and other collaborating European countries. See European Commission (2004).

7   For example, Boyer, Dwight, Miller, Raubenheimer, Stallmann and Vouk (2007: 345) state that 'students can be better served by small class sizes enhanced with active learning approaches'.

8   See Hunger and Wheelen (1996: 9), Ghoshal and Bartlett (2000: 184) and Hodge and Anthony (1988: 768) for example.

9   See www.dit.ie. The DIT is considering changing from a faculty to a college structure. If this change occurs each school will come under a particular college rather than a faculty, as is the case at present.

10 See the full-time courses at www.dit.ie/faculties/tourism/hospitality/full-timecourses. The modules are offered on five of these courses at present.

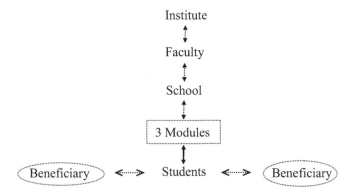

Figure 5.2   Structure: Service-learning modules

Students taking the module decide, in discussion with their lecturer, on the particular charity, school, organisation or community need to benefit from their project. The projects and beneficiaries can vary substantially.[11]

Although the structure level is useful background to our research work it is not our central focus. We now look at the patterns of activity.

Patterns

The service-learning modules rely for their strength and vitality on the activity patterns that underpin their existence. There are two activity patterns worth identifying here – formal and informal.

FORMAL PATTERNS

There are a number of formal patterns including the following: content and teaching patterns as indicated by the syllabi; skill patterns as indicated in the delivery methods; timing patterns as the modules run from start to end.

Syllabi

The three modules are part of the formal School curriculum. They teach project management, leadership and consultancy management using service-learning.

---

11   A small number of project examples are summarised in Appendix 2.

The title of the three modules is the Community Learning Programme (CLP).[12] Each of the three syllabi describes the aims and objectives of the module, the learning and teaching methods, course content and assessment method. In addition, it describes some of the operational features such as the nature of the volunteering project and the related protocol.[13]

In project management, students study some of the concepts and theory of project management, risk management, networking and negotiation.[14] They learn this theory in order to help them manage the volunteering project. In addition, carrying out the actual project can in turn help them to improve their understanding of the theory by reflecting on what happens.

They can then take the leadership module the following year. Here they study leadership, management coaching, and business ethics and these topics help them to lead a volunteering project.[15] Finally, consultancy management includes the theory of management consultancy which students use to carry out a consultancy project for a charity or similar organisation.[16] Each module is assessed by a report which is submitted at the end of the semester.[17]

Delivery methods

These modules use a number of delivery methods. First, there is the standard lecture format. Here the teacher delivers the course material and students take notes, listen, and when necessary, ask questions. Next is the tutorial format. Here the lecturer discusses with the class such things as the course theory or project progress. Students are more involved in this type of activity. Then there is the project mentoring and meeting format. Here the lecturer meets project teams and individuals to discuss project developments and plans. This takes place in class time. Students also plan such things as volunteering activities, team meetings, and study or report preparation. Elaine, as noted previously, arrived during a busy mentoring and meeting session as evidenced by the level of discussion, phoning, debate and activity that was going on.

---

12 This title was given in 2001 when the course content for the original subject was more general. The title reflected the fact that the subject encouraged learning through service in the community. It was only later that it we heard about service-learning.
13 The protocol refers to the etiquette or rules that must be observed in carrying out a project. This refers to issues such as risk, health, safety, finances and costs, and people's well-being.
14 This is called CLP Foundation. See www.dit.ie/anadventureinservice-learning/foundation.
15 This is called CLP Intermediate. See www.dit.ie/anadventureinservice-learning/intermediate.
16 This is called CLP Advanced. See www.dit.ie/anadventureinservice-learning/advanced.
17 See report details in Appendix 1.

The delivery methods and planned activities can be seen as formal work patterns. These can also be classified as skills since they require a complex set of movements with a multitude of integrated parts all requiring some practice. Thus the lecturing, tutorial, and mentoring work patterns require a lecturer with skills in those work areas. In addition, they require students with the skills necessary to effectively operate within these particular formats.

Therefore the physical elements of skills are embedded in this level. The cognitive elements are embedded in the knowledge level below.

Timing

The three modules are available from September to Christmas each year. They begin normally in the third week of September and the first few weeks are used to introduce the relevant course theory. Students are also briefed on how to organise and manage a volunteering project and are given examples of possible projects. Finally, they are advised on their project proposal.

The proposal is normally submitted and accepted by mid-October and the project runs from then to the last week of November – approximately seven weeks in all. Students then have two weeks to submit their report which is due before the Christmas break.

INFORMAL PATTERNS

These relate to such activities as unplanned mentoring, meetings, and discussions between the lecturer and students or between the students themselves. These can occur during unplanned visits, encounters, phone calls, meetings or discussions.

The patterns level is important to us in that it gives the service-learning modules their shape and form.[18] We now arrive at the meaningful objects level.

---

18 Aspects of such behaviour patterns can also be studied by work study and design. See for example, Gunnigle, Heraty and Morley (1997: 109).

Meaningful Objects

We deal with the physical characteristics of the three modules above – the things we can see and observe: the rooms, buildings, equipment, and so on – these things are important for the operation of any activity. Some of these objects, however, can in certain circumstances take on meaning for some or all of those involved.

In a study about the meaning of things it was argued that people contribute to the order in their life when they interact and work with the material world. The nature of this transaction will determine to some extent, the type of person that emerges. Thus the material things that we use and surround ourselves with are in some ways linked to who we are or who we are seen to be. These things give order to our lives. For example, people who have guns in their homes are by this physical fact different from those who do not.[19]

Meaningful objects can also locate us socially – for example, what students or teachers wear or use, what people drive or where they live can indicate differences. Therefore the transactions between people and things constitute an important part of the human condition.[20]

ARTEFACTS

An artefact is an example of a meaningful object. An artefact is used, modified or made by humans and provides an indication of the activity carried out by people. Artefacts can indicate meaning. In drama, for example, artefacts can relate to characters, relationships and contexts. Historical artefacts can give us an insight into times past. For example, the pyramids provide an important insight into ancient Egyptian civilisation.

The Bible can be considered an artefact.[21] The Book of Kells is an illuminated manuscript of the four Gospels produced by Irish monks around 800. As such it is an historical artefact and gives us an insight into times past, just like the pyramids or some other historical artefact.[22]

---

19 See Csikszentmihalyi and Rochberg-Halton (1981: 16) on the above.
20 See Csikszentmihalyi and Rochberg-Halton (1981: ix). See also Manzo (2005) section 4.1. Whereas the former study is about the meaning of domestic objects the latter is about the meaning of particular locations.
21 Dever (1993: 9) in fact says 'it ought not to be controversial to say that the bible is an artefact – that is something fabricated by the human brain and hand'.
22 See www.tcd.ie/about/trinity/bookofkells/#book.

DOMESTIC OBJECTS

People can have meaningful transactions with objects in the home. According to Arendt 'the things of the world have the function of stabilising human life' and people 'can retrieve their sameness, that is, their identity, by being related to the same chair and the same table, the same house'.[23] People who return from a period recuperating in a nursing home often find it nice to be back in their own house. Although they may enjoy the change and rest they often feel much better being at home. Even those who go on an extended vacation can be relieved to get back to their own place and things.

SYMBOLS

Symbols are also meaningful objects. A symbol is an analogue or metaphor standing for some quality of reality that is enhanced in importance or value by the process of symbolisation. It can also be a device for transmitting ideas or meaning between people that are often too difficult to articulate in words. Symbols can include written or visual objects.

Although a symbol may be a single object such as a wedding ring, symbols can appear in clusters and depend upon each other for their accumulated meaning and value. The cross is an important Christian symbol, the crescent moon is a significant Muslim symbol and the lotus flower an important Hindu one.[24]

Only some objects have meaning. Millions of objects are present to our senses but never properly enter our awareness because they do not interest us. People take a variety of meaning from the objects with which they react or none at all. In addition, the same object might be important to some but of little or no consequence to others.[25]

The locations, artefacts and symbols of service-learning may mean little to the participants because of their relative transience. Objects or locations become meaningful through the steady accumulation of experiences. When people have a variety of experiences in a particular place this can add meaning to the place, and people can then be seen to have 'collected' experiences in it.[26]

---

23 See Baehr (2003: 173–174).
24 The above benefited from Encyclopædia Britannica Online (2009e).
25 See Csikszentmihalyi and Rochberg-Halton (1981: xi, 5–6) on the above.
26 See Manzo (2005: 81).

Although students in our school can spend up to three or more years getting their degree the length of time spent on service-learning will be much less. Nevertheless a short service-learning module can be more intense and the objects more meaningful than other similar length modules. Some places or objects can develop meaning because of one or a small number of significant experiences.[27] Classrooms, libraries, or buildings, for example, can develop meaning for people. One particular teacher found that when he looked back at his time in college, he found that 'memories cling to almost every building that encloses the old campus'.[28]

In a similar way, the classrooms, artefacts or locations of service-learning may become meaningful for students. For example, as we saw above, they usually have flat classrooms rather than tiered ones and will have become familiar with particular charities, schools or such places as old people's homes.

The meaningful artefact, symbol or location characteristics of our service-learning modules, although interesting, are not central to this study. Emotions are our next level.

Emotions

Emotions are feelings reflecting fear, anger, joy or sorrow and can be associated with physical symptoms which may be observed. They can also be a quality of consciousness such as sadness or joy. Emotions have been studied by various disciplines such as psychology, biology, and psychiatry.[29]

Some talk about the role of positive emotion in learning. A class's ability to learn can be influenced by the emotions of its members. Here we can talk about the emotional and social harmony that facilitates the full realisation of a group's cognitive capacity. Emotion-based experiences can facilitate learning.[30]

Service-learning can, like any teaching method, generate emotions. However, its range of activity and learning locations is richer than many other methods and the variety and impact of its emotions can therefore be greater.

---

27 See Manzo (2005: 81).
28 See Sewall's comments at www.americanheritage.com/articles/magazine/ah/1991/2/1991_2_88.shtml.
29 See Microsoft Encarta Online Encyclopedia (2009) and Encyclopædia Britannica Online (2009f) on the above material.
30 See Goleman (1996) and Encyclopaedia Britannica Online (2009g).

In Chapter 9 students refer to some of the emotions it arouses such as shock, worry, and stress with one referring to how, at one stage, it felt like 'an absolute nightmare'. They also refer to the enjoyment, fun, inspiration, passion and satisfaction it produces.

Although emotional factors are important and they can sometimes reflect and affect how students learn they are not central to our study. However, the knowledge characteristics of service-learning are central to our study.

Knowledge

Knowledge enables us to do things. It informs and guides our activities and helps us deal with the unexpected. Knowledge, as we saw in Chapter 2, is the awareness and understanding of facts, truths or information gained through experience, introspection or reasoning. In addition, it is the understanding of the interconnections betweens such things. Because we can be mistaken we also define knowledge as the set of beliefs held by people about causal phenomena.

Learning is a flow that changes the stock of individual or organisational knowledge. Some talk about knowledge reservoirs or wellsprings.[31] In this context the three modules can be seen as a knowledge source or pool which students can dip into for one or more semesters.

The knowledge level deals with an important aspect of our study. The next level is meaning.

Meaning

When we acquire new meaning we in fact learn something new. The acquisition of meaning, in this context, is a form of development learning. When something has meaning, it has a special significance or implication for us. The development of meaning is based on experience and our experiences are examined and filtered for meaning in order to help guide our action.

---

31   See Leonard-Barton (1995: 3). These she says are constantly being replenished with streams of new ideas which provide an ever-flowing source of organisational renewal.

Having plenty of experience does not necessarily cause learning. Experiences must be meaningful, if learning and development are to occur. When we extract meaning from an experience, we are better able to understand it. Certain experiences such as those dealing with relationships, autonomy, vulnerability, conflict and mortality can have an important impact on meaning-making.[32]

The service-learning modules provide the opportunity to have new and meaningful experiences. First, students experience the running of a volunteering project and the meaning-making and decision-making that comes with this. In addition, they have the opportunity to have their classroom theory take on deeper meaning as they work their way through and reflect upon their project activity.

The meaning level, although not central to our study, is considered because of its impact on learning in general and knowledge and values in particular. The next level is values which are a central focus of our study.

Values

Values refer to the intrinsic or relative worth, importance or goodness of things. Values are important because they provide a standard which we can use to formulate opinions and judgements. Values therefore provide a general standard for action and living. Values can also refer to the efficacy or capacity of something, as we saw in Chapter 2.

Higher education, according to some, has being encouraged to instil values such as individualism, materialism and competition. Others argue that individualism can increase loneliness, something which is offered only slight relief in hard work, money, and success. It was also suggested that children over nourished on TV and the mass media can lack a sense of values and become rootless.[33]

In Chapter 1 we saw that service-learning could encourage social justice, civic and social responsibility values which are completely different to the individualist, materialistic and competitive values referred to above.

---

32 See our discussion on meaning in Chapter 2.
33 See Chapter 3 for a more detailed discussion of the above points.

In the discussion of our research findings later we distinguish between what we call values of efficacy and values of service. Values of efficacy refer to improvements in personal efficacy through such developments as improved confidence, independence, and increased responsibility. Service values refer to such things as people becoming aware of others, appreciating others or caring for others. The approach to values adopted here therefore distinguishes between what we term the efficacy or capacity type and the altruistic or caring type.

The values level is important to our study. This brings us to our final level, identity.

Identity

Our three service-learning modules (referred to locally as the CLP as mentioned above) can be viewed as an entity and can be seen as the total volume of their characteristics or levels. This refers to the sum total of their physical characteristics, structure, patterns, meaningful objects, emotions, knowledge, meanings and values.

It can more narrowly be defined as the shared or common levels. Most of those involved in the three service-learning modules have common or shared physical locations, structures, patterns, meaningful objects and knowledge. They may also have some shared values, meaning and emotions. This shared element can be defined as the service-learning identity.

Alongside the total volume of patterns lie the shared ones. These shared patterns facilitate people working together.

In addition to the total volume of meaningful objects from the three modules are the shared ones. For example, a particular Microsoft clipart image was used to represent service-learning during the early years. It was incorporated on notices, lecture notes, and elsewhere and became a sort of short-hand symbol for the teaching method.[34]

As well as the total volume of knowledge we have the shared knowledge. This shared knowledge helps people to understand one another. Beneath the variety of individual values, meaning and emotions lie the shared ones. The

---

34   The image cannot be displayed here because of the Microsoft licensing rules relating to clipart. My thanks to Kyle Boyd-Stevenson from Microsoft for his advice on this point.

shared values, meanings and emotions help people to understand and interact with others.

Shared values can arise from a common belief system and may form the basis of such things as a common code of conduct or mission statement.[35] Shared emotions could arise, for example, when some tragic or wonderful news touches a class.[36]

Although the identity level is not a focus of our study it helps to clarify the final depth level and rounds off our discussion of this particular example of service-learning. It also helps to better clarify our particular case for investigation purposes. As we saw earlier a case is a phenomenon or integrated system with working parts that may even be considered to have a 'self'.[37]

Case Unit

Is our case unit the total service-learning phenomenon containing the sum total of its characteristics and levels? Is it, alternatively, the narrower identity with only its shared or common characteristics?

QUESTIONS

We define our case unit by considering the nature of our enquiry and the sort of questions we are interested in answering.[38] We are interested in finding what students learn or discover in service-learning. We are interested in the type of knowledge, skills or values they learn.[39] We are also interested in how well it

---

35 See De Geus (1997: 115). DIT's *Vision for Development 2001–2015* states, among other things, that the Institute must take account of the needs of society and the community it serves (DIT, 2001: 7). This statement gives some encouragement to service-learning.

36 During a second-year economics class a few years ago news broke that a class member had died in tragic circumstances the night before. The shared emotion that developed in that class from the tragedy created a special bond during their remaining time in college. Alternatively, a class win in an institute-wide competition could also strengthen the class atmosphere.

37 See Stake (1995: 2). Stake however, does not clarify what he means by having a self. By contrast we explain what it means and place the self or identity within the context of the CLP structure and levels.

38 These refer to our research questions. See Yin's point here (2003: 23).

39 Chapter 2 states that our main focus was on the advanced forms of learning, knowledge and skills, and the values element of development learning. This focus tallies with the composite role of education which concerns itself with the cognitive, skills and values learning of students as discussed in Chapter 4.

prepares them for the world of work and society?[40]

Therefore our case unit concentrates on knowledge and values. However, we have also considered the patterns level in some detail. This is because of its importance in helping us clarify some of the essential characteristics of the case unit. See Figure 5.3.

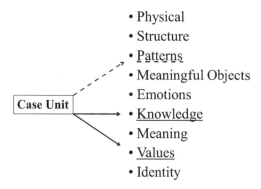

- Physical
- Structure
- <u>Patterns</u>
- Meaningful Objects
- Emotions
- <u>Knowledge</u>
- Meaning
- <u>Values</u>
- Identity

Figure 5.3   Case unit: Service-learning modules

Although other levels can have an impact on our enquiry we concentrate mainly on these three levels.[41]

What information do we use in our enquiry? We investigate our three service-learning modules using different three different information sources as follows:

- 71 interviews from four previous studies.[42]

---

40 This interest corresponds with the composite role of education which focuses on the concerns of the economy and society.

41 We use depth perspective as a heuristic device or analytical framework to help us conceptualise the CLP so we can better identify our case unit and clarify its boundaries. This device allows us to decide that our case unit should significantly focus on knowledge, skills and values. It also clarifies other elements of the CLP such as the physical, structural and patterns elements. In addition, it provides us with a framework for meaning, emotions, symbols and the overall phenomenon itself – what we call the identity.

42 The student interviews are taken from 71 semi-structured, one-to-one interviews from the following four studies: Guinan (2004) (ten interview transcripts); Gao (2005) (15 transcripts), Kieran (2005) (13 transcripts) and Kerins (2008) (33 interviews). Gunian's study is an undergraduate dissertation, Gao's and Kieran's are both postgraduate dissertations and Kerins' is a PhD study. The 71 interviews contain approximately 300,100 words (approximately 82 per cent from Kerins, 7 per cent from Guinan, 6 per cent from Kieran and 5 per cent from Gao).

- A key informant interview.[43]

- Student grades.

The findings from these different sources help us to cross check or triangulate the individual pieces of information. The triangulation metaphor comes from navigation and military strategy where different reference points are used to locate an object's exact position. Given the basic principles of geometry, multiple perspectives may allow for greater accuracy. In a similar way, some argue that researchers can improve the accuracy of their findings by collecting information on the same phenomenon from different sources.[44]

However, triangulation lacks a theoretical framework for identifying the exact manner in which the different methods actually observe, or 'measure' the 'same' object. We cannot, therefore, say that each of the different methods used provide a partial view and together they offer a more complete picture.[45] Therefore, triangulation is nothing more, in our case, than an additional way of reflecting on different sources of information on our topic.

INTERVIEWS

The interviews used a semi-structured approach based on a standard list of question areas or topics. At times, the question order varied depending on the flow of the interview and on occasion, additional questions were asked if additional information was needed.[46]

Guinan's, Gao's, and Kieran's interview transcripts are analysed. These were kindly provided by the three authors. Kerins' interviews are analysed through a study of both the transcripts and the digital recordings.

43 See Kerins (2008). This was a semi-structured interview with Karen O'Sullivan who taught on a team basis for two hours a week (with the present author) from September 2001 to January 2004. Her interview took just over 1 hour and 30 minutes and the transcript contains approximately 15,200 words. O'Sullivan is a key informant. This is because she is a 'knowledgeable source of information' with 'specialised' and 'context-specific' information and 'insight' on the topic. See Tremblay (1957: 689), Johnson, Buehring, Cassell, and Symon (2007: 25), Calantone and Di Benedetto (2007: 7) and Buetow, Adair, Coster, Hight, Gribben and Mitchell (2003: 89).

44 See Jick (1979: 602).

45 See Schröder (1999: 50). The geometric image of data converging on a single point is a little simplistic and researchers can end up with findings that converge weakly or are inconsistent. There are also other difficulties with triangulation. Therefore, although triangulation has some use, researchers must use their judgement to interpret findings. See Murray (1999: 196) and Mathison (1988: 17).

46 Rantz's case study of higher education uses additional questions as 'depth probes' to improve the quality of his study (2002: 459). The interviews took a non-directive approach. Here the information provided to the interviewees in advance of the interviews stated that they were autonomous research participants and were respected for their opinions and insight. They

Therefore, the finding in Chapter 7, for example, that 69 per cent of students indicate it increased their concern for others, does not imply that 31 per cent found it did not. Similarly, the finding that 49 per cent found they learned more about communications does not imply that 51 per cent did not. The semi-structured approach allowed them to bring up the type of things, for example, that they felt they did or did not learn.

Conclusion

This chapter described the nature of the service-learning modules using depth analysis. This analysis along with the discussion in Chapter 4 on the role of education determines that the research will focus on the knowledge, values and skills aspects of the modules. The information sources used in the research are student and key informant interviews and student grades. We now consider the research findings in Chapters 6 to 9.

---

were also reminded of this point at the start of, or during the interview, as necessary. This was important since the interviewees had studied under the interviewer.

PART 2
Research Findings

Part 2 deals with our research findings and is based on an analysis of 71 student interviews, a key informant interview and an analysis of students' grades. The pace and pattern of the language is different here to our previous chapters since much of it is based on what students say about their experience.

Part 2 contains the following chapters.

6.   Knowledge Learning

7.   Values Learning

8.   Preparation for Work and Society

9.   The Service-Learning Experience

6

Knowledge Learning

What do students discover in service-learning? What type of knowledge or skills do they learn? What type of values do they learn? How well does it prepare them for the world of work and society?

To answer these questions we look at what 71 different students say about their experiences. These students have some interesting and important points to make.

We outline what they say about their experiences and quote them directly. We also summarise some of their points statistically.

Organisation of Findings

Because of the variety of findings we organise the points under the following headings – knowledge, values, preparation and teaching method.

In this chapter we summarise what students say they learned in terms of knowledge improvements. Here we find they learn more about communication, team work, organisation and management. They also learn time and event management, interpersonal skills, negotiation, project management and networking. Finally, some of them mention risk management, self-knowledge, self-learning, planning, leadership and life skills.

In Chapters 7 and 8 we look at how it affects their values and how it prepares them for work and society. In Chapter 9 we summarise what they think of their service-learning experience.

To help check some of our findings we compare or triangulate service-learning grades with other grades. We also check our findings by looking at the views of one of the service-learning lecturers who we regard as a key informant.

Students found they learnt more about the following – communications, team/group, organisation and management. This is followed by such areas as time management, event management, negotiation and networking.

We calculate an approximate measure of the numbers of students that indicate the different areas of learning.[1] The results are displayed in Figure 6.1.[2]

Comments on Knowledge Learning

We now look at some of the points made by students on what type of knowledge or skills they learned. Most students quoted below are identified by a pseudonym. In addition, their service-learning project is mentioned and we are told whether they took service-learning once or twice prior to their interview.[3] Some however, are only identified as either male or female.[4]

COMMUNICATION

Communication is the largest result at 69 per cent. Some interviewees made interesting comments here.

Hao admits he was 'shy' communicating with strangers and felt that project helped. Lei made a similar point.[5] Anne says it 'really helped me in communications because [the] communications [class] we did … was all theory based [with] just … one presentation at the end'.[6]

---

1   The data here and in Chapters 7–9 are based on the best interpretation of what the students say in the interviews.
2   The data are: communications (49 students or 69 per cent overall); working in teams or groups (48 or 68 per cent overall); organisation (53 per cent) and management (38 per cent); time management (32 per cent), event management (31 per cent), interpersonal (28 per cent), negotiation (25 per cent), project management (23 per cent) and networking (21 per cent). These areas of learning are followed by indications of risk management (17 per cent), self-knowledge and self-learning (15 per cent), planning (10 per cent) and leadership and life skills (7 per cent).
3   These are from Kerins (2008). See the relevant footnotes and Appendix 3 for the details.
4   These are from Guinan (2004), Gao (2005) or Kieran (2005) where the extra information is not available.
5   Hao, Lei and Zhu ran a day-long Chinese culture festival for staff and students in the faculty. This included information on such things as Chinese tourism, food, and the city of Beijing. It also included a Chinese movie and a table with some Chinese food and tea for tasting.
6   Anne did a charity makeup workshop with Susan for the Children's Sunshine Home (see www.sunshinehome.ie).

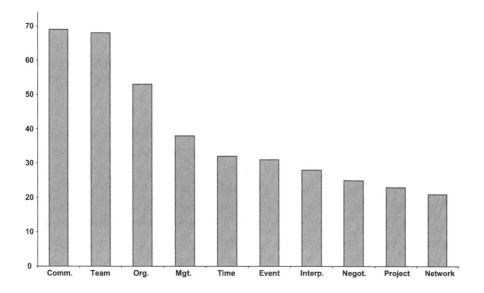

Figure 6.1   Knowledge and skills learning (% of 71 interviews)

Lynn says her first-year communications class was 'not very relevant'.[7] However, 'when you were out there and you had to talk to people everyday and … communicate with them … little things' came back 'like picking up on body language' or the way people present themselves.

Joan by contrast 'took out' her first-year 'communications notes and reread them to make sure that I was actually communicating right with people'.[8] Cindy says it brought her skills as a manager 'together … because you have to constantly communicate… when you're in management'.[9]

---

7   Lynn took service-learning twice. Her first project supported the learning and swimming activities of pupils in the Central Model Infant School. This was carried out with Bill and another student. Her second one on homelessness entailed volunteering in a day centre for young homeless people and running an awareness seminar on the topic (see www.pmvtrust. ie). This was done with Bill.

8   Joan ran a fundraising and awareness project for sick children with two others, one of whom was Holly who we meet below. This entailed planning and implementing a raffle and awareness seminar for Make a Wish Foundation (see www.makeawish.ie).

9   Cindy had taken service-learning twice. Her first project was a fundraiser for Temple Street Children's Hospital in Dublin (see www.templestreet.ie) with three others one of whom was Bridget who we meet here. Her second project was with Mandy and one other and organised fun events for children with cancer in Temple Street Children's Hospital.

In a similar vein, Holly says that 'to be a good manager' you must 'be able to communicate' and 'understand' people.[10] She says she was communicating with 'real people' in her project and says 'you're not going to get that just from studying'. Like Hao and Lei she too admits to being 'shy' and found it 'hard to talk to adults'.

Holly 'hated going in' to shops looking for sponsorship because they always seemed to be 'busy'. Then one day she said to herself 'hang on a second ... we need to help [the charity]... it only takes two minutes out of their day'. After this, she says 'the more I talked to the public the more confidence I got'.

Bridget learned a lot from the group difficulties that beset her first project so she was keen to avoid these the second time around.[11] As a consequence, she encouraged her new team members, who were both doing it for the first time, to meet more often to ensure good communications.

Lynn refers to the importance of listening and says this 'was the biggest skill I learned'. In her primary school project she learned how to 'listen to the child'.

In her homeless project, she learned to listen 'from the heart' even though it 'got to you some days'. She found here that when she sat down with someone 'on a one-to-one basis and asked them a few questions ... it could be upsetting'. Although she 'might be getting upset' however, she found 'they weren't getting upset' because 'they'd turn around and they'd make a little joke' or they would 'lighten the mood a little bit'.

TEAM/GROUP

Teamwork is the second largest result at 68 per cent. Asdis was determined to avoid teamwork at the start and originally proposed a project that she could do on her own. She did not like working in groups and felt that working on her own got 'rid of all the hassle of having to find an appropriate time to meet' others.[12]

---

10 Holly, as we saw above, ran the fundraising and awareness project for sick children with Joan and one other.

11 Bridget took service-learning twice. First, she organised a fundraising event for Temple Street Children's Hospital with Cindy and two others. Second, she did the alcohol awareness project with Cormac and Asdis.

12 Asdis's first proposal was turned down.

As it turned out she worked in a group and found it 'a positive experience'.[13] She was surprised to find that in spite of 'being busy' there are ways of accommodating group working. As a result of her experience she says her teamwork skills improved.

Some compare the team experience here to group assignments. In a group assignment Deirdre says you 'meet up, divide the work, then go off ... meet up the day before it's due and have it all done'.[14] By contrast, this type of teamwork 'is on a different scale ... we were continually doing it ... together'. She says 'we both backed each other up and ... one wouldn't have been able to do it without the other'. In the end 'we both just went for it together'.

Grace says group assessments are 'so easy' since you just 'do your bit the night before ... hand it in, and have it done'.[15] With this however, 'we were constantly on the phone trying to arrange things ... trying to get the whole thing stuck together, so ... we really had to ... gel together'. Grace's team mate Tracy says her other group experiences were not 'as constant'. Here by contrast they had to 'meet up and do something every day'.

The team skill learned here paid dividends for Amy.[16] For example, she found it helped her with an important group assignment in another subject. Here, for the first time ever, she was 'the person to step up and give them a call and go listen why aren't you in, this is our mark [sic]'.

Ellen felt her team operated for an 'awful long time' and 'were constantly meeting up' and 'building on ... each other's ideas'.[17] She found you had to be 'very calm [and] ... keep control' to be an effective team member.

---

13 Asdis did an alcohol awareness project with Cormac and Bridget. This entailed the planning and implementation of an alcohol awareness seminar and two information stands in the faculty.

14 Deirdre did a nursing home project with another student. The project included weekly visits to a nursing home. (Note: the home cannot be identified because of a negative comment later in the text.)

15 Grace ran a rape awareness project with Tracy and one other. This included information stands and a seminar in the main faculty building in liaison with the Dublin Rape Crisis Centre (see www.drcc.ie).

16 Amy did a project with Mary and Theresa on drug awareness. This included a drug awareness day in the faculty incorporating both an information stand and seminar. It also included visits to two drug rehabilitation centres – Merchants Quay Dublin (www.mqi.ie/Home.shtml) and Ballymun Youth Action Project (www.ncge.ie/service.asp?id=CG031005).

17 Ellen did a project with Nora and Sinead (who we meet later) for a city centre primary school. This was a four-person project, three of whom were interviewed. The project supported the learning and swimming activities of pupils in the Central Model Infant School. It also ran a football and music event for the pupils.

Elena says she normally took the 'back seat' in any team assignment.[18] However the 'feel' of the team element was 'different' here, it was 'more active ... more alive' and 'we had more ... deadlines'.

Here she realised she could affect other people's performance unless she carried her share of the work. She also realised that in a group project you 'don't think of ... individuals you think of the outcome of the group'. As a result, she 'stepped it up a gear'.

Eoin admits his group 'could have done a lot more as a team' and feels 'you should be able to trust the people you work with'.[19] Cindy found that people must 'learn to be fair ... working so closely together'.

Anne 'learned how to work as part of a team' although she admits this was a difficult process.[20] This was partly because her team mate held strong views. However, she found the experience taught her 'to be stronger'.

Her team mate Susan confirms Anne's point by admitting to being 'very independent' and saying she 'wanted to do everything' herself. However, by the end of the project, she found she became a better team player and became more reliant on her colleague.

Lucy found you must learn 'how to deal with people's personalities' and 'work through' problems.[21] You must learn 'to deal with other people's attitudes and personalities and how to get through it as opposed to shouting your opinions across at them'. In the end, her group resolved their problems 'otherwise the project would have just collapsed beneath us'.

Aileen confirms Lucy's points.[22] Her group 'learned a lot in the first [project] because we had a lot of conflict'. They eventually sat down and talked rather

---

18 Elena organised a five-kilometre charity walk for the Irish Cancer Society with Cathy and one other. This included an information stand in the faculty, fundraising activities, and a five-kilometre walk in the Phoenix Park, Dublin for the Irish Cancer Society (see www.cancer.ie).

19 Eoin, with two other colleagues, ran an all-day soccer tournament in aid of the Irish Heart Foundation (see www.irishheart.ie).

20 She did a charity makeup workshop with Susan for the Children's Sunshine Home (see www.sunshinehome.ie).

21 Lucy had taken service-learning twice. Her first project was a fundraising 'swimathon' for the Special Olympics with Aileen and one other. This was held in the National Aquatic Centre in Dublin (see www.nationalaquaticcentre.ie). Her second was a charity breakfast with Aileen and Dusan. This was held in the student cafeteria for Childline (see www.ispcc.ie/childline.htm).

22 Aileen took service-learning twice and did both projects, as explained above, with Lucy.

than 'shout at each other'. As a result of this experience they 'knew what to avoid the second time'. The second time around, they decided 'to prevent any problems or confusion' by talking about things and sorting them out and this worked 'a lot better'.

Cormac's points are rather interesting.[23] The project he says starts with 'an idea you come up with ... something that inspires you or ... that you really want to do'. The idea however is 'out there' and you have to 'take it from out there and ... make it real' you have to 'create it'. He found however that it can often be 'out there and you're not quite sure how you're going to make it happen'. He felt at one stage during the project that they 'started being out there as well'. However, in the end they pulled it together and 'suddenly ... when you see the result for yourself it's real, you know you've seen it'. He says 'you couldn't all sit back and ... hope that someone [else] ... organised it'. He found that his 'biggest' learning was team work.

ORGANISATION

Organisation is the third largest result at 53 per cent. Aileen says she is 'more organised now because of it'. However, some students indicate that organising even a relatively small one-semester project is quite a task.

Sinead says students 'don't expect that it's going to be so much work'.[24] Eoin says 'you have to go out on the road ... meet ... different people and [try] to get something off the ground'. He admits he was 'winging it sometimes'.

Grace says her project 'was such a big ... project for us to do, we hadn't done anything this size before' and 'we all really had to ... pull our fingers out and actually work'.

Her team mate Tracy 'would be more confident ... next time' in 'organising something from scratch'. She admits to being 'nervous' in case it 'flopped'. She says that to 'organise it from scratch ourselves ... was actually a lot of hard work'. She was surprised 'how hard ... it was to get started'. She says that 'just to pick our topic and ... organise someone to come in and talk ... was a lot of work'.

---

23 Cormac, as we saw above, did an alcohol awareness project with Asdis and Bridget.

24 Sinead, as we saw above, did a project with Nora and Ellen for a city centre primary school.

Finally, Elena says 'it was definitely a course that I will remember ... so much organisation and then it [did] not ... completely materialise'. She says 'we recruited eighty people ... everybody gave us their word' and 'only seven ... appeared' on the day.

MANAGEMENT

Management at 38 per cent is fourth.[25] Andy found it 'good practice' for management.[26]

Asdis came to college to apply theory to practice as she comes from a family business where 'it's your whole life ... you live and breathe it'. She found she could link her service-learning experience to management theory by reflecting on the different management styles. She also found she could understand her team and leadership experiences through reflecting on the theory and realised that management theory provided 'guidelines' on motivating.

Cindy says 'it brought my skills as a manager together'. She also says she learned 'more managerial skills' in service-learning than in her internship. Amy says she learned 'how to put the management theories that we'd learned in the last couple of years into practice'.

Aileen however, was lukewarm about its contribution to learning management and says you learn 'a little bit ... but not much'. She feels it helped to enliven the management theory on 'leading, controlling, [and] organising' along with 'some of the newer theories'. However, she says that the learning depends on whether or not 'you actually realise it'.

Susan is rather scathing about management as a subject. She said 'Management 1 was a lot about theory, a lot of boring stuff'. She feels it did not teach her how to 'work in a hotel [or] how to manage front line staff, it was more Maslow's hierarchy of needs, you know all the different theories, which

---

25 The 38 per cent refers as normal to the average management result for the 71 interviews. Management lies in third place at 64 per cent in Kerins' study. In contrast it is joint eighth at 16 per cent in Gao, Guinan and Kieran. Although the data variation is sizeable, the real difference may not be as remarkable as it appears. This is because interviewees sometimes used management learning as a catch-all for other outcomes. For example, Joan says it helps 'management skills in the sense of team work ... communicating ... marketing skills and ... accounting'. In addition, Kerins' study was more focused on identifying learning outcomes.

26 Andy did a project with Maeve for Larkin Community College, a secondary school in the centre of Dublin. This supported the physical education teachers and their students (see www. larkincommunitycollege.ie/about.html).

I found a load of rubbish, who cares'. She felt that service-learning 'taught us how to manage per se an event'.

Cathy says the experience helps you 'learn how to manage people'.[27] Without service-learning she would still be 'immature' and 'would not know how to deal with people'. She found it 'helps you manage everything better' including 'your time … your life' and staff. She says 'when you are a manager and something goes wrong you need skills to be able to assess the situation' so as to 'come up with … solutions'. She continues 'everything is not going to go perfect' but service-learning 'prepares you for that because you've got to look at your project and you've got to assess what could go wrong … [and] come up with possible solutions … in the same way a manager has [to]'.

Strategic management theory she says did not prepare her for management 'because it is just airy-fairy and you are falling asleep … you should be there doing [it] and understanding why you are doing it'. Finally, she says you 'learn from your mistakes, because then you can see how it benefits you'.

Bridget makes a similar point when she says it helps management learning because 'you remember what worked for you and what didn't'. In a similar vein, Sinead says you learn about what 'you are responsible for' not what you are told.[28]

Anne found it brings management theory to life and says it was her 'first taste of management' where 'instead of having to write it all down, you actually get to live it'. In a similar vein Lynn says that management theories 'give you the ideal situation' but 'they don't give you … the reality, because there's no feeling there'.

TIME MANAGEMENT

Time management comes fifth at 32 per cent. Grace says 'the biggest thing I learned' was about 'managing your time correctly … returning phone calls' and keeping appointments. She admits missing an important appointment early on in the project and had to wait 'weeks to get another one'. Lin feels her time

---

27 Cathy had taken the CLP twice. Her first project was with three others including Mandy. This organised a four-day cancer awareness project in the faculty. It also included a seminar and fundraising activities for the Irish Cancer Society (see www.cancer.ie). The second involved a five-kilometre walk for the same charity with Elena and one other as mentioned earlier. This was held in the Phoenix Park.

28 Sinead, as we saw above, did her project with Ellen and Nora for a city centre primary school.

management skills improved after the module and says that 'when you deal with stress you deal with time management'.[29]

Asdis admitted being 'a last minute person' and worked 'best under … pressure'. Therefore, she had 'a tendency' to do assessments just before they are due. However, she confesses that staying up 'for forty hours' to get an assessment done on time 'is no fun'.

Having experienced 'breaking' her project 'down into … achievable sections' she realises this 'is a much easier way to approach [tasks]'. She says the experience helped her with other time sensitive activities such as her 'monstrous' thesis which she broke into 'many mini deadlines instead of one massive one'.

Finally, Eoin says when you manage time, money, or people 'your failure was measured on time'. Therefore, he says you have to be 'very economic with your time'.

EVENT MANAGEMENT

Event management comes next with 31 per cent.[30] Zhu had worked two years in marketing and already had event management experience.[31] However, this is the first time he says he had the opportunity to be responsible for a full event.

Tracy found that there was 'a lot of work' in organising an event and 'a lot of preparation'. Cormac says events 'don't come together by chance … you can't hope for [them]'. In a similar vein Bridget says 'oh God we'll never get it done' but then says 'once you get into it … it's better'.

Cathy found that 'whatever problems happen within your event … are your problems … and that's the whole thing about it'. She says 'I never thought I could have ever done an event and I never thought the [charity] would take

---

29 Lin did a project for the Harcourt Nursing Home, Adelaide Road, Dublin with two others. This involved weekly visits to the nursing home and a small event at the end on Chinese culture for the residents.

30 Event management learning in Kerins (2008) scored 45 per cent amounting to 65 per cent of those who ran event-based projects. Examples of an event project are fundraising or information events. Other types of projects, for example, include weekly visits to nursing homes, schools, or shelters. Although such projects may contain a small closure event, they rely mainly on weekly activities.

31 Zhu, as we saw, ran a day-long Chinese culture festival for staff and students in the faculty with Hao and Lei.

... us seriously'. Her surprise seemed to stem from the fact that she 'always thought students were looked at ... as dossers [sic]'.[32]

Finally, Amy says 'I learned that I love planning events'. She says 'we planned a big event' but 'didn't like it at the time'. This was 'because of the pressure ... was it just all going to fall through'. However, she says she 'really loved it when the day went off ... without a hitch it was just a great ... experience'. Amy seems relieved it worked out.

INTERPERSONAL

Improved interpersonal skills came seventh at 28 per cent. Some of the comments were as follows. Lei learned 'how to deal with people' even though she was 'scared' and 'shy' at the outset.

Bill has 'strong views' on how 'to deal with things' and feels he may 'come across as a bit ... cocky and know-it-all'.[33] However, 'to organise your project you have to talk to people and get on with them, you can't be too shy or you'll never do it'. He found his group had to learn to 'work around ... and understand each other'. He says that to get support you have to 'get people on your side' and convince them 'you are doing them a favour'. He found it took time to get the 'confidence to do that and be articulate enough to say ... we are doing you a favour really ... would you like to give us a hand ... we could be promoting your company ... it's helping out the community'.

Although Theresa says she prefers 'doing projects on my own' she now realises the benefits of working with others.[34] Mary one of her team mates says she used to look at things 'from my point of view' instead of from the 'other person's' but she now tries to 'look at it more from their point of view'.

The third member Amy always 'sat in the background'. However, 'I am much better able to deal' with things because the 'project really brought me out

---

32 Dossers refer to lazy people or malingerers. When someone is said to be 'on the doss' they mean they have taken time off without permission. See B. Ryan's use of 'dossers', 'on the doss' and 'dossing', in Seanad Éireann (1982).

33 Bill, as we saw earlier, had taken service-learning twice. His first project, with Lynn and one other supported the learning and swimming activities of primary school pupils. The second entailed volunteering in a day centre for young homeless people and running an awareness seminar on homelessness in the faculty.

34 Theresa did her first service-learning project on her own. This entailed planning and managing a fun and education day in a rural primary school. Her second one was with Mary and Amy on the drug awareness project discussed earlier.

of myself'. She is 'a lot more opinionated' now and by the end of it says 'you weren't looking at … your group anymore as friends, you were looking at them as people doing a project and you had to get it done, so you had to be as happy or nasty with them as needs be'.

Susan and Deirdre were both affected by the people they came across. Susan visited very sick children as part of her project. She found her experience 'teaches you to be able to deal with other people' and says when you come across disabled people in work 'you do not want to be … disrespectful' or 'uncaring'. She feels 'being able to deal with that is a huge skill'.

Deirdre had to deal with elderly people some of whom were terminally ill and says 'it was very hard dealing with people like that'. In the end she says she 'learned a lot about myself and what I can cope with'.

Cindy says she learned 'how to manage myself better with people' and 'deal with conflict'. She found that 'things can change in a second, your plans … [can] be destroyed and you have to come up with something else. … you have to be calm … you cannot just go "ok, I'm going to give up"'.

Cathy had problems with herself in her career but says service-learning 'helped me to get over them'. She admits she has very little patience and finds it difficult to deal with people. She found her two projects helped her to 'develop patience … and learn how to … conduct myself and be more professional'. When she speaks to her managers now 'rather than screaming at them … I talk to them and that was basically from [service-learning] because I got benefits when I spoke to people nicely … I got benefits when I was patient'.

We now consider the less common results. Negotiation, project management and networking, comes next followed by risk management, self-knowledge and self-learning, planning, leadership and life skills.

NEGOTIATION

Negotiation skills have a 25 per cent result. Some of the comments were as follows.

Susan 'learned how to negotiate' and 'take on board other people's opinions'. Lucy's team negotiated 'how to get each other's points across' and how to 'put them all together' and resolve difficulties and 'keep going'. Cindy similarly learned how to negotiate with team members and 'manage myself better with people' and be 'approachable' and 'fair'.

Lynn felt negotiation played an important part in both her projects. She says when you were dealing with people, you 'had to get them to come around to ... your way of thinking'. Aileen admits to being 'very shy' but having done service-learning twice is 'more confident ... negotiating with people'. She explains how her team got the National Aquatic Centre to support their Special Olympics project. The manager said 'he doesn't ... mind giving us the lane for free but he'd like some publicity'. As a result, she says 'we had to negotiate around that ... we got the *Irish Times*'.[35]

It helped Cathy 'understand how to negotiate' and 'go out into the business world and act as a mature adult rather than a student and work with people out there who aren't part of college and aren't going to protect you'. When you go looking for prizes, sponsorship or event speakers she says you need to know your 'bottom line'. She mentions that she was doing another module on negotiation and although 'some people in my class don't get it' she did because of her service-learning experience.

Finally, Amy says she did not realise she had learned negotiation skills until she had to reflect back on her experience when she was writing her report. Up until then, she says 'I just thought I was talking to people'.

PROJECT MANAGEMENT

Project management came next with 23 per cent. Some of the comments here are interesting.

Zhu said that the most important thing he learned was 'how to run a project from the beginning to the end'. Matt explains this point as follows: 'you learn how to take an idea' and identify the 'steps that we need to take to make this work, to manage it, to keep it under control, [and to] make sure it doesn't get too big'.[36]

---

35 Aileen and her group got some coverage for the event in the *Irish Times*.
36 Matt did a project on homelessness in the Capuchin Day Centre, Dublin with two others. This involved weekly visits to help in the centre. See www.churchandhalston.irishcapuchins.com/Day_Centre.html.

Lucy explains that you are the 'general manager' of your project 'so you decide … how it goes and what you want to do'; therefore, 'you have a lot more responsibility to make it work'.

Finally, Amy says her project 'was so big' that if her group had 'sat back … it would have all unravelled'. She found 'you had to really keep on top of it and write down exactly what you needed to do and when you had …[to] have it done by and who was going to do it'. She says that 'we had to keep on top of it all of the time, so project management was a big thing, a really big thing'.

NETWORKING AND RISK MANAGEMENT

Networking and risk management come next with 21 per cent and 17 per cent respectively. Those indicating networking simply noted the information without adding any commentary worth mentioning. However, two interviewees made some interesting comments on risk management.

Cindy says she 'definitely' learned risk management. Although she 'knew about it' she 'never really understood it until' she was 'in a situation where something goes wrong' and you 'have to find a way … out of it'.

Amy's group had to 'assess the risks that we were going to undertake'. Consequently, they 'sat down and discussed was this something we wanted to do, how risky is this going to be'. She says it was 'a giggly experience … sitting there going, "oh God this is something I'd never do on a normal basis", but we'll do it anyway it's for the project and we soldiered on'.

SELF-KNOWLEDGE, SELF-LEARNING AND PLANNING

Self-knowledge and self-learning are next at 15 per cent followed by planning at 10 per cent. There were a few interesting points on self-knowledge.

One student mentions that the project helped 'identify… who [and] what you are and how you cope and … react'.[37] Andy found he learned 'a lot about' himself and talks about the 'disadvantaged school' he volunteered in with 'every kind of race and religion in it'. He admits 'I wouldn't have been used to that at all'. He admits that a 'lot' of his friends 'would have just [said] "no way, get away from me"'.

---

37 When we do not identify the student name the quote is taken from either Guinan (2004) Gao (2005) or Kieran (2005). This quote in fact comes from one of Guinan's transcripts.

Amy says 'I learned more about myself. More about … what I was capable of doing and definitely things I was not capable of doing and that I had to work on'. She found that she was 'very determined'.

Finally, Susan admits she was 'very scared about going into' the children's home where 'children [were] dying' and one kid was 'screaming' when she arrived. However, she 'didn't break down' and said 'no I can deal with this'. She explains how she 'had to kneel down' and 'touch them because they only … respond to touch'. She confesses that she would not 'have been able to do that before'. Her experiences made her realise 'life's not all about you … going out at the weekend, money, drink … there's other things'.

LEADERSHIP AND LIFE SKILLS

Leadership and life skills both score 7 per cent. Those indicating leadership simply noted the point without adding any thing worth quoting. However, two students made interesting comments on life skills learning.

Susan says her boyfriend goes to college where he is 'one of five hundred people'. If he misses classes, 'it's grand' because 'he gets notes off the Internet, Oh happy days'. She does not feel this type of education 'teaches you any kind of life skills' whereas service-learning 'teaches so much, even about yourself'. She says she does management and HRM but 'they're boring … you can't relate them to life, whereas this [you can]'.

Cathy says you can go into an accountancy or economics exam and 'you're regurgitating stuff that you read over the night before … that's not going to help you in your life because the minute you leave that exam that's gone'. However, service-learning 'was much more like stuff you [are] going to remember and skills you are actually going to … use when you're older'. She says 'I can deal with a lot of things now that I couldn't' because of service-learning 'there's a lot of skills in yourself that it teaches you'.

Triangulate

We now check our findings above by triangulating the results with the views of the key informant. We also look at the type of grades service-learning students achieve.

KEY INFORMANT

The key informant says that 'each student ... was different and came away with different experiences'. She found that 'every single one of them had changed' after service-learning and 'those changes could be either positive or negative and would certainly influence the way they developed and progressed further'. She says that no one 'expressed regret at having done it or ... that they didn't come away with some new knowledge about themselves ... about the way they worked or about the things they knew'.

Subjects

She refers to some of the subjects they learn. She mentions time management here and says 'most students never write ... an action list ... what tasks needed to happen first and by what ... deadlines'. However, they begin 'to learn the consequences of ... events' through their project experience. She also indicates they learn management, project management, risk management, networking, and how to develop alternative scenarios.

Integration

Students, she says, learned to 'think outside the box'. She feels that they 'very often' learn other subjects 'in boxes'. However, when they do service-learning they 'realise' that they have to use 'more than one subject ... [to] achieve an end result'. In this way, the modules help to create 'the bridges ... between the boxes' because it 'forces them' to conceptualise the links between subjects 'in order to achieve their ... project'.

They therefore 'integrate' the knowledge, principles and theories learned in different subjects and this process is a bit 'like doing a jigsaw puzzle'. Putting it another way she says they take the 'pieces and fit them together to create ... a different picture ... perspective or ... a new task ... in order to accomplish an overall project'.

GRADE ANALYSIS

We also analysed service-learning grades earned by students over a six-year period. The analysis tells us that the service-learning grade is 9 per cent on average more than the overall average of the relevant year and course.

To the extent that high grades reflect successful learning we can say that the grade analysis, limited and all as it is, supports the knowledge findings above.[38] There are however, some points we need to take into account here.

First, Howard, as we saw in Chapter 1, states that students should get credit for the learning, not for the service. The service-learning modules are assessed by a report as detailed in Appendix 1. The report facilitates the assessment of learning from such resources as lectures, textbooks and research along with that from the service experience. In this respect, part of the assessment is to link the learning from service to the project management, risk management and other theory learned in the service-learning lectures and to other management theory learned in other subjects. While the report, however, is not marked on the service, a critical mass of service is still needed to reflect on, so students can adequately complete the report.

Second, the 9 per cent grade difference mentioned above must be treated cautiously for the following two reasons: (a) I have been involved in grading the reports over the years. Having said that, however, I am part of an examination system that uses external examiners and, where necessary, peer review to check or moderate grades; and (b) the grading instrument used here is not the same as in other modules. Therefore, a direct comparison of grades is not possible.[39]

Conclusion

Our students tell us that our service-learning modules generates learning in a wide variety of important knowledge areas such as communications, team learning, organisation, management, time management and the like.

The key informant in general concurs with these findings and adds that service-learning helps to integrate subjects from different parts of a course. In addition, we find that the service-learning grades are on average higher than the overall average of other subjects taken by the students. We now look at values learning.

---

38 See Appendix 4.
39 Other issues here are referred to in Kerins (2008: 14.2.4).

7

Values Learning

How does service-learning affect students' values? How does it impact on them?

To identify what impact it has on values we summarise what students say on the topic. Here we outline what they say and quote them directly. We also summarise some of their points statistically.

Students indicate that their confidence and concern or care for others improves. They also indicate that their understanding of others and their sense of responsibility increases.[1]

We calculate an approximate measure of the number of students that indicate how values are affected. The results are summarised in Figure 7.1.[2]

Comments on Values Learning

We now look at some of the points made. One student remarked that 'I don't think it creates values … but it can certainly enhance them'.[3]

---

1   In Chapter 5 we distinguished between values of efficacy and values of service. An improvement in confidence or responsibility is a value of efficacy or capacity. By contrast an improvement in a student's ability to understand or care for others is defined as a service value.

2   The data are: an increase in confidence (41 students or 58 per cent overall), those who come to care for others (35 or 49 per cent overall), increased understanding of others (42 per cent) and a greater sense of responsibility (35 per cent).

3   Most of the students that have already been quoted in Chapter 6 are identified by a pseudonym and have their project details mentioned. These details are summarised in Appendix 3. Some students as we saw, however, can only be identified as either male or female.

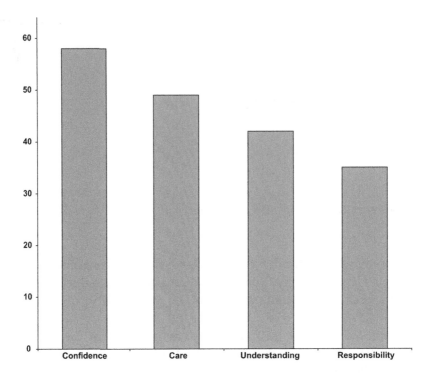

Figure 7.1   Values learning (% of 71 interviews)

CONFIDENCE

Improved confidence at 58 per cent was first. Some were quite blunt on this issue.

One student said it made her more outgoing and determined, 'because we did three projects and only the third one lasted ... it gives you confidence'. Elena says she became 'more confident' where 'normally' she would 'feel intimidated'. Bridget is 'definitely more confident and more assertive' because her project required her to 'go out there'. Theresa admits she was nervous 'in the beginning' but got a 'huge confidence boost' when her project finished successfully.

Susan, who was already 'very confident ... very out there', says it gave her 'a different type of confidence'. She explains that it helped her approach 'people in situations that I didn't feel comfortable in' and admits to being 'very scared about going into the home'. She 'didn't break down and start crying' but decided 'no I can deal with this'.

In more colourful language, Andy admits he would normally be 'laid back' and 'let someone else do it'. Here however, he was 'more raring to go' and says he now has 'more self-belief'.

Lynn admits she was 'right down' during her project and 'didn't know what to do'. However, the experience of bringing 'ourselves back up' strengthened her confidence.

Amy says 'it made me a lot more determined … it made me believe in myself'. She was 'shy' and 'always wanted people to think the best of me'. Consequently, she 'was always striving for perfection … so much so that I … got walked over'. However, after gaining 'more confidence in myself, and learning how to … get my point across without … thinking, "did that sound cheeky?" … I went into my new job and sat there and … went "yes that's fine I'll do my ten hours … but … is it alright if I have the weekend off?"'. She says 'you have to be courteous to people, and … still be strong in getting your point across'. Amy also found it helped with her family and 'can now talk to my parents as equals'.

Finally, one said it gave her 'an opportunity to open up and be myself … to stand up and say, I can do this'. She says 'it has had a big impact on who I am and what I am now'.

CARE FOR OTHERS

Care for others came in second at 49 per cent. Some made interesting comments here.

Deirdre was surprised by her experience in the nursing home. She 'didn't know what to expect' when she first went but thought it might be 'a nice experience'. She found however that it was 'a horrible experience for the people that are there'. After her project, she decided she would 'never ever put any of my family members in a home. I'd rather take them in and look after them twenty-four-seven [sic]'.

Some commented on their experiences with schoolchildren. Ellen, for example, found it 'sad' because the families were 'completely different' from what she was used to and said the children were 'very open … they'd tell you anything'. Nora 'felt sorry' for the children when she saw some of the 'parents coming to collect them … the way they treated them … the state of the parents'.[4] At the start Sinead 'was indifferent' about such children. She now feels however, that some children in disadvantaged schools are 'being brushed under the carpet' and says the experience 'changed me'.

Others made interesting comments on sick children. Cindy says seeing sick children 'changes your perspective on a lot of things'. She says 'it's very sad, but at the same time' she says 'they're trying to be happy and … keep smiling'. She found that her first day 'was really hard … really terrible'. However, 'the more we went in the more we wanted to continue going in'. She found it 'rewarding … in lots of different ways' and says 'you're happy with yourself for starters, you're helping somebody else and you see how happy they are'. She also says 'you have fun at the same time … you have to enjoy it'.

Anne who visited sick children in a home says 'it definitely makes you more caring'. She explains the process as follows. In 'the first week you might … "oh whatever" you know, but … by the end of it … your opinion completely changes'. This she feels is because you 'experience something different [from] any other subject'.

Bridget says 'it was great helping out'. She adds 'not a lot of us would have the opportunity to help out … it wouldn't even come into your mind … all that you were thinking about was college and what we were doing at the weekend'.

Joan says 'everybody is really selfish in our society today'. However, service-learning 'has [a] role … in the sense that it opens your eyes to what else is going on'. She says you are 'still thinking about yourself … and your project but you're also thinking … of wanting to raise as much money as you can for a certain organisation'.

Lucy says 'students are very consumed with their college work'. She feels 'they don't really think about anything else' because 'as soon as you have your assignments finished you've got your exams to worry about' so they 'focus on themselves'. She says it is 'good' to 'focus on … something else' and says 'it felt good to help other people'.

---

4   Nora as we saw earlier did a project with Ellen and Sinead for a Dublin city centre primary school.

Cormac says it gives students 'an opportunity' to do something 'for somebody … less fortunate'. He says 'it's good to do a project and … think of other people rather than thinking about yourself'. He feels it would 'be great if everyone could go out with that frame of mind … because a lot of people leave college and … it's all about me' and 'what can I get for myself'. He says 'the world is a lot bigger than yourself … there's always people less fortunate than you' and 'you can make a difference'.

Cathy took service-learning a second time because it 'changed' her, 'because I came … to care'. She says it made her 'aware that I can do stuff like this'. She elaborates, 'I could have done any other module and just sat and relaxed through it and did whatever, but this' was important to her, this is 'something that I value'.

Finally, Amy says she did her project 'to help people'. However, she feels that in the end 'the only person that I really and truly helped … was myself'.

UNDERSTANDING

Improved understanding comes third with 42 per cent. Some of the comments here are interesting.

Asdis says the alcohol awareness project helped her 'make sense' of the difference 'between me as a foreigner and the Irish'. She 'was very hard on the Irish' but now says 'I understand their perception' of drink. She feels that in terms of what she is used to at home in her own country 'they're still alcoholics but here they're not … and I'm not going to change that'. One of her team mates, Cormac says bluntly that 'people don't take the thing serious enough' here.

Sinead said the standard of teaching and learning in her project's primary school 'isn't up to scratch'. She was surprised 'how much they differed from the children in … the school I went to'. She says 'the focus wasn't on learning' but on 'getting the stuff done … discipline, and trying to [keep] the kids quiet'. She says primary education forms the 'basis for your life' and asks if that is 'not adequate what type of human being are you going to turn into?'

Teachers should inspire children because 'when I was in primary school everybody loved our teacher … it was really engaging … we learned so much'. She feels they 'should be correcting them and helping them … to speak'. She says they are 'growing into little people now and they should [not] be speaking like toddlers'. She found the children did not know 'how to [put] a sentence together' and 'their lack of vocabulary … amazed me'. However, they had 'no problem saying curse words' and knew 'exactly how to … insult somebody'.

After her experience in the nursing home Lin says 'we are in our early twenties … and we just don't have the right to say "oh my God, my life is a mess; I got to give up, I can't do this anymore"'. She says 'you just don't have the right to say that'. This is because there are people in a much worse situation than we are 'and they're still happy'. She says her project showed her 'how to respect old people'. It also helped her understand that 'however stressful your life is somebody out there might be … in a worse situation. It's never give up'.

Some did homeless projects. For example, Lynn says it 'changed my opinion a lot on homeless people … I have more understanding'. She was surprised to find that the homeless centre was 'very happy' and found 'everyone got on really well and there was always lots of chat and … laughing'. She says 'they weren't embarrassed to talk about it, but I think that's the way the centre's run'. She became 'more tolerant and less judgemental of people and their situations' during her project.

When Matt originally saw homeless people on the street, he would have been inclined to 'cross the road'. However, his project gave him 'a better understanding … of life and how cruel it can be'. Another who had done a similar project said that 'seeing… and talking to them … you realise these are people like you'. A homeless person could be a family member, a friend 'it can happen so easily'.

Some did projects on sick children. Lucy admits that 'just seeing' children in hospital 'changes your perspective on a lot of things'. Mandy says 'you don't really understand … until you go in and see them children [sic] … and what they have to go through'.[5]

Three who did a drugs project had interesting things to say. Mary for example, says people often look at those on drugs and 'all they see is the drugs'. They do not realise that someone is 'a different person on drugs'. Theresa says

---

5   Mandy had taken service-learning twice. Her first project with Cathy and two others was on the four-day cancer awareness project for the Irish Cancer Society. Her second one, with Lucy and two others carried out a series of planned activities with children in the playroom of Our Lady's Hospital for Sick Children, Dublin.

she was 'very judgemental' before the project and would say 'Oh! It's only a druggie'. Now however, she would say 'look they have their own problems'.

Amy says it made her look back at her friends who were doing drugs and made her 'stop and think that God that was obviously a really big problem that they had'. She says 'now I know that it's not just as easy as that [to give up drugs]. So ... I don't look at it any more as "oh they're kind of stupid for doing it"'. She now realises 'it's a problem'. She says 'it gives me a better understanding [of] why they were taking them, why some of them ended up ... having ... an overdose and dying and ... it's let me accept it in myself, I'm easier in myself now'.

RESPONSIBILITY

An increased willingness to take responsibility comes fourth with 35 per cent. A number made interesting points here.

Elena admits she has not been as reliable normally as she was in her service-learning module. For example, if she had to telephone someone 'traditionally I would have stuck that number in the bottom of my bag and [lost] it'. However, she made a point of doing her share of the work in her project where she 'felt responsible' for her actions.

Sinead found she could not dodge things and say '"oh I won't go back after lunch, I'll go off into town shopping or something and I'll miss that lecture" but this you couldn't miss'. She explains that it 'invoked a bigger sense of responsibility, I suppose because it was for ... a good cause and you couldn't really let ... people down'. She feels 'the beauty of the thing [is that] you aren't assigned a project ... you find [one] for yourself' so its not 'something ... you're told, it's something ... you are responsible for'.

Bridget says 'it was the first chance we got to have any responsibility really for anything' and 'in the end it was on your own neck if it didn't go through'. In a similar vein, Nora refers to taking 'charge' of her project and feeling more 'in charge as the weeks grew on'. She says 'you have to be mature about it. There will be setbacks and there will be things that won't work out ... which you have to deal with professionally and maturely'.

Andy says he was the 'main man' here rather than being the person 'just … standing there'.[6] In an ordinary class, you 'sit there in the back and scratch your head'. Here however, 'when you have to go out and do it … it has to be done and that's it'.

When Lynn's first project failed they decided to 'pick ourselves back up straightaway and say "right we're going to find something else to do"'. Therefore, 'instead of letting it get to you' and 'being knocked back … you just have to get on with it'.

Students do not usually have anyone to mind, and 'have very little … responsibility' says Susan. So, when people hear you are a student they can say 'oh college, yeah sure, that's for dossers [sic], they don't do anything in there'. However, she could reply, 'no, I'm actually running an event for college … I'm helping [a charity]' and they respond 'Janey Mack! That's brilliant!'[7]

Dusan says 'in work, hey sometimes you have a hangover and you're kind of "oh I don't want to go in"; not that it's happened to me.[8] However, here you cannot call your group members and say "oh I'm sick I can't do it"' because if you do 'the whole armoury … is weakened … and the links are broken'.

Tracy points out that it is different to work placement or food and beverage practicals where students are 'told what to do'. Here they 'did it all' themselves 'from scratch'. She says 'we actually had to take responsibility' and felt that 'if it fails … it's on your back … not on someone else's'.

In placement, Lucy says the company decides 'what you do … when you can do it and how you can do it'. However, here 'you're the general manager of this project, so you decide really how it goes and what you want to do' and 'you have a lot more responsibility to make it work'.

In a similar vein, Cathy says 'internship or work placement problems are not your fault, you do not deal with problems, you give them to your manager'.

---

6   'Main man' is the important, influential, admired person or hero. See *Merriam-Webster Dictionary* (2009) or *Oxford English Dictionary* (2009). It is clear from the context that Andy regarded himself as the important or responsible person in his project.

7   'Janey Mack' is sometimes used instead of 'wow'. See 'Business Travel Report: Irish Have Gift of Gab' *Daily Herald*, Arlington Heights, Illinois, 27 November 2005, p. 9.

8   Dusan took service-learning twice. His first project, with a colleague, was a charity dinner in the faculty's main training restaurant for the Central Remedial Clinic, Dublin (see www.crc. ie). His second one with Lucy and Aileen was a charity breakfast. This was held in the student cafeteria for Childline (see www.ispcc.ie/childline.htm).

However, these problems are yours, 'no one else is going to ... take the blame'. Internship she says is a 'protected environment ... because your college are watching the firm [and] the firm are making sure nothing happens to you'. For example, 'if you go back to college and say ... "I was not treated nicely" they [say] "it is ok ... we will not take on board what they said". But, [this] is real life, there's no protections'.

Triangulate

We now check the above findings by considering what our key informant says about its affect on values.

CONFIDENCE

We found it improves confidence. She corroborates this by saying that it improves 'confidence ... self-esteem ... [and] self-respect'.[9]

RESPONSIBILITY

We found it encourages a greater sense of responsibility. She concurs here and says that 'ultimately the outcome was their responsibility' and since 'they had projected what they were going to do they worked hard at making sure that it happened'.

UNDERSTANDING

We found it encourages a greater level of understanding of others. She concurs and says it changes attitudes 'because they begin to see a perspective beyond their little bubble ... their safety zone' and because 'they are exposed to other societies and cultures' and 'to people not so fortunate'.

As a result, they become 'conscious of their surroundings' and are 'no longer isolated ... [or] privileged'. All of this 'allows them to be more temperate in their attitude ... and ... more tolerant'.[10]

---

9   Confidence and self-respect are synonyms for self-esteem. See Microsoft Encarta World English Dictionary (2009b).

10 A number of interviewees indicate greater tolerance. For example, Ellen, Theresa and Mary talk about becoming more tolerant. Lynn talks about becoming 'more tolerant and less judgemental of people and their situations'.

They also 'begin to develop … empathy for other people … an appreciation that … not everything is always black and white and that what they believe to be right doesn't always follow for someone else'.[11] In this respect, 'they begin to see … and … understand the grey areas'.

CARE FOR OTHERS

We found above that it encourages students to begin to care for others. She concurs here and says they have 'the rough corners eased off them' and become 'more temperate'. She feels there is a 'strong "me" generation' out there where people say 'what's in it for me mate', 'I'm always right', 'when I demand something I'm given it' or 'the teacher will see me through'.

The original motive for taking it can, she feels, be self-interest since some students may be attracted to doing the modules because there is no exam. However, when they get going they tend to become involved and 'become more aware of the project and the reality'. By then some students have said to her 'I really don't care what mark I get because what I've achieved is much more important'. Therefore, although they may 'start out with a … selfish focus … by the end of the journey the student … is now focusing on the outcome for … other people'. They are now thinking 'am I going to get … the speakers … sell the tickets … raise enough money?'

She says they stop thinking 'am I going to be the biggest, the best and the most wonderful' and start thinking about 'how much can I achieve to help this particular charity'. In this way, they start focusing 'on what they achieve for somebody else'. Therefore, what they value in the project can change from a selfish to a less selfish or more caring perspective.[12]

Finally, she says they begin to 'value other human beings … [and their] contribution'. In addition, she talks about how they 'learn about the value of the connection [between] people' and 'begin to realise and value others … human dignity and equality'.

---

11 Empathy is the ability to identify with and understand somebody else's feelings or difficulties. One of its main synonyms is understanding (*Encarta World English Dictionary* 2009).
12 Her view reflects certain aspects of the service spectrum we discussed in Chapter 3.

OTHER VALUES

She also refers to how students learn practical things about 'good and ... bad behaviour'. This she says is 'a little bit of ethics' but she feels it is also about 'protocol', 'etiquette' and 'politics'. She says the 'experience teaches [you] how to ... create a good impression ... for yourself and ... your project' and says however, that while 'some students learn very quickly ... others don't'. We did not discuss these items above. However, there are indications of these points in some of the interviews.[13]

Conclusion

Many found they became more confident after their service-learning experience. Even some who considered themselves confident at the outset seemed to develop a new type of confidence.

They also indicate that became more responsible for their activities. Some in fact indicate that they found their service project place a greater level of responsibility on their shoulders than anything else they did in college including such things as class practicals, work placement or internship.

Some found the experience helped them to be more understanding of other people and more tolerant. They seemed to grow from their contact with whatever group they worked with on their project – whether it was homeless people, sick children, drug addicts, and so on.

Finally, some went further than this and began to care for those they met. Here some realised that they might have been too focused on their own concerns and not realised that there are many out there who are an awful lot worse off.

---

13 These are found in some of the interviews in Kerins (2008). For example, Nora says you 'have to deal with things properly and professionally' since you are 'out there in the real world dealing with professional people'. Lucy found she 'had to be quite professional' and Cathy says she learned how to 'conduct' herself and 'be more professional' and operate in 'business more ethically'. Susan talks about how she can now 'deal with people in a more ... professional way'. Cormac says 'you've got to be professional in your approach if people [are] going to take you seriously' and that sort of thing is 'almost ... on the line of ethics'. Asdis talks about finding out about 'the right way of going about things' and says, 'there's even school politics here, booking an office, things like that, and this is something that was identified in the ... negotiation part of the theory'. Finally, Mandy says 'you could have ... all the qualifications in the world on your CV' but she says 'if you don't have the right attitude there's no point hiring' you if you are 'not going to be an asset to your company'.

8

Preparing for Work and Society

How does service-learning prepare students for operating in the world of work? How does it prepare them for living in society?

To answer these questions we outline what students say on the topics by discussing their opinions or quoting them directly. We also summarise some of their opinions statistically.

Most students feel it helps prepare them for work life and society. The society results are slightly larger than the work life ones. We first look at work preparation.

Most students feel it helps prepare them for work (22 interviewees or 67 per cent). Some have mixed views (six or 18 per cent) and one says it has no relevance.[1]

Among those indicating a positive result, some refer to its sectoral relevance, a few to personality development and one to its effect in developing skills.[2]

Comments on Preparing for Work

We now look at some of the points made.[3] First, there are those who feel it makes some contribution to preparing them for work.

---

1 Kerins (2008) provides this information. Four students offered no comments here. However, two of the quotes used below are from Kieran's transcripts (2005).

2 To be exact 15 (46 per cent) refer to sector, four (12 per cent) to personality and one (9 per cent) to skills.

3 As before most students quoted are identified by a pseudonym. In addition, their service-learning details are mentioned when we first meet the student either here or elsewhere. These details are summarised in Appendix 3.

YES VIEWS

The majority (67 per cent) feels it contributes to preparing for the world of work. Some of these feel it contributes to preparing them for a particular sector.

Sectoral relevance

For example, Maeve says the skills learned will help 'when I'm working out in the leisure industry'. Here she mentions dealing with children, camps, swimming classes and time keeping.[4] Andy who is 'planning on going into PE' says it was useful because it was 'first hand experience'.

Others mention its relevance to the event and conference sector. While Susan mentions this she also refers to its particular relevance in her project for preparing her to deal with disabled people in the workplace.

Others refer to the hotel sector. Hao says the hotelier will choose applicants who did service-learning 'because they can actually do something'.[5] Cormac says 'I could go through the whole project and … relate nearly every bit of it to a scenario in a hotel'.

To work in hospitality Holly says 'you need to be good with people'. She says that 'to be a good manager' is to able to communicate, work with and 'understand … people and identify with their problems and help them out'. She feels that 'if you're not good with people you're not going to get anywhere … it's the most important thing'.

Eoin found it relevant to events, conferences and banquets but 'not relevant' to the accommodation element of the hospitality sector.[6] Bill feels it is relevant to the hospitality sector because it 'is very quick changing'. He says 'you have to keep up with things … and organise them and … try and keep ahead of the game'. He also says it helps prepare you to run a business because 'you're actually out organising yourself which is something I like because I don't really want to … work for someone else I want to be out there trying to have my own business'.

---

4   Maeve did a project with Andy for Larkin Community College as we saw earlier. As before some are only identified as male or female.
5   However, Hao had not yet done his internship, which would have provided him with significant work experience.
6   Hospitality refers to food, drink and accommodation firms. See Medlik (1996: 130–131) and Slattery (2002: 20).

Lucy says it is relevant because it forced her to 'set up something from the beginning and work through it' and 'finish it up properly'. She says 'you have to do that in the business world'.

Elena says 'we're not going to be writing essays on economics or whatever' in work, 'we're going to be doing something like this'. She mentions it in her CV 'because it shows that you can … accomplish a project and work with a team'. She says she has not 'really worked' in the hospitality sector so she uses it to 'strengthen' it.

Some use it on their CV. Grace feels it is an advantage to mention 'on your CV that you were able to run a project'. Cindy says 'it looks good on your CV' because it 'sticks out, it's different'. She says it shows that 'you're self-motivated', have 'a different outlook' and are 'flexible'. If a manager asked her about it she would say 'it was a challenge' and 'it brought my skills as a manager together'. Finally, Aileen mentions it on her CV because it indicates she is 'committed', 'determined', 'organised' and knows how to plan and run events. She says it is important for the hotel sector 'if you're running events … doing marketing or if you're a … manager'.

One student mentions she 'had five interviews before I started the job I am in now … I mentioned that I had organised events and had completed a lot of practical work and this led the interview'. See says that the 'employees could see that I could organise, manage, delegate and I could be a manager … I could be successful. This was a huge bonus'.

Skills relevance

Others answer the question by referring to particular skills that they consider important for working. Mary says that teamwork skills are important because 'most areas of work now are all about team work'. She also says it improved her general people skills. Dusan says 'it is relevant to work' because you have to learn team work, motivation, self-discipline, confidence and leadership.

Personal development

Some refer to personal development issues that arise in the workplace. Nora for example, says it is 'based on those skills' that can be used 'in any career'. She says 'it wakes you up to the realisation that things aren't always easy and you do have to deal with things properly and professionally'. She also says students can experience 'setbacks' and 'things that won't work out' in the project and this is a useful practice for work.

When guest issues arose in work Amy says she would have previously said 'hold on I'm not quite sure how to deal with this problem, I'll go and get my manager'. However, she now says 'I know how to deal with it' and feels 'you have to be courteous to people and … still be strong in getting your point across'. She has now 'learned how to get what I want out of life … out of work and … how to get myself across professionally'.

Cathy says that without it, 'college would not have prepared me for my industry'. She says 'I would still be … immature … and I wouldn't know how to deal with people, deal with managers, negotiate'. She says it 'actually got me to develop patience, be better at my time management and learn how to … conduct myself and be more professional'. She feels it provides 'interpersonal skills … and that's basically what hospitality is about'. She first took service-learning before her internship and found it helped prepare her for it.

One student feels that if you 'can bring something from a classroom and make it work in a real life situation through the process of objective setting, planning, organising, following up and executing the project within 8–10 weeks and making money for charity then they can apply the same principles in business to make money. I think [it] offers a practical element to studies which can prove very valuable for students in the long run.'

Finally, Anne says it is 'the subject that has most … shaped me … for working'. This is because it helps you 'present yourself'. She says it is 'really practical' and says 'you actually get to live it out and it makes it … real for you'.

MIXED VIEWS

Then there are those who have mixed views (18 per cent or six students). Ellen says it has 'nothing to do with tourism' (her sector). She feels however, it is 'useful for building up skills' and provides important experience for employment in general 'because you have to get in there … get your point across … you're on your own'.

Matt says it 'certainly' did not give him 'any new skills' and says 'I don't think I got anything new out of it'. Having said this he then says that the project management material is useful because 'you're always going to have projects to run' in work. He also says it 'improves upon your skills' and says that 'anything that gives you any kind of experience that … the other guy next to you in the queue in the interview room … doesn't have makes … you more employable'.

Zhu feels it is not particularly relevant for his sector. However, he feels it is useful for employment in general in that you need to organise, work in teams, motivate and negotiate in any job.

In a similar vein, Joan says it 'could be more related to working in the industry'.[7] However, she feels the team work skills she learned were useful for her sector 'because you're constantly working in teams'. She found 'some' of it useful for her sector because 'you can't work in this industry and not be good with people'.

Mandy says 'you could have … all the qualifications in the world … but if you don't have the right attitude there's no point hiring that person'. One company she worked for had a 'hire for attitude' policy, believing that if new employees have the right attitude 'you can train them' on doing the 'technical things'.

Finally, Lynn says neither of her two projects dealt with her sector. However, they were 'relevant' for 'working with people in the industry … working with customers'. She refers to it in her CV because she learned 'a lot from it'. Finally, she feels it helps with preparation for work only if students 'put the time and effort into it'.

Comments on Preparing for Society

We now look at how students feel it helps prepare them for society. The responses are interesting. Most feel it helps prepare them for society (25 students or 76 per cent overall). Some however, feel it has no benefit for society preparation (four students or 12 per cent).[8]

---

7   This point refers to her group's experience of having a charity race night and ball proposal turned down. This was mainly because of alcohol availability. Projects with alcohol are generally not allowed unless under special circumstances.
8   As with the work relevance question above four interviewees offer no views.

YES VIEWS

In all 76 per cent refer to how it prepares them for operating in society. We discuss below comments made on maturity, awareness, tolerance, ethics, volunteering and other sundry factors.

Maturity

In referring to how it prepares them for society some refer to its impact on maturity and responsibility. For example, Tracy says it encourages you to 'be a lot more responsible for your actions'. Joan says it helps you mature 'because it opens your eyes to what else is happening [in] the world … and what's more important'.

Eoin says 'it gives a person responsibility… it makes people … more aware of things like the Irish Heart Foundation'. In addition, Lucy says it helps 'you look at other people in different ways'. She says 'they may not [have] had your opportunities and may not [have] been able to do what you've done'. However, 'you realise that … they have different opportunities that mean … a hell of a lot to them'.

Amy says it made her 'grow up' a 'little bit' and says she can now talk to her parents 'as an adult'. It also helped her in her 'social life' because 'I didn't know much about drugs'. However, now she says 'it doesn't scare me, whereas before I probably would have went "that doesn't look too nice, I think I'll go home"' when she came across drug taking. Now she can say 'that's fine just move away from it'.

Awareness

Others refer to how it helps to increase people's awareness of issues in society. Grace for example, refers to it helping her develop a 'better grasp of … the real world'. Dusan says that it makes you 'look around … and not take things for granted … it opens your eyes'.

Holly says it 'broadens your views' about everything, 'all the dimensions of life'. She feels 'you're not going to get that from your accounting … [or] economics'. She says 'you're going out there in the real world … meeting real people … hearing real people's problems, you're not going to get that just from studying'.

Nora refers to the increased understanding it gives her of 'Dublin society… and working with children'. In a similar vein, Mary says you can 'overlook things' like 'teenagers … drinking and smoking' because 'it's not … registering with you'. She now realises that 'what's actually happening' is that 'there's a child walking down the street smoking' and says 'it makes you think differently about that'. Finally, Bridget says 'the alcohol awareness programme … opened … people's eyes'

Tolerant

Some refer to how it made them more tolerant. Anne says 'it makes you realise' how people have difficulties and as a result you 'become more … sensitive to other people'. Ellen says she 'felt sorry' for the inner city school children in her project. She feels 'we weren't really helping them' but were 'just there … to change a couple of days of their week'. Lynn says it prepares you for society 'especially the projects that I did, especially the homeless one, because … I've become more tolerant'.[9]

Ethics

Others refer to ethical factors when talking about how it helps to prepare them for society. Cathy refers to how it prepares you to be more ethical in business. She says 'when you … study accountancy it's all about finance and profit'. However, when you do this it's about 'helping others' and as a result 'you're going to conduct yourself better in society'.

Similarly Cormac says it provides an opportunity 'to go and do something for somebody … less fortunate' and says 'it's good to do a project and … think of other people'. It would he says be 'great if everyone could go out with that frame of mind' because 'a lot of people leave college' and just think about themselves.

Sundry

Zhu refers to how it helps to make people less lonely and stronger and feels it can help develop independence, decisiveness, and character. He says character is something that is 'really hard to practice'.

---

9   Lynn as we saw took service-learning twice. Her first project supported the learning and swimming activities of pupils in a city centre primary school and her second one was on homelessness.

Sinead says 'it does more … than prepare you for your work life'. She says it is 'very important … that you … see the problems in society' and 'be aware that … you can help'.

Finally, Susan mentions that it prepares people for society without elaborating any further. Later on in the interview however, she talks about her interest in volunteering.[10]

NO VIEWS

Some feel it has no impact on preparation for society. For example, Hao says it has no impact and is just like any other subject whereas Elena says 'it was too small' and 'it wasn't long enough'. However, Bill says it will not affect how he operates in society as he has 'strong views on what way to deal with things'. He says, however, that 'it would maybe give me more understanding of people' and he would 'try and look at what they're trying to say and negotiate with them'. However, in the end he has his own 'way of doing stuff'.

VOLUNTEERING

Some students said that the experience created an interest in future volunteering.[11] Of those who developed an interest in volunteering, some did so because of the knowledge, enjoyment or confidence they gained.[12]

---

10 We discuss her comments under the confidence section below.
11 These only refer to those interviewed by Kerins (2008). Here some answered the society question by referring to volunteering. Therefore, Kerins decided to introduce a question directly on the topic. The volunteering question was asked of the twelfth interviewee onwards (except in two cases). In total 22 were asked whether they had an interest in volunteering or independently brought up the topic during the interview. This amounts to 67 per cent of those interviewed. Nineteen of these expressed an interest in volunteering, and this amounts to 58 per cent of all 33 interviewees. Of the 19 expressing an interest in volunteering, 18 or 55 per cent indicated that this was due to their CLP experience. By contrast, 3 or 9 per cent will not volunteer again either because they will have no time or do not see it as helpful. Finally, 2 or 6 per cent say it depends on whether they will have time to volunteer or not.
12 Of the 55 per cent in Kerins (2008) who developed an interest in volunteering, 15 per cent did so because of the knowledge, enjoyment or confidence they gained, with 9 per cent expressing no reason. See the results here in Table 8.1.

Table 8.1   Service-learning encourages volunteering (% of 33 Interviews)

YES:	(Knowledge)	(Confidence)	(Enjoyment)	(Other)	Depends	NO
55:	(15)	(15)	(15)	(9)	6	9

Note: The knowledge, confidence, enjoyment and other categories when rounded up come to 55 per cent in total. Only 70 per cent of interviewees commented on this issue.

Knowledge

Sinead developed an interest in helping in the future because aspects of her project 'shocked' her and she would 'like to try and make a ... difference'. Dusan says the experience 'made me think of other people and how I can help'.

Now that Lucy has 'learned about the Special Olympics and Childline ... it would encourage me to volunteer'. She says 'it changed my attitude towards volunteering and people that help charities'. She used see them as 'do-gooders' who 'won't leave you alone ... when you're walking down the street ... it does change your attitude towards that a lot'.

Theresa found it 'showed me something ... that I've always wanted to deal with ... something ... social ... some kind of care' and 'you know it didn't turn me off'.

Confidence

Some refer to how the confidence gained from doing service-learning has encouraged an interest in volunteering. Aileen now realises she can volunteer 'because I did two projects and nothing really went wrong ... it gives you more confidence'. Another said it 'makes you see you can do things to help people'.

Bridget became involved in a cystic fibrosis charity event 'two or three weeks' after her project had finished and says 'I don't think we would have ... had the confidence to ... pull it off if we hadn't [done service-learning]'.

Andy refers to how he developed the confidence to help in his local football club. He says he now has 'the balls to do it' and can say 'right boys do it' and they 'listen to you because you're ... not shy ... you're positive '.

Cathy is 'going to work' for the Cancer Society or the Irish Guide Dogs for the Blind 'once every year'. She says 'I'd have no problem now ringing up a ... charity and going "look I want to do work for you" ... but before I never would have picked up the phone to do anything like that because I would have been too scared and wouldn't know how to do it'.

Susan says it 'taught me how to think about other people and about what I have to offer' and 'what I can do to make a ... difference'. Had she not done service-learning she would have wondered 'how I can help society … how I can have an impact'.

When asked has it encouraged her to volunteer she says 'definitely I'd do that … tomorrow'. However, she would not volunteer when 'I was having a bad week' and she 'wouldn't want to … be just dealing with hard stuff'.

She also says 'when I started I would have said "I can't volunteer and that's it". I couldn't do it' because she would 'get too upset'. However, it 'taught me … how to be compassionate and … go home and not dwell on it … empathise with them, but not let it affect you'.

Enjoyment

Some refer to how their enjoyment of helping others encouraged an interest in future volunteering. Grace says you 'feel good after you do it' which she 'really liked. I mean I was glad to have helped and to have done what we did and I was also glad for the fact that I was so happy when I'd done it'. In a similar vein, Cindy says 'I'd do the likes of that again definitely … it's rewarding … in lots of different ways … you're happy with yourself for … starters, you're helping somebody else and you see how happy they are … what they get out of it, and you have … fun at the same time'. She says that after doing her project she did a 60-mile cycle for the Irish Guide Dogs for the Blind.

No

Two are unable to volunteer again because of time constraints. First, Elena says 'I don't think I'll be able to [volunteer] again because life is too frigging busy'.[13] She gives money to charity every month. She explains 'they came to my doorstep' and although she 'wasn't emotionally attached to it' she 'felt … guilty … because I haven't done anything before … so I might as well donate'. One reason she took service-learning is 'because it gives me time to volunteer … slotted time … emotionally it feels better, even though you're not necessarily attached, you just feel better that you've done something good for someone else … you just sleep [better]'.

Matt says he cannot volunteer in the future because 'I've a lot of commitments … I barely even get time to volunteer for myself let alone to go volunteering

---

13 Frigging is a meaningless intensive in this context. See *Merriman-Webster Dictionary* (2009).

for other people'. He says 'I'm absolutely knackered [sic].[14] I've just worked six days straight, it's my first day off and I have to go all the way to Westmeath to ... see my daughter'.

Bill indicates he will not be volunteering again as follows. He says 'some ... aren't that interested in being helped ... you have to understand them, they probably have their own reasons'. He also says 'you'd probably be better off not helping them, because you could be giving them the wrong sort of help'.

Triangulate

We now check the above findings by triangulating the results with the views of the key informant.

WORK

Concerning the workforce, she says 'that all students have a part-time job so ... before they even come to third level education [they] know about the work environment'. However, these jobs are often 'mundane' such as 'clearing tables or washing ... dishes'. Service-learning by contrast, 'gives them a taste of ... authority which ... [can give] them the inspiration, the motivation, to aspire to becoming ... manager ... [or] CEO of an organisation'. This experience helps them 'realise ... there is a light at the end of the tunnel' because they have had 'a taste [of] being the boss'.

Following the experience she says that 'some of them want' to be a manager and 'some of them don't' and are 'quite happy being an assistant'. She says the experience helps them 'realise ... what their particular forte is'. As a result, the student can perform better at interviews and can now for example, say 'I enjoyed [the] planning ... financing ... marketing ... advertisement' or 'the implementation was brilliant ... I was on a high all day' or 'I came up with the innovated ideas, but I couldn't follow through on it'.

SOCIETY

She feels it helps prepare students for society because it 'strengthens ... values and attitudes'. It also gives them an appreciation of community and says they

---

14 Knackered means tired or exhausted. See *Merriman-Webster Dictionary* (2009).

are 'more conscious of what exists out there … their blinkers have been taken off'.

Finally, on volunteering, she says 'it puts them in a better … position to … step forward to contribute' in the future and 'it might … help them to volunteer'. She explains this point by saying 'if you ask someone to volunteer for something that they have never done … before they … [might] say no because they [might] be uncomfortable in that foreign environment'. However, if they have done it in 'college they might be more inclined to say "oh yes I did something like that in college there's no reason why I can't do it again"'. However, she warns that the relationship between cause and effect is not simple and it is not certain 'that this is going to make them more socially responsible'.

Conclusion

Learning project management and leadership through service-learning helps to prepare students for the work world and the economy. However, it also helps to prepare them for participating in society. They are not just learning new knowledge and skills for employment and business. Their values and attitudes are being affected.

Management courses normally focus on preparing people for business, employment and the economy. They never really pay much attention to the needs of community and society. They have from time to time provided courses on ethics and such issues and discussed some of the scandals of our corporate world.

However, they never really provide an opportunity for students to develop their understanding, tolerance, empathy and care for others. There is plenty of 'I' in college subjects but little or no 'Thou'.

Service-learning allows us to prepare students for the work world and the economy while making some contribution to preparing them for citizenship, community and society. It can also do this in a way that facilitates deeper learning, which brings us to our next topic – the response of students to this new teaching method.

9

The Service-Learning Experience

What do students think of service-learning? How do they feel about this new teaching method? To answer these questions we discuss what they have to say about their service-learning experiences.[1] We also summarise some of their opinions statistically.

The most surprising finding here is how many find it both enjoyable and challenging at the same time. One would have expected them to either enjoy or feel challenged by the experience but not both. Some also found it had a significant impact on them whereas a smaller number say it introduced them to a different world.

A relatively larger number were attracted to the practical nature of the method and some referred positively to the balance it provided to their college education. Others refer to the theory learning aspect and some were struck by the freedom it gave them.

We now consider the results on the teaching method and summarise the findings in Figure 9.1.[2]

Comments on Service-Learning Experience

We now look at some of the comments made by students on service-learning.

---

1   We take the points on teaching method from the 71 interviews used in Chapter 6.
2   The data are: enjoyable (50 students or 70 per cent), challenging (47 students or 66 per cent) nature of the method, those who refer positively to its practical element (58 per cent) and those who say it had an impact on them (39 per cent). Some refer to how it brought them into contact with a different world (24 per cent) and indicate their engagement with the theory element of the method (20 per cent). Finally, a few refer to the freedom of the method (14 per cent), the balance it provides in the course (13 per cent) and the learning responsibility it encourages (8 per cent).

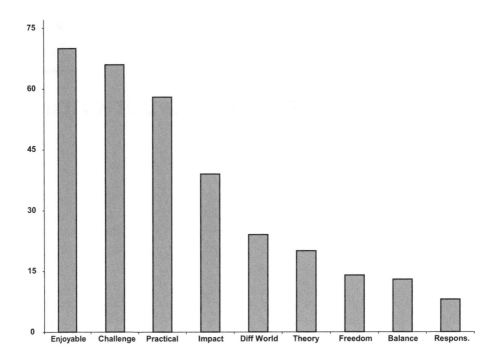

Figure 9.1   The service-learning experience (% of 71 interviews)

ENJOYMENT

Despite the challenges faced, the service-learning experience was mentioned as enjoyable by 70 per cent of students (or 50 in all). Nora says you 'feel better as a person' having done the project and Joan says 'you feel better that you're helping somebody'.

Maeve says she benefited because 'I was giving back to the community as well as going through a process of learning'. She also 'felt better' about herself 'going out and helping'. Overall, she 'didn't find it hugely stressful, because I enjoyed doing it'.

Cindy says 'it's rewarding ... in lots of different ways'. She says 'you're happy with yourself for starters, you're helping somebody else and you see how happy they are ... what they get out of it' and 'you have ... fun at the same time'.

Lucy felt 'it was different' from anything she had done and was 'worthwhile because it was for somebody else and for people that really needed it'. She says 'it was very satisfying to be able to help them'.

Aileen, who took it twice, says she 'enjoyed it' although 'it was time consuming'. She says 'it's nice to actually organise an event and do something good ... for an organisation ... and to have got a good mark'.

Holly says she 'grew as a person' and says 'you don't know until ... you've actually done volunteering work' whether or not it is possible. She found it 'so fulfilling'.

Cormac, who took it in final year for the first time, says 'there should be more' of it, 'it's a refreshing change'. He felt 'a sense of achievement' because he 'made it happen' and feels 'inspired by thinking I could do a project'.

Mary says it was 'fun', 'enjoyable' and 'stressful' all at the same time. She says it was 'fun because you get to do something that you are interested in and something that ... you might be passionate about or have views upon ... and want to learn more about'. She feels this type of thing 'keeps you grounded' and 'makes you look ... outside the college'. She says from her experience service-learning 'is relevant to everyone'.

Amy did her drugs project 'because it was something I wanted to do' and 'enjoyed' and therefore 'wanted to get in and get it done, and ... do it really well'. She found she was 'really keen to learn' and her attitude 'was to go out, get the work done' and 'be really positive about it'. Consequently, the course material 'didn't become something that you [just] read, it became something that you discussed and that you talked about'. She 'found it a great way of learning' and in the end, her grade 'was irrelevant'.

Anne found it 'really enjoyable' and says 'even doing the report was enjoyable'. She was 'gripped' by 'what went on in the ... hospice' and 'talked about it loads at home'.

Bill says it was 'more enjoyable' than the standard option and added that 'you get more out of it and you see the benefits of what you're doing'. When asked why he took it twice having found it so challenging the first time he says 'I couldn't really imagine myself doing anything else'.

Lynn says 'it was a huge amount of work'. Nevertheless she 'really enjoyed' it 'because it was different … it wasn't just a classroom and you were being told … this is the way it's going to be'. Instead, 'you got out there and you got to experience things for yourself'. She 'loved that it was hands on … work'.

Cathy was significantly challenged by both projects. However, she found it 'takes you away from … being a student and puts you more into being an adult'. She says 'if college life was all fun and games' this is 'serious'. She refers to the 'buzz' after it when she stood back and realised, 'I actually did something valuable in society'. She says 'I don't care what people say about students in newspapers … I'm actually going out and doing something proper with my life'. Finally, she says 'it was the best course' she did and feels 'it should have been compulsory'.

Susan who was surprised by the amount of work involved. Yet she says 'I loved doing it, it was brilliant … best thing I've ever done in college, by far.' She then says 'I'd make it compulsory in all colleges, especially for men … definitely … sorry, I just wanted to say that to someone'.

Finally, Theresa says 'I love [service-learning] … it was about helping people'. She describes it as 'a brilliant adventure'. She was interested in both projects and 'was inspired the whole time to go at them'. She, like others, laced her positive commentary with the challenges faced. She says for example, that it was time consuming 'because I was so interested in it'. She also says her log 'was the bane of my life'.[3]

CHALLENGE

Service-learning is very challenging according to 66 per cent of students (47 in all).

One student said that 'a lot of people see it as … easy… and then when they get in they're kind of shocked.' Even in her own case, she said there were times 'I'd say I'd never ever do it again'. However, 'when you're finished … you look back [and] say well you know I did learn from it.' Another said that 'we had three failed projects before we actually got to proceed with our final choice'.

Cathy says it was more stressful 'than anything I did', whereas other subjects 'were only stressful at one point, [the exam]'. It is stressful she says because

---

3   Every student must keep a project log.

you have 'to organise things' just like 'when you go out into your career'. By comparison, she feels college generally 'is such a doss [sic], you go around, you have a laugh for four years and then you get stressed for your finals'.[4]

Lin and Holly both agree. The former says simply that it is 'very time consuming [and] stressful'. Holly expands somewhat and says it was 'a huge project' and 'took up most of our time'. She found it 'hard getting knocked back so much ... especially [since] it was for such a good cause'. She says 'a lot of days' were spent doing things for the project. For example, 'it would take a full day to walk around town ... asking the managers to donate prizes ... then ringing around because people weren't getting back to us'. She says it was 'the little things that you don't even think of ... it's not necessarily the project itself, it's the actual getting out there, walking around ... trying to convince people'.

One student found it 'a culture shock' and had to 'give it 100 per cent'. She found it 'very time-consuming' but felt 'this may have been because we were not used to having to do this kind of thing on a regular basis'.

Some said the initial weeks were difficult. One felt this was because it can take 'a while to figure out what it is all about'. Another said it was because students were trying to decide on their project proposals. The latter also said that although this period was 'time wasting' she 'knew people had to make up their minds' on their proposals. She also felt the experience makes 'you realise the importance of decision-making skills'. Supporting this point, another said he 'became more dependent and reliant' on his own decision-making ability during the project.

The challenge factor caused some at least to baulk at the idea of taking it. One said 'a lot of us ... were afraid to choose it ... because we didn't know what it entailed'.' He was 'concerned about it being difficult'. In spite of this, he indicates he was attracted to it because others 'had got a lot out of the course and were glad they had done it'. He also said that 'the hardest part is to work out how you are going to get people involved' as 'you are just a student' and you have to really 'work on your ability to talk to people'.

Another said that in a lecture 'all the work is [by] the lecturer, the student can just sit there, say nothing and just walk out again. [Here] the student has to give 50 per cent and the lecturer ... 50 per cent ... it needs a strong lecturer, it's challenging for both sides.'

---

4   Cathy was in her fourth and final year and had also taken service-learning in her third year.

One felt that it is easier 'to write 2000 words on the effectiveness of management than it is to actually get up and organise it'. Another said 'if you spent 20 minutes [on] any other subject … you could come out with a first'. She felt 'you had to spend about ten hours a week. It was never about getting a grade; it was always about the project.' She said it was 'all on your own back. You had to set your own time frames [and] targets … [and] become very real about everything.'

Aileen likewise found it 'very time consuming'. After other classes she says 'you go home' and 'don't really do anything, unless you have an assessment'. However, with this 'the minute you leave class you have to go and organise something … it's on going'.

Eoin says it was 'hassle' at the start because 'we kept on coming up with these proposals' that 'just didn't work'. He found it 'a worry'. For example, he would be 'at home on a Sunday night thinking … I have to get this proposal written up for the fourth time'. He says you have 'three hours in the class every week but you have about ten hours outside of the class doing stuff'.

Grace 'hadn't done anything this size before'. Consequently, her group had to 'pull our fingers out and actually work'. By comparison other assessments are 'easy' because you just 'do your bit the night before'. However, with this 'we were constantly … trying to arrange things … trying to get the whole thing stuck together'.

Tracy was 'enthusiastic' to get started 'because I wanted to do something different'. However, 'once I got into it, I was surprised how hard … it was … it's on your back'. She says it was 'an absolute nightmare … trying to get started' and was 'a complete nightmare' trying to arrange meetings with the charity, 'every time we wanted to meet them they weren't there'.

She feels however, that her group did not put in 'as much effort as we actually should have in the very beginning'. Overall, she found it was 'constant [work] which was something that we hadn't done before'.

Matt's group was 'messing a bit too much' at the start and 'were getting along so well, we didn't get stressed about [it]'.[5] Consequently, 'our proposal was late'.

---

5   Messing arises here from the particular meaning of the word mess – to make a mess of, to cause to be spoiled by inept handling; to muddle or mishandle. See *Oxford English Dictionary* (2009).

His group 'didn't take the classes as seriously as we possibly should have'. Consequently, 'I don't think I took too much away from the actual lectures … but certainly … I took a greater experience and understanding away [from the project]'. However, once he got going on his homeless project he found it 'was very daunting'. Overall, he feels it is 'a lot of work' but does not complain because he believes 'you don't get a degree for nothing'.

Nora explains its stressful nature as follows. She says things 'cropped up that we hadn't planned for, that we had to deal with … on the spot'. She feels that 'even though there's no exam … it's still a very busy few weeks … because you have to be there and alert and ready to work'.

Mary says her group were 'calm and collected at the start'. However, 'when it came round to doing it, it was so much more difficult' and 'the final few weeks' were 'so stressful'. Part of the stress is because 'if it goes wrong there's people there to see it. Whereas if you go into an exam and you bomb at it, there's no one there looking at you'. Although she says she 'probably worked more' on it than on 'a lot of other subjects' she was not being told 'what you have to do' and concludes that although 'it was stressful … it wasn't like you couldn't cope'.

Bill says it was 'hard work' and stressful and feels 'you need to be very motivated to get it done'. He found it 'hectic' trying 'to fit it in' to his life and points out that 'you can cut here and there' with other modules but with this 'you had to be there and you had to do it'.

Maeve felt that the 'getting out and about and … getting started is the toughest part' and 'is the biggest learning part'. Although she found it difficult, she still prefers the 'type of stress' where you have to come up 'with your own solutions to problems'.

Although Lynn says it is a 'huge amount of work', she feels it was only 'hassle if you made it hassle'. This happened 'if you didn't pull your weight' or if you let other team members 'drift off and you were left on your own'.

Susan says she found some of it 'worrying because I was putting myself in a situation where I haven't been before'. She says however, that the worry helped her in that 'it actually gave me a lot of adrenaline'.

Amy says that if she 'sat back' at all her 'big' project would have 'unravelled around' her and therefore 'had to really keep on top of it all the time'. In spite of this, she feels it is not the 'most pressurised' module because 'anybody could get their head around [it]'. This is partly because she was involved in picking and working on a project that she was interested in and understood. Although she felt 'pressurised trying to get things done' she found subjects like accounting 'a lot more pressurised, because I haven't a clue'. For her it 'was a pressure in a good way … a motivational pressure'.

Lucy says 'it is very, very involved' and takes 'a lot of time'. She says 'you have to be doing something every single day … to keep it going' and her group would even 'be in contact at the weekend talking about what we were going to do'.

She feels her first group 'took on too much' and 'it became a lot bigger than we anticipated'. In the end, she decided 'you have to have a balance'. As a result, she 'kept it a bit smaller for the second one so it was a lot easier to manage'. This helped ensure that the second one was 'more managed because we knew what we were doing'.

PRACTICAL LEARNING

We now look at comments on the practical element of the method. In total 58 per cent (41 students) refer positively to its practical nature.

One student cautioned that although it 'is a good teaching method' you must be 'disciplined to ensure you do actually learn from the process'. Echoing this point, another refers to its 'set time frame' and the fact that 'our tasks and objectives were set at the beginning'. As a result, she said, 'we always had something to work towards and it was regimental [sic]'.

A number say they learned better by doing than by reading or listening. One of these said 'it's the best way to learn, get your hands dirty and get stuck in … you are then ten times better off and you don't forget the good and the bad'. Another says that learning by doing allows you 'to learn it for yourself' rather than sitting in lectures and 'trying to soak up the notes'.

One says 'I prefer practical work to theory work … it gives you more control'. Another says 'I remember [it] because I had to do it. I remember the process ... In marketing, you do a marketing plan, but it does not matter if you get it wrong.'

Bill found it useful going 'out there meeting people and talking ... and working with them and trying to understand what they're doing. Rather than just being in a classroom and ... maybe not learning anything, you know just falling asleep.' He says 'the research and organising was the best ... you're out doing it, making mistakes, learning from it'.

Like Bill, Lynn talks about the 'benefits of being out there' and 'experiencing things yourself'. These 'totally outweigh' the process of the lecturer 'telling you the way things should be'.

Aileen feels 'you learn a lot more from it, because in a lecture you ... sometimes ... daydream if you're not interested in the topic'. However, you are interested in learning here 'because you picked the organisation ... and you want to do well for it. So you're going to listen to everything that you need to know for it and you keep doing whatever you need to do.' By contrast, during internship she 'felt like a robot' because 'they told me what to do ... it gets very boring ... it becomes a routine'.

This is only one of a number of experiential methods students come across. Some have already spent relatively longer periods in work placement and others have taken food and beverage practicals.[6] Although Deirdre favours 'more practical courses' she would have preferred to have used her time here in extra internship and says she 'learned more in placement' than in service-learning.

Cindy says 'it depends on what kind of a person you are'. She is 'not the type of person that just sits down ... all day ... I have to be out and doing things ... It gives you scope.' In internship she says you do 'the crappy jobs' whereas this is 'your idea'. She feels you learn 'more managerial skills' here than in internship which is 'very straightforward and ... I don't like sitting at a desk and being straightforward ... It wasn't ... real responsibility there was always somebody checking up on you.'

Lucy compares it to her restaurant practical where she had two days' management experience 'one in the kitchen as head chef and one in the

---

6   Food and beverage practicals take place in a classroom kitchen or restaurant whereas work placement or internship takes place in a company for a period of weeks or months.

restaurant as manager'. She says it is 'very limited as to what you can do and … you always have the lecturer … [with the] final say'. By contrast, here 'you're dealing with it, you're managing it … it's your project'.

She also compares it to internship. Here 'you're working for a company and they decide what you do … when you can do it and how you can do it'. By contrast, here you are like 'the general manager of this project, so you decide really how it goes and what you want to do'.

One particular student says it was a 'proper learning experience' since the learning in work placement was 'on someone else's terms' whereas here it was 'on your own terms'. Another says that in a restaurant practical, 'you're very much protected; you're told what to do every step of the way' and in work placement you 'have a few friends around you and everyone is doing the same thing'. By contrast, here 'no one is making decisions without you'.

PERSONAL IMPACT

In addition, to those who found it challenging and enjoyable, 39 per cent indicate it had an impact on them.

Seven use the term 'eye opener' to explain their experience. Nora says it was 'an eye opener' and made her 'appreciate what I have'. She says she 'grew from the experience'. Cormac refers to it as 'a big eye opener' while Joan comments that it 'opens your eyes to what else is happening [in] the world'. Sinead refers to how it opened her eyes and says her project experience was 'completely outside the box' and led her to realise she had been living in a 'goldfish bowl'.[7]

Others say such things as 'it really did something to me', and 'it had a personal … hold on us … people I met I would never forget'. Other comments were 'it's meaningful', 'it took over everything else … it was really important we did it' and 'it's so much fulfilment'. Where Bridget says it 'brought a lot of things home … it does hit you', Lucy says 'it does change you a bit', and Cathy says she 'realised a lot more after [it], I think I matured'.

---

7   A goldfish bowl means a place or situation with little or no privacy (*Oxford English Dictionary*, 2009). However, the interviewee here was metaphorically referring to it as a relatively protected place.

Theresa says it 'taught me to make the most of life' and not to 'sit back or ... ruin your life'. On her drugs project she says she came to realise that 'things are really, really bad ... what they have to deal with, so, so bad ... it's terrible'.

Mary mentions 'realisation' and being able to 'see things when you're walking down the street' that previously she had not noticed. After she had been to the drug centre, she said 'when we walked out of there we saw so much more'. She says 'I always thought I was a very observant person, but ... it strengthened by ... a million'.

Anne says her first visit to the children's home 'shocked me a bit' because she 'came face to face' with kids who 'are going to die really young'. She found the experience 'really does ... bring things home for you'.

Bill says some of the schoolchildren in his project 'were crazy' and 'was completely taken aback by it'. He also says that some of what he came across in his homeless project was 'fairly extreme'.

Asdis had to write her report 'maybe eight times' and says she 'wasn't sure how honest to be ... I was on this journey'. She says her project 'made me realise ... you have to also adapt'. She says her experience helped her address certain issues in her life and helped her make 'sense of the whole journey since my first arrival here'.

Amy was 'about halfway through the project' when she 'began to be passionate about it'. Her 'attitude towards it changed' because 'it wasn't just ... a college project' and she 'started to love doing' it. At one point, 'my mum turned around and said ... "are you actually doing this for college anymore or is this something that's a little bigger to you?"' and she admitted that it was 'more important than college at this stage'.

In the end 'it made me believe in myself' and 'it was a really great experience'. She wanted to 'do it really well because it was something ... I was really interested in' and she eventually came to the point where 'the value I had for it was really ... a devotion'.

Matt found it a 'bit of an eye opener' and came to realise that homeless 'are real people' with 'serious problems'. For example, that 'guy over there in the corner. He's here ... everyday ... he has that bag which he's very protective about, you know Jeez [sic] what's that all about'? He was surprised to find that if he missed a week they would notice and say '"you weren't here last week, took the day off did you?" … and you'd be like "Jesus these guys noticed that I wasn't here"'.

On his first week 'one guy walked up to me and … said, "I find it hard walking up the hill because every time I walk up … I slip and I fall down to the bottom, that's why I wear these boots"'. Matt did not 'have the faintest clue what he was talking about, the only thing I could think of to say to him was "nice boots" … I never got my head round him, but … he was there every week and I actually see him around town the odd time'. He was 'a real character, probably not … all with it upstairs [sic],[8] but … that's the sad reality of some of these people ... You're living on the streets all of the time, you're lonely, you have no one to look after you, care for you and you know you might go a bit odd'.

He feels 'a lot of them are on the streets' because 'they've been on their own for so long … they've lost the social skills … to … be reintegrated … you don't exist' on the street. To elaborate he says 'if you don't have a bank account … you don't exist and you can't get a bank account unless you have a billing address … it's actually scary how hard it is to open a bank account'.

In the middle of this, he admits he is 'absolutely' exhausted and refers to his work and other pressures. However, 'it could be worse I could be … in a cardboard box …. I know things are tough for me but they could always be tougher. You know … somebody could come along and throw a real spanner in the works and things could get real tough'. He says we are 'balancing on a knife edge and … if you fall one way you can fall into homelessness, if you fall the other way you can … have a happy life but you're always tinkering on that knife edge [sic]'.[9] This is especially the case 'at my age, my time of life, I think that whole experience helped mature me' and 'made me … more … grateful'.

He says, 'I have a roof over my head … a job, I go to college … most of my college is paid for … at the end of the day, I'm a very lucky individual'. He says homeless people 'have real problems and … just need a helping hand … [and] people to talk to'.

---

8   'Upstairs' in slang can refer to how one is mentally and is mainly used in phrases indicating weak (or abundant) mental capacity (*Oxford English Dictionary*, 2009).

9   Tinkering means working at something clumsily or imperfectly or doing something in a trifling or aimless way (*Oxford English Dictionary*, 2009).

Finally, one says it gave her 'an opportunity to open up and be myself ... to stand up and say, I can do this ... it has had a big impact on who I am and what I am now' whereas another found it 'was a total life changing experience'.

DIFFERENT WORLD

Next, 24 per cent refer to how it brought them into a different world.

One says 'it was totally outside college [and] ... really broadened your learning experience'. Another says 'you will be mainly dealing with complete strangers' and feels that 'life isn't about being in a classroom surrounded by four walls'.

Theresa says it takes you 'out of college' to a 'different kind of world' although 'we had a report to write and all of that ... brought us back into it'. Aileen feels 'it opens your eyes a bit more and you realise what's actually going on out there'. She says the normal theory based subject 'doesn't prepare you for the actual outside world' but with this 'you learn ... more about what's out there'.

Susan says it takes you 'out into the big wide world on your own' and helps to provide you with the capacity to 'actually do something, rather than just pass exams'. More colourfully, Sinead says it was 'completely outside the box for me'. She says it introduces students to 'a world out there past ... doing our assignments, going out and getting drunk at the weekend and going to our little part-time jobs'.

Lei says the 'real world' of her project is 'a little bit scary because you never know what things [are] going to happen next'. In a similar vein, Cathy says this 'is real life, there's no protections [sic] ... if you fail nobody's going to let you start again'. She says 'the world's not going to stop when something bad happens, it's got to keep going so you've got to find out how to ... benefit from that'.

Holly who 'went to a private school' and lives in 'a well off area', feels she has been 'growing up in a bubble' and regards herself as 'lucky'. As a result she says 'it's very hard to ... know what's happening in the real world ... when you're not in it yourself; it's very hard to ... imagine it'. This however, took her 'out there in the real world ... meeting ... real people ... hearing real people's problems'. Finally, Nora says it brought her into 'a very different world ... totally different'.

THEORY

Only 20 per cent overall indicate a reasonable level of engagement with the theory element of the method.[10] There is a variety of responses here. These vary quite a bit and for discussion purposes we summarise them under different headings.

Class only

First, some indicate they did not read the theory outside class. Of these for example, Deirdre says the theory 'didn't mean anything ... I didn't need it'. Instead, she says 'I put my own skills ... into ... the project'. Matt says 'what theory did I take away ... Not a whole lot'.

No exam

Others indicated they did not pay as much attention to theory, as they would have, had they faced an exam.

Report

Some used the theory to help prepare the report. Here Grace admits that her 'project just ... happened' indicating that she did not use theory to guide or manage her project. Hao 'found some mistakes' that he could have avoided had he paid more attention to theory during his project.

Aileen used her class slides to help prepare her report during the first module. In level two however, she also read the theory to 'see what part I could put into ... the report'.

Mary by comparison used the theory 'mainly when I was doing the report' and feels it is important to review the theory when doing the report so 'you can relate' one to the other. She found she was relatively 'disconnected' from the theory because she 'was so focused' on her project. Because it was 'completely' different to other subjects 'when I got to the classroom ... I wasn't as focused

---

10 Theory scored only 11 per cent on average with Guinan (2004), Gao (2005) and Kieran (2005) and 45 per cent with Kerins (2008).

as I should have been'. However, she 'sat exams where [it] has popped into my mind … and I'd reference it as an experience'. For example, she says 'I remember sitting in a few [management] exams and being able to relate back to service-learning'.

Project and report

Some use the theory for both their projects and reports. Lucy read the theory while doing her project because she needed to know how to do things. In her case, she 'had to apply the negotiation, conflict resolution' to her project. This makes it 'clearer in your head' because 'you're applying it to something that you're doing as opposed to writing out an essay' that 'you're going to forget … as soon as you've handed it in'. By contrast, 'you always remember doing something, when you did it and the things that you did'.

Joan says it 'made you want to go out and learn' the theory. She says 'it made you use what you'd learned from the other subjects and if you hadn't learned it, it [made] you go and look for it'. For example, she says 'I couldn't really remember a lot from marketing and it really made me root out the notes and then go and research it all over again … [to] find out what we had to do'.

Maeve says you can learn theories but one cannot really understand them 'unless you … practise them'. Here she says there was theory, practical work, and 'time … to discuss it'. In an ordinary class, she says, 'you rarely get to do that ... because you come in, the lecturer starts, you take your notes … it's finished'. She feels it is a 'better way of learning' because 'you're working directly with … the theory' and 'you're doing it yourself'.

Maeve says the theory was 'substantial' but 'useful' because if she had no theory she would not 'have been able to approach the actual project as well as' she did. She says the theory 'was quite specific to the project we were doing'.

Finally, Amy says the theory did not just 'become something that you read, it became something that you … talked about'. She says 'I knew everyday when I was going into … class, that yes I was going to learn something that I probably never would have heard of before'. She also says 'I knew that when I left the class that I would learn something new, but I wouldn't have even realised, because I applied it to something I already knew'.

She says if she were only doing the theory on its own 'it probably would have went completely over my head'. However, 'because I was sitting there and I was actually going "oh I did that", and "oh I need to do that". I was actually putting it into action and ... going "yes this is the best way of going about it"'.

Comparison

Sinead compares her learning here with other modules. Talking about her course generally she says 'I don't remember learning much last year ... I forgot it all after the exams'. She feels she 'wouldn't be able to talk for this [length of time]' if she was being asked about another subject. She lists a number of things she learned from the module and says 'it's something that's stuck with me'.

Sundry

Some students made other points on theory. Holly admits she only 'skimmed over' the theory as she had 'enough to be doing with my other exams'. Nora did not spend a lot of time on the theory, except for risk management, which she found useful for her project. She says this was 'more project based' and the 'theory is the minor side'. She feels 'a lot of stuff' in other lectures or books 'goes over your head' and concludes by saying that 'being practical with something, you'll always remember it'.

Asdis says it links 'theory and practice'. She says that 'instead of just reading about how to do project management ... we did it as well'. She feels that when you learn theory in class 'it doesn't necessarily mean that you've fully registered it' and says you learn more effectively when you are 'putting it in practice'.

One particular student says she 'tried to follow' the theory 'as far as possible but at the end of the day it worked out that when you look back and reflect on it that's where you learned most'. Another refers to the experience of group dynamics and the related learning. He says that 'group dynamics is something that you see afterwards, you don't see it as [it happens], it is a little bit like the wind, you can measure where it comes from and where it goes, but you know there is nothing else you can do'.

There was also some criticism of the theory. For example, one student says 'it wasn't very relevant to what we were doing' and another says that the lectures are 'very long, very boring and completely unnecessary'. Another states that 'there was too much useless information, it was time wasting'. 'The classes tended to be a bit tedious and I know it was background to what we were doing but [it] is all about hands on and I think its just that they weren't too closely linked together' says another student.[11]

Finally, one interviewee says that since 'the project was a big part of it ... [it] took over. Although you ... learn the academic side, you don't always remember it'.

FREEDOM

A small number (14 per cent) refer to the freedom the method provides. On being asked what impressed her most, one mentions 'the freedom of it. Not being told what to do ... there is a timeframe for the lectures, but there is ... flexibility'. Others said it gave 'freedom to ... develop your own project under certain limits' and it provided 'a lot more room than other courses'.

Freedom was explained as being able to say, 'look, I do not agree with that, and for someone to take on your opinion'. Another referred to the freedom 'to go out and do something that you want to as long as it is not too radical ... to get an idea and to mould it'.

In a similar vein, one said that 'other courses spoon-feed you' but here students have to think for themselves and 'take control of the situation ... and you're really out there, facing the real world'. It was also said that 'your project becomes very much your own thing' while someone else referred to the fact that 'you are actually living it'.

BALANCE

A small number (13 per cent) refer to the importance of balance in the methods used. One feels there is a need for balance and says that 'it helps to break the monotony of ... normal lectures'. Another felt a balance of methods suited her but it may not suit others because 'it depends on the type of person you are'.

Another says a balance of teaching methods produces the 'best calibre of ... students for the industry'. One admits that 'lectures are excellent for some

---

11 The negative comments in this paragraph come from Guinan (2004), Gao (2005) and Kieran (2005) and lead shortly afterwards to a tightening of the course content and a better linkage between theory and project activity.

subjects but I find them a bit draining'. By contrast, she feels you 'absorb more information' here as it is 'a self-learning experience'.

Another says you need lectures to 'cover the vast amount of learning material' and small group teaching to enable you 'to question, discuss and share experiences'. He feels it achieves both these aims because 'it brings together the theory with a real life situation/project'. Realising this one day he said – 'Wow! This is where we use all the information from other subjects to put this plan in place ...'

Finally, one said that although lectures can be boring they are still a 'good means of collecting all the necessary information on a subject'. By contrast, small group methods are useful because 'they allow you to gain a better understanding of what was taught in the lecture'. She said however, that service-learning 'combines the theory with the practical' and 'a combination of all three methods works best for me'.

LEARNER RESPONSIBILITY

Finally, 8 per cent of students refer to how it encourages personal responsibility for learning. One says it leaves the 'learning responsibility to the student'. Another refers to a change in lecturing style from teaching to 'facilitating us in ... learning that had now become our responsibility'. Another mentioned that she gained a lot more here than elsewhere because she took 'responsibility for [her] own learning'.

However, it was pointed out that taking responsibility for one's learning could create adjustment difficulties because 'you are so used to having the lecturer responsible for your learning needs'. Another felt people 'need to be mature enough for this type of learning otherwise they may not benefit as much as they should'.

Making a different but related point, another said she was at first 'confused as to where the learning was' and 'what it was I was learning'. She said that 'it was only when we had completed [the project] ... when I was writing up the report and reflecting on what we had done ... that I truly realised what I had learned'. This comment indicates that people's ability to adjust to becoming responsible for their own learning may be due not just to maturity and engagement issues but also due to the novelty of the method.

Triangulate

We now check the above findings by triangulating the results with the views of the key informant.

CHALLENGE

The key informant feels it is a challenge not just for the student but also for the lecturer. She says it is 'interactive' and can be 'emotionally' demanding and 'time consuming' for the student. Here they are 'dependent on their ability to think on their feet' and the 'participation in their learning' is a challenge for them. She found that some students were 'unhappy' with the experience and 'did not see the rosy picture'.[12]

However she found it is also a challenge for the lecturer. She describes the student as a trapeze artist with the lecturer 'spotting all the time to catch that student ... don't let ... the trapeze artiste fall'. It is also a challenge being consistent with students and 'you need to be fair to every student ... do you give this person more time than that person or ... are you available to every one of them equally?'

She also mentions a lack of infrastructural support for the method to 'back up both the teaching staff and the students'. Here she feels there could be a room where students and staff could have access to project resources. She also suggests that since 'different projects have different ... elements that need to be addressed' it would help if 'expert knowledge' could be made available to the lecturer.

She suggests team teaching so different teachers can 'complement each other' and says it can be a 'strain on one individual' and feels that 'because

---

12 She elaborates this point as follows. Many students have lived relatively sheltered lives and are often unaware of the hardships faced by others. Service-learning can broaden their awareness of such realities and can force them to face the hardship of the real world where disappointment is commonplace. In this respect, she feels it may sometimes be the first opportunity to deal with significant failure or disappointment. For example, students have had to abandon different projects because they could not get insurance, Garda (police) clearance, or school or hospital support for their idea. They then have to develop a new one. (Project failure has normally happened early in the semester and often before a project proposal has been submitted or passed. There has then usually been time for students to develop an alternative.) In some cases students may have been disappointed with elements of their project. Here for example, they may not have achieved an adequate turnout in their charity walk or awareness seminar despite putting a lot of time and effort into the project.

there's so much being pulled in together here the responsibility is probably better ... shared'.

PRACTICE

She talks about the practical aspects. She says that the students have 'been given an opportunity to begin to put the theory into practice, and the more practice the stronger they are going to become'.

IMPACT

She refers to the emotional aspect of learning and says that students need 'to feel what they're learning ... to learn it'. She feels for example, that they are 'removed' from a case study because 'they can make a decision about the case ... but the impact has no affect on them'. She says 'we can't control ... the emotional learning the student has ... we have no way of controlling how that's going to take place'.

FREEDOM

She also mentions the freedom of the method and refers to how it gives 'them the freedom to develop and to learn'.

LEARNING RESPONSIBILITY

She says they work hard 'at making sure that it happened' and normally produced a '110 per cent commitment, which is something rare'. She says 'ownership was a huge element' and 'if something went wrong ... they weren't going to blame the ... lecturer'. This was because the project 'was theirs, and ultimately the outcome was their responsibility'. For this reason, she says 'attendance was extremely good' and they tend to work at their report 'constantly' and always hand it in 'on time'. She says the fear 'about loss of face' was important here and feels the students 'were never going to let this fail ... because they couldn't blame somebody else'.[13]

---

13 She does not refer to the enjoyment or different world finding. This may be because these findings may be more pertinent to the consciousness of students than teachers.

Theory

Why did such a low number refer to theory learning? Some students were overpowered by the project whereas others decided that since there was no exam they would not bother with the theory. Some of the earlier student comments led, as we saw above, to changes in the way the theory was delivered.[14]

However, theory is significantly learned here through the interaction of practice and reflection during the project and when the report is being written up. Praxis is a useful concept in this context.

PRAXIS

Praxis means integrating theory and practice and is a learning process that happens when we reflect on our experiences.[15] In this respect praxis happens when theory becomes part of lived experience. Therefore rather than the theory just being learned intellectually in a classroom or library, it is now experienced and realised in the real world.[16]

Nora, one of the service-learning students links theory and practice as follows. She says 'a lot of stuff you do in other lectures ... goes over your head'. However, by being 'practical with something you'll always remember it'. She says you learn theory 'to help you through your project'.

Amy talks about learning theory by linking it to practice. She feels that the theory 'probably would have went completely over my head' had she not 'found it relevant'. However, because she could relate the practice to the theory and say 'oh I did that', and 'oh I need to do that' she says she could learn better.

When she was writing her report 'it made me look back on say what I did and how I dealt with things ... and think "oh well God that actually was negotiation". Whereas, while I was actually doing it I just thought I was talking to people.'

---

14 As mentioned above a small number of negative comments from Guinan (2004), Gao (2005) and Kieran (2005) led to a better linkage between theory and project activity.
15 See Totikidis and Prilleltensky (2006: 48).
16 See, for example, Stephenson and Christensen (2007) on practice-centred learning.

Maeve refers to 'working directly ... with the theory' She says when you 'practice something you absorb it, better than just sitting there constantly reading over ... your notes'. She says 'you can learn about organisation skills' in class 'but until you practise them you're not going to fully understand them'.

Finally, Asdis says she knew 'theoretical time management' as she had done courses on it. However, she admits she did not really learn how to manage her time until she experienced the 'benefits of actually managing time' while doing her project.

Conclusion

According to our findings in Chapters 6 to 9 this is a highly challenging but enjoyable group of service-learning modules that provides a range of important knowledge, skills and values learning.

Should we not be happy? A challenging, high impact and balanced teaching method that students, beyond all expectations, seem to enjoy. What's the hitch?

We must be cautious. Taking service-learning is not like taking medicine. It is neither a remedy nor a cure. It is a place, method, and process where students are given certain information, theory, and learning opportunities, and which, depending on their experiences and response, can lead to important learning.

This learning however is not a causal effect. Its occurrence depends on certain things including the students' engagement with the course, what they bring to it and the happenings they engage in and allow to take shape.[17]

The method therefore provides certain structures, processes, and opportunities, which students can respond to in particular ways. To this extent, and this extent only, can it generate significant and important learning.

In our final chapter we look at the lessons learned and where we should go from here.

---

17 See also the points made in our evaluation of the findings in Appendix 5.

PART 3
The Future

Part 3 looks to the future. In doing so, it discusses how service-learning can contribute to higher education. It also mentions how our three service-learning modules can enhance business and management courses along with a wide variety of other ones. Finally, it refers to how it can contribute to needs that lie well beyond the normal remit of higher education.

Part 3 contains the following chapter:

10.   How to Strengthen Education

10

How to Strengthen Education

This chapter summarises our findings and makes suggestions for the future.

Higher education has two roles according to the main international bodies in the area.[1] First, it should prepare students for the world of work and for operating in and supporting the economy. It should do this by contributing to the knowledge and skills development of the student. We call this the dominant role of education.

Second, it should prepare students for society and the economy by encouraging the development of relevant values. This facilitates the development of a more ethical graduate. We call this the ancillary role.

Findings

The findings indicate that our service-learning modules can encourage different types of learning. First, they can encourage the development of a range of knowledge and skills learning. Students here learn more about communications, team working, organisation, management, time management, event management, interpersonal, negotiation, project management, networking, and other topics.[2] These types of knowledge and skills can help prepare students for the world of work and society.

Second, they also can encourage confidence and a sense of responsibility. In addition, they can encourage an understanding of others and a capacity to

---

1   See Chapter 4.
2   The type of learning that are experienced by students could differ somewhat if the modules were part of other courses. For example, if the project management module was part of a social work, science or engineering course the types of learning identified by the students themselves could differ.

be concerned for, or care for, those in need. These values and qualities can help prepare students for the economy and society.[3]

MODELS

The service-learning modules provide students with the opportunity to enhance their knowledge, skills and values. Consequently, they meet the requirements of both the dominant and ancillary roles of higher education.

They can, therefore, be considered useful models for higher education as follows. First, some or all of the three modules (project management, leadership and consultancy management) could contribute to any business or management course. Second, they could contribute to other courses. The project management module, for example, could enhance planning, architecture, real estate, construction, engineering, science, social work, health or other programmes. Courses involved in preparing students for delivering activities, for example, art, design, drama, media, education, and social work, could also consider using the project management module. In all cases above, the exact module format and syllabus content can be amended to suit local needs.

In addition, the general service-learning method can be used to enhance the learning in any subject from architecture right through to zoology. As long as the theory is properly integrated with the service activity the subject can benefit and knowledge, skills and values learning can occur. When the service and theory components are integrated and suitably balanced neither is swamped by the other.[4]

THE LEARNING IN SERVICE-LEARNING

The boundaries of what we can learn in education have been changed by service-learning. In the traditional classroom method we expect to learn new knowledge. In experiential learning such as practicals, lab work, internship, or the like we expect to learn new skills. Service-learning however, provides us with the added opportunity of learning personal, civic or caring values. In addition, insight, meaning, and on very special occasions, metanoia, can become part of the learning process.[5] See Figure 10.1.

---

3   Both statements above are tentative findings. If any philosophy comes near to clarifying the assumptions underpinning them it is critical realism. See Kerins (2008: Chapter 7).
4   See Chapter 1.
5   Bloom's taxonomy is weak on the development learning gained from insight, meaning or metanoia and leaves us with a conceptual gap for analysing the possibilities of service-learning.

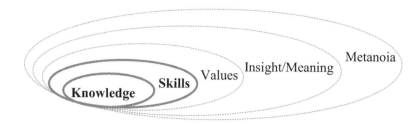

Figure 10.1 The learning in service-learning

Although an exciting lecture or tutorial can have an impact on students, it is mainly in experiential learning, and in particular the service part of service-learning that a more complete range of development learning can occur. The additional types of learning that can occur in service-learning also allow it to contribute to other social and personal needs.

Therefore, we find that higher education can be made more relevant to both work life and society preparation through a judicious use of service-learning. If service-learning is integrated wisely and effectively into the curriculum it can improve the quality and range of learning. This is the main outcome of our study and this is where we should conclude.

However, embedded throughout the study and its findings are pointers to other issues that need to be at least mentioned in this conclusion. To consider this point we discuss things not through the lens of economic and societal needs but by focusing on things at ground level.

Ground Level

What are students really concerned about on the ground? The maintenance of self is primary and grand objectives do not normally evoke much interest. While these are the concern of academics, policy makers and the like, students are much more concerned about things that directly and individually affect them.

At ground level they have to get out of bed every day. They have to organise themselves and do their college work. Mostly they try to get ahead – by studying, taking notes and preparing for exams and assessments. They normally blend college work with leisure and social activity and may also work part-time.

The predominant urge is to survive and thrive: to get good grades, enjoy a social life, maintain their leisure interests, and if necessary have a part-time job to help them pay their way or to pay for the extras. And in the end they hope to get a good job or start their own business.

What does service-learning feel like at ground level? Although our findings allow us to distil its use for higher education in general, a lot of the ground level detail is also there. Students for the most part found it tough going and were hard pressed at times to get it finished. There was not much philosophy here and very little poetry.

However, to be fair, there was a certain amount of excitement and sometimes students became quite involved in their project. This was picked up in the unexpected level of enjoyment the modules generated and in some cases the impact it had on students.

In addition, the grades were higher than average. We should not read too much into this finding, however, except to say that the higher grades are most likely due to the hard work they found themselves putting into the module. In addition, the enjoyment levels may have been part relief at getting through, part joy at a job well done and part satisfaction from doing something useful.

Is there anything else we should say about service-learning? Is there something else we should mention on our way out the door as it were?

Giving students a curriculum-based opportunity to help others may contribute to their development as people. There are several layers to this point. First, we look again at the issue of community.

Need for Community

We need community to help us identify who we are. Without being connected to some community or other we run the risk of being adrift and having a weakened sense of self.[6]

---

6   See Pinkard (1994: 165).

At a deeper level, however, we need community for our well-being. Community in this sense is a place of belonging, caring and personal growth. It is where people care for, and are cared for, by others. People often join a community to be happy but end up staying when they find that happiness comes from helping others. A group of friends become a community when, little by little, they begin to look after each other.[7]

There is, however, a certain resistance to community. This is because people can be reluctant to commit themselves to others. They want to be flexible, try things out and keep their options open. However, if they go on living like this they can end up rootless and may regret not being more decisive in their attachments. Instead of the free spirit and intense life they had once hoped for, they may have become insecure travellers in a changing world.[8]

Change is good – however too much change is not. Toffler, writing as far back as 1970, refers to future shock as 'the disorientation and stress brought about by trying to cope with too many changes in too short a time'.[9] He says we must not overload individuals, organisations, or even countries with too much change. When this happens, it can disorient us and weaken our ability to make intelligent decisions.

Future shock can undermine the familiar ways of thinking and doing and can affect people's social and mental well-being. Depression, for example, is more common among people who have to deal with continual change and adjustment. When we keep changing and cannot easily adjust, our mind can react against all this change.[10] Research indicates that the rate of depression has increased tenfold over the last half century and has become a pervasive feature of countries such as the US.[11]

Toffler has little advice to offer on future shock except to tell us to slow down.[12] But what else can we do to solve the difficulties that can arise from the constant change that surrounds and entices us? In today's world of multiple

---

7   See our discussion on community in Chapter 3.
8   See Grun (2006: 50) for some of the above material.
9   See Tracy (2008: 34) and Toffler (1970).
10 See Grun (2006: 50). See also Khouzam and Singh (2006: 132) who refer to there being a weak positive relationship between life changes and depression and Rahe (1979) who says recent life changes appear to be an important element in explaining illness onset.
11 See Tracy (2008: 35).
12 See Tracy (2008: 34–35) on the above points. Depression is summarised in Turner, Foster, and Johnson as loss of the familiar (2002: 249).

adjustments, fixed points and stability are important for our well-being. In this context, community stability has been offered as a strategy for difficult times.

STABILITY AND COMMITMENT

Stability and a sustained sense of commitment is said to have contributed to the strength of the Roman Empire.[13] For example, the Roman army benefitted from the soldier's lifelong commitment to his legion and the body politic from the senators' commitment to the Senate. This approach originated in the Graeco-Roman system of family life. Here the extended family provided commitment, stability, and the essential ingredient of a cohesive organisation.

This type of organisational commitment was adopted and expanded as *stabilitas loci* by Benedict, the founder of Western monasticism. Prior to this, monks and hermits would wander around joining and leaving different communities as they wished. They might stay for a week, month or longer but then could move on. Benedict's approach to monastic life changed all this.[14] According to Grun, this approach became a 'medicine for the restless era of the great tribal migrations' and today takes on a new immediacy in the context of the amount and variety of local, national and global change.[15]

Stabilitas loci is an unspoken contract between community members confirming their commitment to each other and promising to perform to the best of their abilities. It encourages fairness and tenure and supports a sense of belonging and security. Fairness means there are no favourites and everyone can expect the same rules and rewards. Tenure means the community is not a revolving door and people commit themselves to its well-being and stability.

Grumbling and dissent are discouraged by community. Grumbling can indicate we are dissatisfied with ourselves and a constant desire to improve can stem from an unrecognised dissatisfaction with certain personal weaknesses. Only when there are extreme difficulties with certain people is someone asked to leave – anything less is a violation of the fundamental principle of a stable community.[16]

---

13 See Galbraith and Galbraith (2004: 56–57).
14 See Galbraith and Galbraith (2004: 56).
15 See Grun (2006: 44, 49).
16 See Galbraith and Galbraith (2004: Chapter 7) on the above discussion.

A community of people can be a source of great strength for its members. It can also facilitate peace and harmony among people. This is because a precondition for peace is that each of us is able to deal with our own needs and weaknesses. Here our needs can be expressed and given time to be dealt with one way or the other. Rather than being presented, therefore, as demands, they are allowed to be ventilated. Rather, therefore, than forcing people to make peace, it may be better to first build peace in our own community and then provide it as an example and support for others.[17]

THE NEED TO HELP

Walking down a side street one cold day I saw two homeless men sitting in a doorway. As I got closer I noticed how distressed and unwell one of them was. As he shook and cried he was being held closely and comforted by the other man. They were both very unkempt and worn out and neither seemed to have eaten or slept properly in a long time. I stood there in shock until it dawned on me that the only one in the whole world this very distressed man had to turn to was his homeless and unkempt friend.

People like to help others. Have you noticed how pleased some people can be when they sort out someone else's problem? Or how happy parents can be when they eventually solve a child's problem?

A business negotiation book says 'our very deepest animal instincts remind us that we have a need to help other people'. Although this need may be greater for some than for others, in the end we all want to protect our family and friends.[18]

One of the benefits of relationship is being needed for care and love and being able to nurture and help someone else.[19] Breggin, the psychiatrist, says that 'of all the gifts given to us … being able to help others is among the greatest'.[20] Few experiences in life, he says, are as fulfilling as this. People are grateful, he says, to be parents, teachers, health professionals, religious ministers, volunteers, coaches, or big brothers and sisters. Friends, he says, can feel privileged to help each other.

---

17 See Grun (2006: 45–49, 55–59) on the above material.
18 See Nixon's book on mastering business negotiation in Asia (2005: 128–129).
19 See Cutrona (2004: 992).
20 See Breggin (2006: 167).

Confucius's social philosophy largely revolves around the concept of love or what he calls *ren*. This condition is the ideal state of humanity and needs self-discipline to be achieved.

People with the characteristic of *ren* work to help others. Helping others does not just mean giving them money or food. It also means helping them to become better people themselves. Confucius regards loving others as a calling and a mission for which we should be ready to die.[21]

Ren is a quality that everyone should strive to achieve, but it is so exalted that he is wary of attributing the quality to anyone. Thus for Confucius, the good life is really the endless aspiration for ethical perfection.[22]

In the Christian tradition when we help others we improve and develop ourselves. According to Luke the Gospel writer the more we give, the more we receive: 'give and it shall be given to you'.[23]

In the Islamic tradition 'Sufism', or Islamic mysticism, encourages the selfless love of others. It also encourages meditation, prayer, chanting and the renunciation of certain aspects of the material world.[24] Sufism plays a significant role in the attitude of the individual Muslim towards life. It also plays an important role in Islam's ethical system, and in its history.[25]

We need people who can help others, in the home, at work, in the neighbourhood and on the street. If not, who will fill the cracks in our world? Who will visit the sick, old, indigent or cranky? Who will care for the kids, especially when they go bad? Who will think kindly of, or help the unemployed, the vagrant, or the prisoner?

Students

Students go to college to learn. They can spend long hours sitting in classes, listening, and taking notes. In applied subjects, like engineering or medicine, they do a lot of practical work. They then have to spend time studying or practising what they have learned.

---

21 See Liu (2006: 57–58) and Riegel (2006) on the above.
22 See Microsoft Encarta Online Encyclopedia (2009a).
23 See Luke 6:38; Acts 20:35.
24 See Saeed (2003: 69).
25 See Ghorbal (1987: 66), Hourani (1992: 40), and Merriam-Webster (2000: 1557).

Most of them have being doing this type of thing since secondary school or earlier. This is a long process for which there seems to be little remedy except to look forward to leaving college when they can hope to do real things with what they know.

In the meantime what happens to all this learning? In most cases it seems to be used for no other reason than to do assignments or sit exams.

No one seems to get any immediate benefit from it apart from the students themselves. Much as they might enjoy and benefit from it they are rarely, if ever, given the chance to help others with their learning. Even when they occasionally get to help a sibling or friend with their knowledge this only gives temporary respite from the process.

Surely, there is a better way of doing things? Surely there can be some other purpose to college learning than waiting for graduation and the real world?

This situation is changed by service-learning. Here students are given the opportunity to use their college learning to help others. Now it can be used for more than just grade enhancement or personal advancement.

FINDINGS

The satisfaction that students get from helping others and doing something useful comes up again and again in our own findings. Although most students refer to the challenging and trying nature of service-learning, many refer to the enjoyment and satisfaction they get from doing the projects and helping others.[26]

I remember a difficult conversation I had with a student who wanted to minimise her time spent on her project. The conversation went like this.

> 'Now look here' she said. 'I have absolutely no interest in spending an extra two hours in that old folks' home. I mean to say no one cares whether I'm there or not. I'm in my final year and you guys want me to just put in time. This is not first year for God's sake.'
>
> 'They really need help' I said.

---

26 See Chapter 9.

Silence.

'Some of them get absolutely no visitors at all' I said.

She seemed to be cooling down while she scrutinised me intently.

'They really don't' I said.

Silence.

'Mmmh, that's different …' and she stood thinking.

'Ok then!' and off she went.

When she realised she was really needed she changed position.

HELPING OTHERS

Helping others is not easy. However, some of the great doers and thinkers of our civilisation suggest it is the essential ingredient of a worthy person. There may in fact, be a deep need in us to be able to help people. Helping others may be part of the higher order of our being when we get beyond independence, competence and achievement.[27]

Service-learning gives students a structured and supported opportunity to engage with the community and help others. While most of us work our way through school, college and the work world, the pressure to survive can be significant and sometimes things can get so difficult that we may be tempted to walk over others to reach the far bank. So much so that even thinking about other people's needs may be difficult.

Eventually, however, life intrudes with its demands and a sick parent, child or close friend may be the first real call on our caring capacity. But some may have had to help out when they were younger because they had a sick sibling or lived in a poor area where hardship was quite common.

One way or the other, service-learning can be a mechanism for providing people with an early opportunity to use their learning and skills to help others.

---

27 See for example, the brief comments on Maslow's 'humanistic' theory of motivation in Pincus (2004: 379).

It can also provide them with the chance to engage with their community. Our research indicates that some students were so affected by their experience that they volunteered after they had finished their module.

However, learning to help others is not like learning to ride a bicycle and one or two service-learning modules are not likely to change things dramatically. Being able to help others in difficult circumstances can call for great determination. Confucius says that *ren* needs much discipline and Christ is said to have spent 40 days and nights in the desert preparing himself for his difficult task.[28] Similarly, the Sufi path of Islam is developed through a variety of exercises and practices which help the person to refine their soul and reach God.[29]

Service-learning must not become a mere device or social engineering project. Neither should it create uncalled for expectations. For example, asking service-learning to encourage a volunteering cadre to fill gaps in a government's efforts to meet some of our social needs may need to be done with caution.

A thriving service-learning sector in higher education may indeed lead to a cadre of later life volunteers whose activities support the government's social goals and society's needs. However, there is much more at work than this. Matt's comment in Chapter 8 that he barely gets time to volunteer for himself 'let alone go volunteering for other people' is worth repeating. Matt has little space for volunteering. In fact, one of his main tasks at present is to make sure he is strong enough to look after the obligations on his own doorstep.

Having said this, however, service-learning can fulfil an important community and human development role that is additional to the important role it can play in higher education. This role has its own separate integrity and is worth supporting. To clarify this point we could remind ourselves of what Matt says about his homelessness project in Chapter 9.

Although he is 'absolutely' exhausted he says 'it could be worse, I could be … in a cardboard box …. You know … somebody could come along and throw a real spanner in the works and things could get real tough'. He says, 'I have a

---

28 See Luke 4:1–13.
29 See Saeed (2003: 69–70). See also Porterfield (2008: 10–11) who says that Muslims around the world acknowledge the role that Sufi approaches to Islam plays in encouraging kindness and other desirable traits.

roof over my head … a job, I go to college … most of my college is paid for … at the end of the day, I'm a very lucky individual'.

It is all a matter of perspective. The homeless man might well have walked past his distressed colleague to get to the soup kitchen. Matt might similarly have ignored his daughter to deal with the ample challenges that arise from his job and college activities.[30]

Everyone is challenged in one way or the other and getting out of bed is a difficulty for some. Infants begin life in a state of total physical helplessness. As they grow and develop they become more and more autonomous.

By the time they go to college they have reached an advanced stage of autonomy and are often in the final stages of preparation for work life and the economy and on the cusp of independent living.

They are also ready to move more definitely from helplessness and reliance to independence, autonomy and beyond. Being able to help people is the fullest flowering of human and spiritual development. The Confucian concept of *ren* and the Christian concept of love is the highest form of human achievement.

It is not to the North Pole or Mount Everest we must go to see real heroes. It is in the hard neighbourhoods, the difficult marriages, the homeless shelters, the prisons, the awful homes, and the mean streets that we may see them operate. They may also be found in our ordinary homes when adversity comes knocking and in the workplace when things go bad.

The psychiatrist Breggin says that helping others is impossible without first being able to help ourselves. As we find confidence and comfort within ourselves, we are better able to provide it to others.[31] Matt's responsibility to his daughter is mentioned in Chapter 8. However, this is not always the case as the example of the two homeless men above shows. Even the weak and beaten down can be heroic.

---

30 Matt's responsibility to his daughter is mentioned in Chapter 8.
31 Breggin says that 'as we find confidence and comfort within ourselves, we will *spontaneously* provide it to others' (2006: 75). This is wishful thinking. Helping others is not a spontaneous reflex and sometimes can be very challenging – no matter how well we are. However, his point that we need to be strong to better help others is correct.

Conclusion

Service-learning can contribute to the improvement of higher education. Here it can be sold as transformational and paradigm shifting.[32]

However, one should not get carried away with this sort of thing. Fundamentally important as it is, we should realise that changing the format and pattern of the higher education curriculum is no easy task. Before calling for a significant use of service-learning we should recognise the slow rate of change in higher education.[33]

When service-learning has been clarified at institute level and its potential clearly identified, its introduction should be well planned. Here the effective use of piloting, where helpful, should be seen as a natural part of the slow but sure improvement in higher education.

However, it can do more than this. A service-learning approach that encourages students to help others may allow them to have some curriculum-based experience of what it is to care for others. In doing so it may help introduce them to that area of life where human greatness is most heavily tried, tested and achieved.

---

32 See for example, Nucci and Narváez (2008: 489).
33 In Ross (1973: 108) it was stated that higher education does not respond adequately to short-term fluctuations in social or economic conditions.

Postscript

Book writing is a challenging activity and requires much time and effort. Although some writers can think fast and write quickly, I find it a slow and detailed process. Rice says the commitment necessary for book writing is 'enormous' and says it is a 'lonely' activity requiring 'much fortitude of spirit and personal reflection on life'.[1] Some compare book writing to sending out messengers: to go where we cannot, to speak to people we would never meet and to encourage ideas that might otherwise have died on the vine of our own locality. Ecclesiastes, however, warns us that 'of making many books there is no end; and much study is a weariness of the flesh'.[2]

Writing as Discovery

Writing this book was not a logical or linear process. Although the general outline of the book was anticipated at the outset, the writing process was a reflective process of discovery that continued right throughout the study.

The text was structured and restructured both within and across chapters a number of times as things became clearer. The writing and rewriting of this text has been part of the learning process and has provided me with an additional space for analysis and discovery. In this respect, I often improved my understanding of things by reading and reflecting on the evolving text.

Writing is normally seen as a way of telling readers what we have discovered. Researchers sometimes see the writing-up process as a mechanical activity that functions simply to deliver information and discoveries. When this is the

---

1   See Rice (1997: 38). I took roughly six years to prepare this book, one of which was full-time.
2   See Ecclesiastes 12:12 and http://loud-time.blogspot.com/2008/12/of-making-of-books-there-is-no-end.html located on 7 October 2009 on above the points.

case, and when the writing-up process shuts down the creative and receptive capacity, it may lead to a boring text.[3]

Researching and Writing in an Age of Endless Information

We live and write in an age of endless facts, data, opinion and argument. What are we to do with all this detail? How can we survive the press of information that seeks our attention?

The academic world has a structured search process that facilitates engagement with the available information on any particular topic. Some writers refer to the importance of a well planned literature search strategy. Others go further and suggest a particular search order such as dictionaries and encyclopaedias, books, articles, newspapers, government publications, theses, conferences proceedings, and so on.[4]

The methodology of fashion forecasting is worth mentioning. Edelkoort says that fashion forecasters are like electrical cords taking down the market's message. They are plugged into the flow of relevant information in the fashion world and are, therefore, better able to identify the early trends.

Identifying fashion trends often calls for an eclectic approach. For example, people need to continually watch for new developments by keeping a close eye on what is bought in the shops and worn on the street. They also look for information in fashion fairs and exhibitions, magazines, newspapers, TV and wherever else useful information is available.[5]

IMMERSION

Wright Mills says it is important to be 'soaked in the literature'. He says you do not really have to study a topic since 'once you are into it, it is everywhere'. By becoming immersed in the literature you become sensitive to its themes and you hear and see them everywhere, often in unrelated areas. Even the mass media, with its movies, novels, glossy magazines and so on 'are disclosed in fresh importance to you'.[6]

---

3   See Richardson (2000: 923, 925) on the above material.
4   See Wilkinson (2000: 71) and Hussey and Hussey (1997: 89).
5   See Kerins (1999: 234–236) on the above points.
6   See Wright Mills (1970: 232, 236) on the above material.

Wright Mills exaggerates in saying that once you are into a topic it is everywhere. It is not everywhere. It does, however, have the happy habit of popping up when you least expect it and you can sometimes find yourself making unexpected linkages.

The various strategies for doing a literature search and review can now be summarised as lying between two extremes. At one end is the standard academic approach and at the other is the full immersion approach of Wright Mills. These are outlined in Figure P.1.

Search Strategy

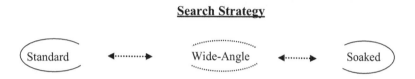

Figure P.1   Literature search strategies

The standard approach may be more than adequate for the busy world we live in. Telling researchers to become soaked in the literature may be off-putting, especially for those who like a healthy work–life balance. Wright Mills is also aware of the difficulties of this approach and cautions against becoming 'too soaked' in case we drown in the literature.[7]

Offering a middle strategy may be more acceptable. This we call the 'wide-angle' approach. Here researchers supplement the standard approach by developing a frame of mind that facilitates them picking up information elsewhere.

I initially took a standard approach. However, over time I unknowingly began to take the wide-angle approach. Because of this, such activities as leisure reading, coffee breaks with colleagues or watching TV became opportunities for useful leads, information, or realisations. However, when work was finished I avoided the topic unless something relevant popped up, in which case I left a note on my desk for the next working day.

---

7   See Wright Mills (1970: 236).

SOCIOLOGICAL IMAGINATION

Wright Mills calls for the development of a sociological imagination. Information, he says, can dominate our attention and overwhelm our ability to assimilate it, in what he calls our Age of Facts. The skills of reason, he admits, are important but we also need the qualities of mind that helps us use information and develop reason in order to achieve lucid summaries of what is going on in our world. Wright Mills proposes a number of ways of stimulating the sociological imagination.[8] Among these he mentions that general notions we come across may be cast into types as we think about them. Here a new classification can initiate a fruitful conceptual development and in this context refers to the skill of thinking up types.

This study develops a small number of new types to enlarge and improve our understanding of the material discussed. For example, the search strategy concepts above helped summarise for me the alternative approaches to the literature review. Other examples are available elsewhere.[9]

He advises the development of themes when writing up our material. These are different to topics which he suggests can easily be covered in a chapter or section. Themes, by contrast, are master conceptions or signal trends. Some books do not have themes, says Wright Mills, just a string of topics. He says topics on their own are 'indispensable to the writing of books by men without ideas'.[10]

Finally, the sociological imagination can be stimulated by rearranging files. Here we dump out heretofore disconnected folders and then set about re-sorting them. I did not follow this advice.

INTEREST

Wright Mills neglects something critical which can hinder or help a study. This is the issue of excitement, or lack of it, in one's topic. And this, in our world of endless information, is an important gap.

---

8   See Wright Mills (1970: 11, 22, 233–238).
9   See Figures 2.1 and 3.2 on types of learning and the service impulse spectrum for example.
10   See Wright Mills (1970: 238). Wright Mills also suggests we develop an attitude of playfulness towards our key words and phrases by looking up synonyms for them. We did not follow Wright Mill's advice here.

Emotional considerations are important in any venture and can matter more than IQ. In addition, the energy needed to sustain effort, endure frustration and think creatively flows most readily from passion for the topic. This passion provides the energy necessary to propel a project forward.[11]

A study is strengthened when it is interesting to the writer. Those who lack a real interest in their topic may need to stick to the standard search approach if they are not to wear themselves out. Here their leisure time can help them gather the energy and resolve needed for their work task.

For this reason researchers should, where possible, allow their hearts to influence their choice of topic. If this is not possible, they should hope that the actual engagement with the topic generates interest or excitement. My interest in the study was a welcome relief from the daily grind involved in preparing this book.

CONCEPTUALISING TOPICS

Service-learning is a relatively new topic. My understanding of the topic would have been weakened had I just focused on the service-learning literature and not additionally focused on the related concepts of learning and service.

Similarly, my analysis of learning would have been rather limited had I narrowly focused on its meaning and disregarded closely related areas such as learning locations, experiential learning, motivation, responsibility and personal centring.

Analytical mosaic

I used, therefore, what can be called an analytical mosaic approach to analysing phenomena. The mosaic approach helped me to better understand the complex nature of service-learning and its components learning and service by reflecting on their adjacent hinterlands.[12] The opposite can, for discussion purposes, be referred to as the focused approach where we consider the particular concept in question and ignore contiguous elements.

---

11 See Goleman (1996) and Veroff (1992: 156).
12 A mosaic fits a variety of small pieces together in a design. For example, the adjacent hinterland of service included volunteering, community, society developments, location (internal or external community) and so on.

The mosaic approach helped me deal with some of the complexities of my topic. However, it could also create difficulties. For example, how do we define the components of the mosaic and what are its borders? I have taken a particular approach to the mosaic method. Others may dispute the delineation of the learning and service components. However, I at least brought greater clarity to my own thought processes and took my understanding of learning, service and service-learning further than I found to be the case in the available literature.

I also improved my understanding of the topic by taking a multidisciplinary approach. Education in general and service-learning in particular does not easily fit under any one of the traditional disciplines. Therefore relevant material from disciplines such as sociology, psychology, psychiatry, philosophy, business management, politics, and elsewhere are drawn upon in the analysis.

In addition, material outside the standard disciplines is used. For example, O'Shea's pottery story is used because the standard literature accessed did not readily provide this complex but important point.[13] Complex or novel points can sometimes be best dealt with through parables or stories and sometimes I felt more comfortable using raw dialogue to make certain points.

End

The writer John Banville once said that all he wanted to do in writing a book was to make a small, finished, polished and beautiful object. He said he had 'nothing to say about the world, or society … or anything else … apart from the object itself' and 'just wanted to get the damn thing done'.[14]

His comments helped me realise the change I underwent while doing this study – from teacher, to researcher, and on then to writer. Although I had plenty to say about the topic, it was mostly based on what I discovered others had to say through a detailed research and reflection process. Therefore, although the finished object is mine, it is fundamentally everyone else's, in that I have travelled through their territory, their experiences, their opinions, and writings.

---

13   See O'Shea (1992).
14   See Banville at http://marksarvas.blogs.com/elegvar/2005/06/were_back_from_.html located on 8 April 2009.

However, in spite of the fact that the details are everyone else's, I am responsible for the finished product which in the end is in harmony with how I feel after the journey – which has now ended.

Appendices

Appendices

1

Report Requirements

Title Page[1]

Contents Page

Executive Summary[2]

Background[*]   – *Why I choose the CLP elective*[3]
                      – *Why I chose my particular project*

Introduction[*]   *Objectives; Beneficiaries;*

Work Phases[**]   *Identify the project's critical development phases.*[4]

Analysis[5][**]   Do an analysis of your project as follows:

1. Reflect on your *course subjects* since first year and discuss where your project experience has given you a deeper understanding of your course material.

2. Reflect on the *material discussed* in this course and relate it, where useful, to your project experience.

---

1   Title (explanatory), author, group or individual project, date submitted, first or final draft.
2   Maximum ½ a page for the summary. Each section runs on to one another.
3   Where an asterisk (*) is located after a section of the report it indicates how many pages approximately that section should take. Therefore, one asterisk indicates a *maximum of one page* and two asterisks (**)indicates *no more* than *two pages*. Pieces without asterisks are to be less than a page and where possible only a few lines.
4   Outline critical development phases *from the start to the end* including this report stage and include any project changes. Use your log book to help you.
5   Even if your project is a group project you are required to do your own analysis component although you may like to discuss with your group colleague(s) your preparation for the earlier parts of the report.

3. Would your project have happened without CLP? If not why not?

4. If useful you can break your project into its planning, implementation and evaluation stage. Here you could discuss what you have learned about planning, implementation and evaluation of a project.

Evaluation[**] Please evaluate as follows:

1. Evaluate your project impact on the beneficiaries.

2. Evaluate *your strengths and weaknesses* in doing professional project work and outline the lessons you have learned.

3. Outline the *pros and cons* of the CLP from your perspective.

Recommendations[*] – Professional self development;
– Community Learning Programme

Appendix Activity log; evaluation sheet

End Week	ACTIVITY	HEADING
		If possible provide a simple category heading for each week or work phases.

Note: All material must be *accurate, brief and to the point*. Long-winded and poorly edited material is not advised. Type your report on A4, typesize 12pt, single spacing. Appended material should be the bare minimum.

2

Examples of Service-learning Projects

There has been a large variety of volunteering projects carried out by service-learning students. Below are some of many different examples.

1.   *Special Olympics*: There have been a number of Special Olympics projects including a faculty based awareness and recruitment campaign for the 2003 Special Olympics in Ireland.

2.   *Homelessness*: There have been a number of homelessness projects some of which included fundraising, participation on a Simon Community soup run on the streets of Dublin and a presentation in the faculty on homelessness. Another combined a weekly visit to a local homeless shelter to help with the mid-day meal and an awareness seminar in the faculty.

3.   *Blindness*: One project planned, organised and ran an evening dinner for visually impaired people in the college restaurant with the support of the National Council of the Blind of Ireland.

4.   *Homework Support*: nine students in different projects have assisted children from disadvantaged backgrounds with their schooling. Here for example, four students worked with the children in the St Vincent de Paul Society Homework Club and also helped recruit volunteers in this area.

5.   *Terminally Ill Children*: three students helped plan and implement a charity lunch in Clontarf Castle Hotel to provide funds for the Share a Dream Foundation. This charity supports the work being done with terminally ill children.

6. *Senior Citizens*: this involved a number of separate projects including the following two examples:

    – Two students helped out in a nursing home at meal time and during recreation periods. In addition, they helped out with the annual Christmas fund raising fair. This project was linked to the Little Sisters of the Poor, Dublin.
    – Three students helped out in a nursing home by visiting during recreation times. In addition, they introduced the residents to some of the interesting aspects of Chinese culture. This project was linked to the Harcourt Home, Dublin.

7. *Third World AIDS*: two students planned and organised a fundraising event for Third World AIDS relief, and organised a student information presentation on the topic of Third World AIDS.

8. *Bosnia Relief*: one student planned and organised a Bosnia Relief fundraising project with an Applied Leaving Cert class in a local secondary school.

9. *Depression Awareness*: one student planned and organised an information seminar on depression for students. This created awareness of depression and outlined the type of supports and services open to those who suffer from it. This project was linked to Aware.

10. *Model Infant School*: two students supported the local Model Infant School in a fundraising exercise for the Samaritans Purse International. This was for the Operation Christmas Child Project. This project involved a number of fundraising activities with a class of infants including a Christmas Carols event in the student common room of the college.

11. *Children's Christmas Activities*: one student planned, prepared for, and ran a Christmas Nativity Play, and a Carol Service event, with a first-year group of infants in a local primary school.

12. *Charity Parachute*: A number of projects organised a charity parachute jump for such beneficiaries as Tallaght Children's Hospital and Aware.

3

The 33 Interviewees in Kerins' Study

Name		PROJECTS
1.	ELLEN	Primary School Support
2.	SINEAD	"
3.	NORA	"
4.	MAEVE	Secondary School Support
5.	ANDY	"
6.	CORMAC	Alcohol Awareness Project
7.	ASDIS	"
8.	HOLLY	Fundraising/Awareness for Sick Children
9.	JOAN	"
10.	DEIRDRE	Nursing Home Support
11.	LIN*	"
12.	HAO	Chinese Culture Festival
13.	LEI	"
14.	ZHU	"
15.	MATT	Homeless Project
16.	ELENA	5k Charity Cancer Walk
17.	EOIN	Charity Soccer Tournament
18.	GRACE	Rape Awareness
19.	TRACY	"
20.	ANNE	Charity Makeup Workshop
21.	SUSAN	"
22.	AMY	Drugs Awareness Project
23.	MARY	"
24.	THERESA (2)[†]	Primary School Support and Drugs Awareness
25.	BILL (2)	Primary School Support and Homeless Youth
26.	LYNN (2)	"
27.	CATHY (2)	Cancer Awareness and Fundraising and 5k Cancer Charity Walk
28.	MANDY (2)	Cancer Awareness and Fundraising and Fun Events for Children with Cancer
29.	DUSAN (2)	Charity Dinner and Charity Breakfast
30.	BRIDGET (2)	Fundraising for Children's Hospital and Alcohol Awareness
31.	LUCY (2)	Fundraising for Children's Hospital and Fun Events for Children with Cancer in Hospital
32.	AILEEN (2)	Special Olympics 'Swimathon' and Charity Breakfast
33.	CINDY (2)	Fundraiser in College for Children's Hospital
		Fun Events for Children With Cancer in Hospital

[*] Lin was the pilot interviewee. She took the service-learning module three years before the interview.
[†] The (2) denotation indicates those who, at the interview date, had already taken both the project management and leadership modules. The rest had taken the project management module.

4

Analysis of Student Grades

We analysed student grades over a six-year period and compared them against the average student grade for the relevant year and course.[1]

The average service-learning grade between the 2001/02 and 2006/07 academic years was 66.37 per cent with a 14.89 per cent coefficient of variation (CV).[2] As Table A.1 below indicates, the average annual service-learning grade varied during this period from 61.16 per cent to 70.1 per cent and the CV from 8.91 per cent to 21.21 per cent.

The average grade of the 33 students interviewed for this study was 62.8 per cent with a coefficient of variation of 14.8 per cent. Therefore, those interviewed had a slightly lower grade than the 2001–06 average and a slightly higher CV.

Table A.1   Service-learning grades (%)

YEARS	2001/2	2002/3	2003/4	2004/5	2005/6	2006/7	Av.	Interviewees
Number	12	20	21	65	45	37	33.33	33
Average	65.67	70.1	68.95	67.26	61.16	65.05	66.37	62.79
Coeff. of Var.	8.91	11.19	14.38	15.65	18.09	21.12	14.89	16.90

Note: The above figures are rounded up to the nearest 0.01 per cent. The analysis of grades is only available up to 2007 unlike the service-learning numbers in Table 5.1 which include the 2008/09 data.

---

1   The exam grades below are extracted from the relevant examination results in the faculty exams office. The data were analysed using Excel. Other relevant points are referred to in the material below.

2   My thanks to Stuart Wilson and his colleagues in the exams office for their help and advice. See http://intranet.dit.ie/mis2/FAQs/Banner%20FAQs.htm#link1A for information on the DIT's web-based information source that contains among other things the relevant exam results used.

Comparison

The above grades can be placed in context by comparing them to the annual average grade for the relevant year and course of the above student cohort during each of these years. This information is provided in Table A.2.

The average service-learning grade at 66.37 per cent is 9.01 per cent higher than the overall average of the service-learning student cohort at 57.36 per cent. The difference during this period varies from 5.09 per cent in 2005/06 to 11.69 per cent in 2002/03.[3]

The above comparison is graphically displayed in Figure A.1. The service-learning grades are on the left and the overall averages are on the right.

Table A.2   Comparing service-learning (SL) grades to average grades (%)

YEARS	2001/2	2002/3	2003/4	2004/5	2005/6	2006/7	Av.
SL Average	65.67	70.1	68.95	67.26	61.16	65.05	66.37
Overall Average	57.69	58.41	57.74	58.21	56.07	56.04	57.36
Grade Difference	7.98	11.69	11.21	9.05	5.09	9.01	9.01
% Difference	14.00	20.02	19.42	15.55	9.07	16.09	15.70

Note: The above data are taken from an Excel analysis calculated to 6 or more decimal places. (This explains why, for example, the percentage difference in 2001/2 is 14.00 rather than the 13.83 it would be if we used only the data listed above.)

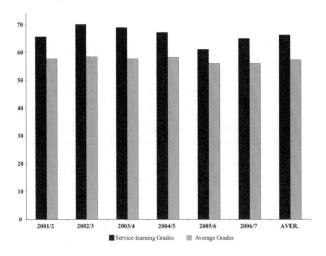

Figure A.1   Comparing service-learning grades with average grades (%)

---

3   The relative difference is 15.7 per cent and this varies from 9.07 per cent to 20.02 per cent.

5

Evaluation of Research Findings

How solid are our research findings? The findings are based on an analysis of 71 interviews from four different studies, one key informant interview and an analysis of student grades.

The analysis of the 71 student interviews required a translation of meaning across four different studies. To help avoid difficulties we use a standard methodological and reporting format to analyse and report on these findings. This includes writing up our findings using the four thematic areas of knowledge, values, preparation for work and society and teaching method.[1]

Student Interviews

There are however, certain points we should take account of when we use the findings from the student interviews. Although the interviews provide a rich source of information we need to be cautious with this type of evidence. Some suggest that self-report is a relatively weak measure of learning and can confuse student satisfaction with the actual learning itself.[2] This is why we cross check where possible the findings with the opinions of the key informant and the results of an analysis of student grades.

Second, students may not know they have learned certain things such as tacit knowledge. This is the type of knowledge that people do not know they have and which they cannot articulate. However, it is important for organisational

---

1   The knowledge findings are dealt with in Chapter 6, values in Chapter 7, preparation for work and society in Chapter 8 and the teaching method findings are covered in Chapter 9.

2   Eyler says we should instead develop measures that require us to show evidence of learning, rather than rely on the opinions of students. In spite of her suggestion, however she admits that cognitive scientists have been 'struggling' with such measures 'for some time' (Eyler, 2000: 13). Steinke and Buresh similarly support the need for such measures. However, they too admit the difficulties with such methodologies (2002: 5).

and individual success and is one of the key factors distinguishing successful managers from others. Since most tacit learning occurs through activity this learning mostly occurs through the service component of service-learning.[3]

Third, the findings reflect the students' capacity to explain their experiences in ways that can be understood and analysed. The findings for example, may be influenced by the concepts available to students in their course. What they say about learning (communications, teamwork and so on) might differ if they were taking a different course. For example, if they were studying community work, sociology, economics or political science their identified learning could differ from the above.[4]

Fourth, the concepts used in the findings are not always as watertight as the results imply. For example, the distinction between event and project management learning may not be as distinct as implied. This is because some interviewees may believe their project gave them *event* knowledge rather than *project* knowledge depending on their understanding and use of the terms. Even within a particular course, concepts may come and go. Take event management again. This concept has become more commonly used since 2005.[5]

Thus, environmental or societal factors may affect the types of learning identified. If, therefore, the same questions were asked ten years ago or ten years hence some of the learning concepts used for the exact same projects, course content and experiences might be different.

---

3   See Armstrong and Mahmud (2008: 189, 201) on the above material on tacit knowledge.

4   For example, community work students might mention facilitating, supporting, promoting and persevering as relevant learning. This might especially be the case if they had read Andrews (2006) whose work lists the skills mentioned. Sociology students might refer to cross-cultural understanding, dealing with social problems, and community relations skills, especially if they studied in the Sociology Department of Belmont University. See www.belmont.edu/sociology/skills/index.html. Economics students might mention efficiency, resource allocation and competitive skills along with social entrepreneurship. Political science students might mention political understanding, partnership working and local leadership skills, especially if they had read Silvester (2007: 7).

5   A significant change here was the introduction of an event management degree in the school in September 2005. Although an event management module has been running since 1997, event management moved centre stage when the degree started in September 2005. The original interviews for Guinan (2004) and Gao (2005) and Kieran (2005) took place before this date (where it scored 18 per cent). Students may have mentioned it more often in Kerins (2008) (45 per cent) partly at least because they are in an environment where the term is in greater use. The level of event management learning however, also reflects the type of service-learning projects. Projects with events are more likely to contain event management learning than those with only small event activity. However, this factor does not appear to explain the noticeable difference between this and the earlier studies.

Fifth, the findings reflect our ability to interpret the concepts used by interviewees. This was not always an easy task. For example, when interviewees say they learn communications, it was not always easy to identify whether they developed more communications knowledge, better skill, or some combination of both. Therefore, it is sometimes difficult to discern whether learning outcomes refer to knowledge, skill or a combination of both.

Finally, the challenge of avoiding error is not just to do with the conceptual capacity of the researcher or students but can relate to the distinctiveness of words. The philosopher Locke says that 'the very nature of words makes it almost unavoidable for many of them to be doubtful and uncertain in their significations'.[6] We need not go this far to agree that the words available to both the researcher and interviewees are not always as watertight and conceptually distinct as we would wish.

Therefore we cross check or triangulate the 71 interview findings with the key informant interview and the grade analysis. Even here we must be wary. For example, the finding that service-learning students earn 9 per cent on average more than the overall average of the relevant year and course is interesting. However, we must remember that service-learning students had a relatively high attendance and this might have contributed to the higher grade.[7]

---

6   See Locke (1854: 309).
7   See the evaluation of the grades in Kerins (2008: 14.2.4).

References

Abes, Elisa S., Golden Jackson and Susan R. Jones (2002) 'Factors That Motivate and Deter Faculty Use of Service-Learning', *Michigan Journal of Community Service Learning*, Fall, Vol. 9, No. 1, pp. 5–17.

Ainley, Mary, Suzanne Hidi and Dagmar Berndorff (2002) 'Interest, Learning, and Psychological Processes that Mediate their Relationship', *Journal of Educational Psychology*, Vol. 94, No. 3, pp. 545–561.

Andrews, Dave (2006) *Compassionate Community Work: An Introductory Course for Christians*, Carlisle: Piquant Press.

Annette, John (2002) 'Service Learning in an International Context', *Frontiers*, Winter, pp. 83–93.

Applegate, James L. and Sherwyn P. Moreale (2001) 'Creating Engaged Disciplines: One Association's Effort to Encourage Community Involvement', *Campus Compact Reader: Service-Learning and Civic Engagement*, Fall, Vol. 2, No. 2, pp. 2–6.

Armstrong, Steven J. and Anis Mahmud (2008) 'Experiential Learning and the Acquisition of Managerial Tacit Knowledge', *Academy of Management Learning & Education*, Vol. 7, No. 2, pp. 189–208.

Arnason, Arnar (2001) 'Experts of the Ordinary: Bereavement Counselling in Britain', *Journal of the Royal Anthropological Institute*, Vol. 7, pp. 299–313.

Arnett, Jeffrey Jensen (2000) 'Emerging Adulthood: A Theory of Development From the Late Teens Through the Twenties', *American Psychologist*, May, Vol. 55, No. 5, pp. 469–480.

Arnett, Jeffrey Jensen (2007), *Adolescence and Emerging Adulthood: A Cultural Approach*, Third Edition, Upper Saddle River, NJ: Prentice Hall.

Arnold, Karen D. (2007) 'Education on the Appalachian Trail: What 2,000 Miles can Teach us About Learning', *About Campus*, November–December, Vol. 12, No. 5, pp. 2–9.

Baali, Fuad (1988) *Society, State and Urbanism: Ibn Khaldun's Sociological Thought*, Albany, New York: SUNY Press.

Baccaro, Lucio and Marco Simoni (2007) 'Centralized Wage Bargaining and the "Celtic Tiger" Phenomenon', *Industrial Relations – A Journal of Economy and Society*, July, Vol. 46, No. 3, pp. 426–454.

Baehr, Peter R. (Editor) (2003) *The Portable Hannah Arendt*, Harmondsworth: Penguin Classics.

Banner, James M., Jr. and Harold C. Cannon (1997) *The Elements of Teaching*, New Haven and London: Yale University Press.

Barab, Sasha, Michael Thomas, Tyler Dodge, Robert Carteaux and Hakan Tuzun (2005) 'Making Learning Fun: Quest Atlantis, A Game Without Guns', *Educational Technology Research and Development*, Vol. 53, No. 1, pp. 86–107.

Barak, Gregg (2005) 'A Reciprocal Approach to Peacemaking Criminology: Between Adversarialism and Mutualism', *Theoretical Criminology*, Vol. 9, No. 2, pp. 131–152.

Battistoni, Richard M. (2001) 'Service-Learning and Civic Education', *Campus Compact Reader: Service-Learning and Civic Engagement*, Summer, Vol. 2, No. 1, pp. 6–14.

Becker, Anne (2008) 'Rise of the TV Shrink, Why New Shows on Psychotherapy Sessions Keep Viewers on Edge of Couch', *Broadcasting & Cable*, 24 February, located at www.broadcastingcable.com/article/CA6534744.html on 5 March 2009.

Berman, Sally (2006) *Service Learning: A Guide to Planning, Implementing and Assessing*, Second Edition, Thousand Oaks, CA: Corwin Press.

Bhatnagar, S. Rani (1970) 'From Charity to Taxes: Observations on the Sociology of Religious and Secular Giving', *Scientific Study of Religion*, Fall, Vol. 9, No. 3, pp. 209–218.

Bloom, Benjamin S. and David R. Krathwohl (1956) *Taxonomy of Educational Objectives: The Classification of Educational Goals, by a Committee of College and University Examiners, Handbook I: Cognitive Domain*, New York: Longman Green.

Blunsdon Betsy, Steven McEachern, Nicola McNeil and Ken Reed (2003) 'Experiential Learning in Social Science Theory: An Investigation of the Relationship Between Student Enjoyment and Learning', *Higher Education Research and Development*, Vol. 22, No. 1, pp. 43–56.

Boyer, Kristy Elizabeth, Rachael S. Dwight, Carolyn S. Miller, C. Dianne Raubenheimer, Matthias F. Stallmann and Mladen A. Vouk (2007) *A Case for Smaller Class Size with Integrated Lab for Introductory Computer Science*, in the Proceedings of the 38th SIGCSE Technical Symposium on Computer Science Education, Covington, Kentucky, 7–10 March, New York, NY: ACM Press, pp. 341–345.

Bowes, John (1998) 'Service-Learning as a New Form of Catholic Action', *Review of Business*, Fall, Jamaica, Vol. 20, Issue 1, pp. 26–29.

Breggin, Peter R., (2006) *The Heart of Being Helpful: Empathy and the Creation of a Healing Presence*, New York: Springer Publishing Company.

Brown, John Seely and Paul Duguid (2000) 'Organisational Learning and Communities-of-Practice: Toward a Unified View of Working, Learning, and Innovation', in Rob Cross and Sam Israelit (Editors), *Strategic Learning in a Knowledge Economy: Individual, Collective and Organizational Learning Process*, Woburn, MA: Butterworth Heinemann, pp. 143–165.

Bucco, Diana A. and Julie A. Busch (1996) 'Starting a Service-Learning Programme', in Barbara Jacoby and Associates, *Service-Learning in Higher Education: Concepts and Practices*, San Francisco: Jossey-Bass, pp. 231–245.

Buetow, Stephen, Vivienne Adair, Gregor Coster, Makere Hight, Barry Gribben and Ed Mitchell (2003) 'Key Informant Representations of Maori and Other Patient Fears of Accessing General Practitioner Care for Child Asthma in Auckland, New Zealand', *Health Education*, Vol. 103, Issue 2, pp. 88–98.

Butin, Dan W. (2006) 'The Limits of Service-Learning in Higher Education', *The Review of Higher Education*, Project Muse, Vol. 29, No. 4, pp. 473–498.

Cacioppo, John T., Louise C. Hawkley, Edith M. Rickett, and Christopher M. Masi (2005) 'Sociality, Spirituality, and Meaning Making: Chicago Health, Aging, and Social Relations Study', *Review of General Psychology*, Vol. 9, No. 2, pp. 143–155.

Calantone, Roger J. and C. Anthony Di Benedetto (2007) 'Clustering Product Launches by Price and Launch Strategy', *Journal of Business & Industrial Marketing*, Vol. 22, No. 1, pp. 4–19.

Calvert, Pamela (2006) 'Media and Metanoia: Documentary "Impact" Through the Lens of Conversion', *Journal of Pastoral Psychology*, Vol. 55, No. 2, November, pp. 145–166.

Campus Compact (2002) *Building the Service-Learning Pyramid*, located at www.compact.org/faculty/specialreport.html on 3 March 2009.

Campus Compact (2007) *2006 Service Statistics: Highlights and Trends of Campus Compact's Annual Membership Survey*, Providence, RI: Campus Compact located at www.compact.org/about/statistics/2006/service_statistics.pdf on 3 March 2009.

Campus Compact (2009) *Glossary of Terms*, located at www.compact.org/help/glossary accessed on 3 March 2009.

Cantillon, Peter and Maeve MacDermott (2008) 'Does Responsibility Drive Learning? Lessons from Intern Rotations in General Practice', *Medical Teacher: An International Journal in the Health Sciences*, Vol. 30, No. 3, pp. 254–259.

Carr, Edward G. and Robert H. Horner (2007) 'The Expanding Vision of Positive Behavior Support: Research Perspectives on Happiness', *Journal of Positive Behavior Interventions*, Vol. 9, No. 1, pp. 3–14.

Carr, Patricia (2000) *The Age of Enterprise: The Emergence and Evolution of Entrepreneurial Management*, Dublin: Blackhall Publishing.

Chapman, Judith G. and Joseph R. Ferrari (1999) 'An Introduction to Community-Based Service Learning (CBSL)', in Joseph R. Ferrari and Judith G. Chapman (Editors) *Educating Students to Make a Difference: Community-Based Service Learning*, New York: The Hawthorn Press Inc., pp. 1–4.

Charon, Joel M. (1992) *Sociology: A Conceptual Approach*, Third Edition, Needham Heights, MA: Allyn & Bacon.

Cheng, Eddie W.L. and Ian Hampson (2007) 'Transfer of Training: A Review and New Insights', *International Journal of Management Reviews*, Vol. 10, No. 1, pp. 1–15.

Chickering, Arthur W. and Linda Reisser (1993) *Education and Identity*, Second Edition, San Francisco: Jossey-Bass.

Clancy, Gareth (2008) 'Employment of Foreign Workers in the United Kingdom: 1997 to 2008', *Economic & Labour Market Review*, July, Vol. 2, No. 7, pp. 18–30.

Clancy, Paula, Ian Hughes and Teresa Brannick (2005) *Public Perspectives on Democracy in Ireland: Topline Results*, 20 June, Democratic Audit, Dublin: TASC.

Clark, Donald (1999) 'Learning Domains or Bloom's Taxonomy' created 5 June, updated 6 November 2007, located at www.nwlink.com/~donclark/hrd/bloom.html accessed on 5 March 2009.

Cohen, Jeremy (1994) 'Matching University Mission with Service Motivations: Do the Accomplishments of Community Service Match the Claims?' *Michigan Journal of Community Service Learning*, Fall, Vol. 1, No. 1, pp. 98–104.

Collins, Tom (2002) Community Development and State Building: A Shared Project, *Community Development Journal*, Vol. 37, No. 1, pp. 91–100.

Cooke, John and Matt Smith (2004) 'Beyond Formal Learning: Informal Community eLearning', *Computers and Education*, CAL03 Special Issue, Vol. 43, No. 1–2, pp. 35–47.

Cooney, Thomas M. (2008) 'Celtic Tiger Found in Education Jungle', *Education & Training*, Vol. 50, No. 1, pp. 64–66.

Cooper, David, (2000) 'Service with Others', *Campus Compact Reader: Service-Learning and Civic Engagement*, Fall, Vol. 1, No. 2, pp. 6–7.

Crews, Robin J. (2002) *Higher Education Service-Learning Source Book*, Westport: Oryx Press.

Cronk, George (2005) *George Herbert Mead (1863–1931)*, located at www.utm.edu/research/iep/m/mead.htm accessed on 5 October 2009.

Csikszentmihalyi, Mihaly and Eugene Rochberg-Halton (1981) *The Meaning of Things: Domestic Symbols and the Self*, New York: Cambridge University Press.

Cuban, Sondra and Jeffrey B. Anderson (2007) 'Where's the Justice in Service-Learning? Institutionalizing Service-Learning from a Social Justice Perspective at a Jesuit University', *Equity and Excellence in Education*, Vol. 40, No. 2, pp. 144–155.

Cutrona, Carolyn E. (2004) 'A Psychological Perspective: Marriage and the Social Provisions of Relationships', *Journal of Marriage and Family*, November, Vol. 66, pp. 992–999.

Davies, Ian (1996) 'Education for Citizenship' in Rosemary Webb, *Cross-Curricular Primary Practice: Taking a Leadership Role*, London: Falmer Press, pp. 116–128.

Davis, Andrew and Kevin Williams (2003) 'Epistemology and Curriculum', in Nigel Blake, Paul Smeyers, Richard Smith, and Paul Standish (Editors), *The Blackwell Guide to the Philosophy of Education*, Malden, MA: Blackwell, pp. 253–270.

De Geus, Arie (1997) *The Living Company: Growth, Learning and Longevity in Business*, London: Nicholas Brealey.

Deans, Thomas (1999) 'Service-Learning in Two Keys: Paulo Freire's Critical Pedagogy in Relation to John Dewey's Pragmatism', *Michigan Journal of Community Service Learning*, Fall, Vol. 6, pp. 15–29.

Dell'Olio, Fiorella (2005) *The Europeanization of Citizenship: Between the Ideology of Nationalism, Immigration and European Identity*, Aldershot: Ashgate Publishing.

Dell'Olio, Fiorella (2007) 'Citizenship: Superseding a Claustrophobic Concept', Networking European Citizenship Education Conference: *Rethinking Citizenship Education in European Migration Societies: Political Strategies – Social Changes –Educational Concepts*, Lisbon, Portugal, 26–28 April.

Dench, Sally (1997) 'Changing Skill Needs: What Makes People Employable?' *Industrial and Commercial Training*, Vol. 29, No. 6, pp. 190–193.

Department of Social, Community and Family Affairs (2000) *A Framework for Supporting Voluntary Activity and for Developing the Relationship between the State and the Community and Voluntary Sector*, Dublin: Government Publications.

Dever, William (1993) *Recent Archaeological Discoveries and Biblical Research*, Seattle, WA: University of Washington Press.

Dewey, John (1933) *How We Think: A Restatement of the Relation of Reflective Thinking to the Educative Process*, Lexington, Massachusetts: D.C. Heath and Company.

Dewey, John (1963) *Experience and Education*, New York: Collier Macmillan.

Dewey, John (1990) *The Child and the Curriculum,* London: The University of Chicago.

Dingle, Alan with Wojciech Sokolowski, Susan K.E. Saxon-Harrold, Justin Davis Smith and Robert Leigh (2001) *Measuring Volunteering, A Practical Toolkit – 2001 International Year of Volunteers,* A joint project of the Independent Sector and United Nations Volunteers located at www.independentsector. org/programs/research/toolkit/IYVToolkit.PDF on 3 March 2009.

DIT (2001) *Dublin Institute of Technology Strategic Plan: A Vision for Development 2001–15,* Dublin: DIT.

Donaldson, Lex (2007) 'Ethics Problems and Problems with Ethics: Toward a Pro-Management Theory', *Journal of Business Ethics,* Vol. 78, pp. 299–311.

Donati, Pierpaolo (2003) 'Giving and Social Relations: the Culture of Free Giving and its Differentiation Today', *International Review of Sociology – Revue Internationale de Sociologie,* Vol. 13, No. 2, pp. 243–272.

Dore, Ronald P. and Mari Sako (1989) *How the Japanese Learn to Work,* London: Routledge.

Du Gay, P. and G. Salaman (1992) 'The Culture of the Customer', *Journal of Management Studies,* Vol. 29, No. 5, pp. 615–633.

Ellison, Nicole B., Charles Steinfield and Cliff Lampe (2007) 'The Benefits of Facebook "Friends": Social Capital and College Students' Use of Online Social Network Sites', *Journal of Computer-Mediated Communication,* Vol. 12, No. 4, pp. 1143–1168.

Emery, Lee and Adele Flood (2003) 'Visual Literacy', in Joan Livermore (Editor) *More Than Words Can Say: A View of Literacy through the Arts,* Braddon, Australia: National Affiliation of Arts Educators Australia.

Encyclopædia Britannica (1999) *Knowledge for the Information Age: International Version,* Encyclopaedia Britannica CD Multimedia edition.

Encyclopædia Britannica Online (2009) '*John Dewey*' located at http://search. eb.com.elib.tcd.ie/eb/article-9030186 on 4 March.[1]

Encyclopædia Britannica Online (2009a) '*Learning Theory*' located at http:// search.eb.com.elib.tcd.ie/eb/article-9108413 on 4 March.

Encyclopædia Britannica Online (2009b) '*Axiology*' located at http://search. eb.com.elib.tcd.ie/eb/article-9011479 on 4 March.

Encyclopædia Britannica Online (2009c) '*Charity*' located at http://search. eb.com.elib.tcd.ie/eb/article-9022536 on 4 March.

---

1   The Encyclopædia Britannica Online article web references used here are based on the TCD library web access system. Therefore the article title and number are the relevant identifiers. Also some of the articles have a number of relevant sub-articles which can be accessed by going to the next page of the article or by scrolling along the table of contents.

Encyclopædia Britannica Online (2009d), *'Religion'* Table I: 'Worldwide Adherents of All Religions by Six Continental Areas, Mid-2007', in *Britannica Book of the Year, 2008*, located at http://search.eb.com.elib.tcd.ie/eb/article-9442242 on 4 March.

Encyclopædia Britannica Online (2009e) *'Symbol(s)'* located at http://search.eb.com.elib.tcd.ie/eb/article-9070715 and from the communications article at http://search.eb.com.elib.tcd.ie/eb/article-21930 on 4 March.

Encyclopædia Britannica Online (2009f) *'Emotion'*, located at http://search.eb.com.elib.tcd.ie/eb/article-9106029 and http://search.eb.com.elib.tcd.ie/eb/article-59204 on 4 March.

Encyclopædia Britannica Online (2009g) *'Contemporary Approaches to Emotion: Emotions and Adaptation'* located at http://search.eb.com.elib.tcd.ie/eb/article-59214 on 4 March.

Eshac, Haim (2007) 'Bridging In-school and Out-of-school Learning: Formal, Non-Formal, and Informal Education', *Journal of Science Education and Technology*, April, Vol. 16, No. 2, pp.171–190.

European Commission (1997) *Promoting the Role of Voluntary Organisations and Foundations in Europe*, Communication from the Commission, Brussels: European Commission.

European Commission (2000) *A Memorandum on Lifelong Learning*, Commission Staff Working Paper, Sec (2000) 1832, 30 October, Brussels: European Commission.

European Commission (2002) *A New Impetus for Youth: European Commission White Paper*, Brussels: European Commission.

European Commission (2003) *The Role of the Universities in the Europe of Knowledge*, Communication from the Commission, Brussels: European Commission.

European Commission (2004) *European Credit Transfer and Accumulation System (ECTS) – Key Features*, Luxembourg: Office for Official Publications of the European Communities.

European Commission (2008) *Growing Regions, Growing Europe: Fifth Progress Report on Economic and Social Cohesion*, Communication from the Commission to the European Parliament and the Council COM(2008) 371 final, Brussels: European Commission.

Eurydice (2005) *Citizenship Education at School in Europe*, Brussels: Eurydice.

Eyler, Janet (2000) 'What Do We Need to Know About the Impact of Service-Learning on Student Learning?' *Michigan Journal of Community Service Learning*, Fall, pp. 11–17.

Eyler, Janet and Dwight E. Giles, Jr (1999) *Where's the Learning in Service-Learning?* San Francisco: Jossey-Bass.

Fagan, Kieran, (2008) 'So What are they Worth', *Innovation, The Irish Times*, Issue 17, December, pp. 34–35.

Faulks, Sebastian (2002) *On Green Dolphin Street*, London: Vintage.

Felstead, Alan, Duncan Gallie and Francis Green (2002) *Work Skills in Britain 1986–2001*, January, London: DfES Publications.

Fisher, Douglas and Nancy Frey (2008) *Better Learning through Structured Teaching: A Framework for the Gradual Release of Responsibility*, Alexandria, VA: Association for Supervision and Curriculum Development.

Foos, Catherine Ludlum (1998) 'The "Different Voice" of Service', *Michigan Journal of Community Service Learning*, Fall, Vol. 5, pp. 14–21.

Friedman, Maurice (1976) *Martin Buber: The Life of Dialogue*, London and Chicago: University of Chicago Press.

Fromm, Erich (1956) *The Art of Loving*, New York: Harper & Row.

Galbraith, Craig S. and Oliver Galbraith (2004) *The Benedictine Rule of Leadership: Classic Management Secrets You Can Use Today*, Avon, Massachusetts: Adams Media.

Gale, Colin and Jasbir Kaur (2004) *Fashion and Textiles: An Overview*, New York: Berg Publishers.

Gao, Shan (2005) *Is the CLP an Effective Teaching Pedagogy for Using in the Education of Hospitality Management and Tourism Students?* Minor Postgraduate Dissertation submitted to the School of Hospitality Management and Tourism, DIT, September.

Ghorbal (1987) 'Ideas and Movements in Islamic History', in Kenneth W. Morgan (Editor) *Islam, the Straight Path: Islam Interpreted by Muslims*, Delhi: Motilal Banarsidass, pp. 42–86.

Ghoshal, Sumantra and Christopher A. Bartlett (2000) *The Individualised Corporation; A Fundamentally New Approach to Management*, Sydney: Random House Business Books.

Giddens, Anthony (2001) *Sociology*, Fourth Edition, Cambridge: Polity Press and Blackwell Publishing.

Giles, Dwight E. Jr and Janet Eyler (1994) 'The Theoretical Roots of Service-Learning in John Dewey: Toward a Theory of Service-Learning', *Michigan Journal of Community Service Learning*, Fall, Vol. 1, No. 1, pp. 77–85.

Gillespie, Paul (2009) Making a Virtue out of a Moral Impasse, *Irish Times*, 14 March.

Glennon, Fred (2008) 'Promoting Freedom, Responsibility, and Learning in the Classroom: The Learning Covenant a Decade Later', *Teaching Theology and Religion*, Vol. 11, No. 1, pp. 32–41.

Godfrey, Paul C. and Edward T. Grasso (Editors) (2000) *Working for the Common Good: Concepts and Models for Service-Learning in Management*, Washington: American Association for Higher Education.

Godsey, R. Kirby (2005) *Centering Our Souls: Devotional Reflections of a University President*, Macon GA: Mercer University Press.

Goleman, Daniel (1996) *Emotional Intelligence: Why it Can Matter More than IQ*, London: Bloomsbury.

Gopal, Anandasivamand and Sanjay Gosain (2009) 'The Role of Organizational Controls and Boundary Spanning in Software Development Outsourcing: Implications for Project Performance', forthcoming in *Information Systems Research*, located at www.rhsmith.umd.edu/faculty/agopal/Controls%20Bo undary%20Spanning%20ISR%20Final.pdf on 5 March. See www.informs. org/site/ISR/article.php?id=126.

Gordon, Rick (Editor) (2000) *Problem Based Service Learning: A Fieldguide for Making a Difference in Higher Education*, Second Edition, Sponsored by Campus Compact for New Hampshire.

Granott, Nira (1998) 'We Learn Therefore we Develop: Learning Versus Development', in M. Cecil Smith and Thomas Pourchot (Editors) *Adult Learning and Development: Perspectives from Educational Psychology, The Educational Psychology Series*, Mahwah, NJ: Lawrence Erlbaum Associates, pp. 15–34.

Granovetter, Mark (1985) 'Economic Action and Social Structure: The Problem of Embeddedness', *American Journal of Sociology*, November, Vol. 91, No. 3, pp. 481–510.

Gray, John (2002) 'Fame is the Filthy Lucre of a Celebrity Economy', *The Sunday Times*, 27 October, London.

Griswold, Wendy (1994) *Cultures and Societies in a Changing World*, California: Pine Forge Press.

Grun, Anselm (2006) *Benedict of Nursia: His Message for Today*, Linda M. Maloney (Translator), Collegeville, Minnesota: Liturgical Press.

Guinan, Michelle (2004) *Do Teaching Practices in Hospitality and Tourism Management Education Meet the Needs of Industry and the Career and Development Needs of Students – A Case Study on the Community Learning Programme*, Undergraduate Dissertation submitted to the School of Hospitality Management and Tourism, DIT, April.

Gujarathi, Mahendra R., and Ralph J. McQuade (2002) Service-Learning: Extending the Curriculum, *The CPA Journal*, New York, February.

Gunnigle, Patrick, Noreen Heraty and Michael Morley (1997) *Personnel and Human Resource Management: Theory and Practice in Ireland*, Dublin: Gill and Macmillan.

Hager, Paul and Terry Hyland (2003) 'Vocational Education and Training', in Nigel Blake, Paul Smeyers, Richard Smith and Paul Standish (Editors), *The Blackwell Guide to the Philosophy of Education*, Malden, MA: Blackwell, pp. 271–287.

Handy, Charles (1999) *Understanding Organisations*, Fourth Edition, London: Penguin Books.

Haralambos, Michael and Martin Holborn (1995) *Sociology: Themes and Perspectives*, Fourth Edition, London: Collins Educational.

Harrow, Anita J. (1972) *Taxonomy of the Psychomotor Domain; a Guide for Developing Behavioral Objectives*, New York: McKay.

Hatcher, Julie A. (1997) 'The Moral Dimensions of John Dewey's Philosophy: Implications for Undergraduate Education', *Michigan Journal of Community Service Learning*, Fall, Vol. 4, pp. 22–29.

Hartman, Diane B., Jan Bentley, Kathleen Richards and Cynthia Krebs (2005) 'Administrative Tasks and Skills Needed for Today's Officer: The Employees Perspective', *Journal of Education for Business*, July/August, pp. 347–357.

Hartnett, Daniel (2000) 'Service-Learning and Justice: Setting Higher Standards for Higher Education', *Solutions*, an internal publication of Loyola University Chicago, October, located at www.luc.edu/experiential/pdfs/Hartnett,_S-L_ and_Justice.pdf on 3 March 2009.

Heine, Steven J., Travis Proulx and Kathleen D. Vohs (2006) 'The Meaning Maintenance Model: On the Coherence of Social Motivations', *Personality and Social Psychology Review*, Vol. 10, No. 2, pp. 88–110.

Heinemann, Mark H. (2005) 'Teacher–Student Interaction and Learning in Online Theological Education. Part II: Additional Theoretical Frameworks', *Christian Higher Education*, Vol. 4, No. 4, pp. 277–297.

Heller, Agnes (1982) *A Theory of History*, London: Routledge and Kegan Paul.

Hidi, Suzanne (2001) 'Interest, Reading, and Learning: Theoretical and Practical Considerations', *Educational Psychology Review*, Vol. 13, No. 3, pp. 191–209.

Hodge, B.J. and William P. Anthony (1988) *Organisation Theory*, Third Edition, Massachusetts: Allyn & Bacon Inc.

Hourani, Albert (1992) *Islam in European Thought*, New York: Cambridge University Press.

Howard, Jeffrey (2001) *Service-Learning Course Design Workbook*, Michigan Journal of Community Service Learning, Summer, OCSL, University of Michigan.

Hunger, David J. and Thomas L. Wheelen (1996) *Strategic Management*, Reading, MA: Addison-Wesley Publishing Company International.

Hurd, Clayton A., (2008) 'Is Service Learning Effective? A Look at the Current Research', in Shalini, S. (Editor) *Service Learning: Perspectives and Applications*, Punjagutta, Hyderabad, India: ICFAI University Press, pp. 44–60.

Hussey, Jill and Roger Hussey (1997) *Business Research: A Practical Guide for Undergraduate and Postgraduate Students*, Basingstoke, Hampshire: MacMillan Press.

Illeris, Knud (2003) 'Workplace Learning and Learning Theory', *Journal of Workplace Learning*, Vol. 15, No. 4, pp. 167–178.

Jacoby, Barbara and Associates (1996) *Service-Learning in Higher Education: Concepts and Practices*, San Francisco: Jossey-Bass.

Jacoby, Barbara and Associates (2003) *Building Partnerships for Service-Learning*, San Francisco: Jossey-Bass.

Jick, Todd D. (1979) 'Mixing Qualitative and Quantitative Methods: Triangulation in Action', *Administrative Science Quarterly*, December, Vol. 24, No. 4, Qualitative Methodology, pp. 602–611.

Johnson Foundation (2009) *Principles of Good Practice for Combining Service and Learning* by Ellen Porter Honnet and Susan J. Poulsen, The Johnson Foundation, located at www.johnsonfdn.org/principles.html on 5 March 2009.[2]

Johnson, Phil, Anna Buehring, Catherine Cassell and Gillian Symon (2007) 'Defining Qualitative Management Research: an Empirical Investigation', *Qualitative Research in Organizations and Management: An International Journal*, Vol. 2, Issue 1, pp. 23–42.

Kahne, Joseph, Joel Westheimer, and Bethany Rogers (2000) 'Service-Learning and Citizenship: Directions in Research', *Michigan Journal of Community Service Learning*, Fall, Special Issue, pp. 42–51.

Kaptein, Muel (2008) 'The Relationship between Ethical Culture and Unethical Behaviour in Work Groups: Testing the Corporate Ethical Virtues Model', *Erasmus Research Institute of Management Report Series*, July, No. ERS-2008-037-ORG, pp. 1–31.

Katz, Idit, Avi Assor, Yaniv Kanat-Maymon and Yoella Bereby-Myer (2006) 'Interest as a Motivational Resource: Feedback and Gender Matter, but Interest Makes the Difference', *Social Psychology of Education*, February, Vol. 9, No. 1, pp. 27–42.

Kayes, D. Christopher (2002) 'Experiential Learning and Its Critics: Preserving the Role of Experience in Management Learning and Education', *Academy of Management Learning and Education*, Vol. 1, No. 2, pp. 137–149.

Kearsley, Greg (2009) *Taxonomies*, from the Theory into Practice Database located on http://tip.psychology.org/taxonomy.html on 5 March 2009.

---

2   There is no date on the web location of the Principles so the latest access date is used.

Kearsley, Greg (2009a) *Andragogy: M. Knowles*, from the Theory into Practice Database located on http://tip.psychology.org/knowles.html on 5 March 2009.

Kendall, Jane C. and Associates (1990) *Combining Service and Learning: A Resource Book for Community and Public Service: Volume 1*, Raleigh, North Carolina: National Society for Internships and Experiential Education.

Kenworthy-U'Ren, Amy L., (2000) 'Management Students as Consultants: A Strategy for Service-Learning in Management', in Paul C. Godfrey and Edward T. Grasso (Editors) *Working for the Common Good: Concepts and Models for Service-Learning in Management*, Washington: American Association for Higher Education, pp. 55–68.

Kerins, Anto T. (1993) *Learning Societies and Low Unemployment*, Dublin: Irish Management Institute.

Kerins, Anto T. (1999) *Sole Survivors: How Exceptional Companies Survive and Thrive at the Edge*, Dublin: Oak Tree Press.

Kerins, Anto T. (2008) *Service-Learning: The CLP Case*, Submitted to the University of Dublin, Trinity College Dublin in fulfilment of the requirements for the degree of Doctor of Philosophy, 17 September.

Keynes, John Maynard (1936) *The General Theory of Employment, Interest and Money*, New York: Harcourt, Brace and Company.

Khan, Maryam and Ken W. McCleary (1996) 'A Proposed Model for Teaching Ethics in Hospitality', *Hospitality and Tourism Educator*, Vol. 8, No. 4, pp. 7–12.

Khouzam, Hani Raoul and Fiza Singh (2006) 'Religion, Spirituality and Psychiatry' in Sylvan D. Ambrose (Editor) *Religion and Psychology: New Research*, New York: Nova Science Publishers.

Kidd, J.R. (1973) *How Adults Learn*, Chicago: Association Press and Follett Publishing Company.

Kieran, Yvonne (2005) *What are the Most Effective Ways of Delivering Education to Third Level Hospitality Management and Tourism Marketing Students from the Students' Perspective?* Minor Postgraduate Dissertation submitted to the School of Hospitality Management and Tourism, DIT, September.

Kinman, Gail and Russell Kinman (2001) 'The Role of Motivation to Learn in Management Education', *Journal of Workplace Learning*, Vol. 13, No. 4, pp. 132–143.

Knowles, Malcolm (1978) *The Adult Learner: A Neglected Species*, Second Edition, Houston Texas: Gulf Publishing.

Koike, Kazuo (1989) 'Human Resource Development on the Shop Floor in Contemporary Japan', *Japanese Employment in the Context of a Changing Economy and Society*, OECD Conference, Paris 30–31 October.

Kolb, David A., (1984) *Experiential Learning: Experience as the Source of Learning and Development*, New Jersey: Prentice Hall.

Kolb, D. (2000) 'The Process of Experiential Learning, Strategic Learning in a Knowledge Economy: Individual, Collective and Organizational Learning Process' in Cross, Rob and Sam Israelit (Editors), *Strategic Learning in a Knowledge Economy: Individual, Collective and Organizational Learning Process*, Woburn MA: Butterworth Heinemann, pp. 313–331.

Korczynski, Marek (2005) 'Skills in Service Work: An Overview', *Human Resource Management Journal*, Vol. 15, No. 2, pp. 3–14.

Kracher, Alfred (2006) 'Meta-Humans and Metanoia: The Moral Dimension of Extraterrestrials', *Zygon: Journal of Religion and Science*, June, Vol. 41, No. 2, pp. 329–346.

Krathwohl, David R. (2002) 'A Revision of Bloom's Taxonomy', *Theory in Practice*, Autumn, Vol. 41, No. 4, pp. 212–218.

Krathwohl, David R., Benjamin S. Bloom and Bertram B. Masia (1964) *Taxonomy of Educational Objectives: The Classification of Educational Goals. Handbook II: Affective Domain*, New York: David McKay Company Inc.

Laroder, Aris, Deborah Tippins, Vicente Handa and Lourdes Morano (2007) 'Rock Showdown: Learning Science through Service with the Community', *Science Scope*, March, Vol. 30, No. 7, pp. 32–37.

Larragy, Joe (2001) *International Approaches to Volunteering: Executive Summary*, A Report to the National Committee on Volunteering, Ireland, November.

Lave, J. and E. Wenger (2000) 'Legitimate Peripheral Participation in Communities of Practice' in Cross, Rob and Sam Israelit (Editors), *Strategic Learning in a Knowledge Economy: Individual, Collective and Organizational Learning Process*, Woburn MA: Butterworth Heinemann, pp. 167–182.

Law, Jonathan (2006) *Oxford Dictionary of Business and Management*, Fourth Edition, Oxford: Oxford University Press, Market House Books Ltd.

Leonard-Barton, Dorothy (1995) *Wellsprings of Knowledge: Building and Sustaining the Sources of Innovation*, Boston: Harvard Business Press.

Lewis, David K. (1983) *Philosophical Papers: Volume 1*, Oxford: Oxford University Press.

Libreria Editrice Vaticana (2005) *Compendium of the Social Doctrine of the Church*, Pontifical Council for Justice and Peace, Vatican City located at www.vatican. va/roman_curia/pontifical_councils/justpeace/documents/rc_pc_justpeace_ doc_20060526_compendio-dott-soc_en.html on 19 March 2008.

Linn, Marcia C., Catherine Lewis, Ineko Tsuchida and Nancy Butler Songer (2000) 'Beyond Fourth-Grade Science: Why Do US and Japanese Students Diverge?', *Educational Researcher*, Vol. 29, No. 3, pp. 4–14.

Linnenbrink, Elizabeth A. and Paul R. Pintrich, (2003) 'The Role of Self-Efficacy Beliefs in Student Engagement and Learning in the Classroom', *Reading & Writing Quarterly*, pp. 119–137.

Litke, Rebecca A. (2002) 'Do All Students Get It? Comparing Students' Reflections to Course Performance', *Journal of Community Service Learning*, Spring, Vol. 8, No. 2, pp. 27–34.

Liu, JeeLoo (2006) *An Introduction to Chinese Philosophy: From Ancient Philosophy to Chinese Buddhism*, Malden, MA: Blackwell Publishing.

Locke, John (1854) *Locke's Essay: An Essay Concerning Human Understanding and a Treatise on the Conduct of the Understanding (Complete in one volume with the author's last additions and corrections)*, Philadelphia: Hayes & Zell Publishers, Original from Oxford University. Digitized 16 May 2007 located at http://books.google.co.uk on 16 April 2008.

Lonergan, Bernard J. (1958) *Insight: A Study of Human Understanding*, Revised Students Edition, London: Longmans, Green and Co Ltd.

Löwgren, Jonas and Erik Stolterman (2004) *Thoughtful Interaction Design: A Design Perspective on Information Technology*, Cambridge: MIT Press.

MacNeela, Pádraig (2008) 'The Give and Take of Volunteering: Motives, Benefits, and Personal Connections among Irish Volunteers', *Voluntas: International Journal of Voluntary and Nonprofit Organizations*, Vol. 19, pp. 125–139.

Mant, Jenny, Helen Wilson and David Coates (2007) 'The Effect of Increasing Conceptual Challenge in Primary Science Lessons on Pupils' Achievement and Engagement', *International Journal of Science Education*, Vol. 29, No. 14, pp. 1707– 1719.

Manzo, Lynne C. (2005) 'For Better or Worse: Exploring Multiple Dimensions of Place Meaning', *Journal of Environmental Psychology*, Vol. 25, pp. 67–86.

Marchel, Carol A. (2003) 'The Path to Altruism in Service-Learning Classes: Big Steps or A Different Kind of Awkwardness?', *Michigan Journal of Community Service Learning*, Fall, Vol. 10, No. 1, pp. 15–27.

Martens, Rob L., Judith Gulikers and Theo Bastiaens (2004) 'The Impact of Intrinsic Motivation on E-learning in Authentic Computer Tasks', *Journal of Computer Assisted Learning*, Vol. 20, pp. 368–376.

Masella, Richard S. (2005) 'Critical Issues in Dental Education: Confronting Shibboleths of Dental Education', *Journal of Dental Education*, October, pp. 1089–1094.

Mathison, Sandra (1988) 'Why Triangulate?', *Educational Researcher*, March, Vol. 17, No. 2, pp. 13–17.

McLean, Kate C. and Avril Thorne (2003) 'Late Adolescents' Self-Defining Memories About Relationships', *Developmental Psychology*, Vol. 39, No. 4, pp. 635–645.

McLean, Kate C. and Michael W. Pratt (2006) 'Life's Little (and Big) Lessons: Identity Statuses and Meaning-Making in the Turning Point Narratives of Emerging Adults', *Developmental Psychology*, Vol. 42, No. 4, pp. 714–722.

Mead, George (1967) *Mind, Self and Society from the Standpoint of a Social Behaviourist*, Chicago: University of Chicago Press.

Meade, Rosie and O'Donovan, Orla (2002) 'Editorial Introduction', *Community Development Journal*, Vol. 37, No. 1, pp. 1–9.

Medlik, S. (1996) *Dictionary of Travel, Tourism and Hospitality*, Second Edition, Oxford: Butterworth-Heinemann.

Meier, Stephan and Alois Stutzer (2008) 'Is Volunteering Rewarding in Itself?' *Economica*, Vol. 75, Issue 297, pp. 39–59.

Merriam-Webster (2000) *Merriam-Webster's Collegiate Encyclopedia: The Ultimate Desk Reference*, Illustrated Edition, Merriam-Webster Inc.

Merriman-Webster Dictionary (2009) in *Encyclopædia Britannica Online* located at http://search.eb.com on various dates.

Microsoft (1999) *Microsoft Bookshelf*, Microsoft Corporation.

Microsoft (1999a) *Encarta Encyclopaedia Deluxe 99*, Microsoft Corporation.

Microsoft Encarta Online Encyclopedia (2009) '*Emotion*', located at http://uk.encarta.msn.com/encyclopedia_761569718/Emotion.html on 14 April.

Microsoft Encarta Online Encyclopedia (2009a) '*Confucianism*', located at http://encarta.msn.com/encyclopedia_761553693/confucianism.html on 14 April 2009.

Microsoft Encarta World English Dictionary (2009b) located at http://uk.encarta.msn.com/encnet/features/dictionary/dictionaryhome.aspx on 24 November.

Mintz, Suzanné and Garry W. Hesser (1996) 'Principles of Good Practices in Service-Learning', in Barbara Jacoby and Associates, *Service-Learning in Higher Education: Concepts and Practices*, San Francisco: Jossey-Bass, pp. 26–52.

Mitchell, Tania D. (2005) 'Service-Learning and Social Justice: Making Connections, Making Commitments', PhD Dissertation, University of Massachusetts, Amherst, September.

Mitchell, Tania D. (2007) 'Critical Service-Learning as Social Justice Education: A Case Study of the Citizen Scholars Program', *Equity & Excellence in Education*, Vol. 40, No. 2, pp. 101–112.

Mitchell, Tania D. (2008) 'Traditional vs. Critical Service-Learning: Engaging the Literature to Differentiate Two Models', *Michigan Journal of Community Service Learning*, Spring, Vol. 14, No. 2, pp. 50–56.

Moely, Barbara E. and Devi Miron (2005) 'College Students' Preferred Approaches to Community Service: Charity and Social Change Paradigms' in Susan Root, Jane Callahan and Shelly H. Billig (Editors) *Improving Service-*

Learning Practice: Research on Models to Enhance Impacts, Greenwich, CN: Information Age Publishing, pp. 61–78.

Morelli, Mark D. and Elizabeth A. Morelli (Editors) (1997) *The Lonergan Reader*, Toronto: University of Toronto Press.

Morgan, Mark, Rita Flanagan and Thomas Kellaghan (2001) *A Study of Non-Completion in Undergraduate University Courses*, Dublin: Higher Education Authority.

Morrison, Alison (Editor) (1998) *Entrepreneurship: An International Perspective*, Oxford: Butterworth-Heinemann

Morton, Keith (1995) 'The Irony of Service: Charity, Project and Social Change in Service-Learning', *Michigan Journal of Community Service Learning*, Fall, Vol. 2, pp. 19–32.

Morton, Keith (1996) 'Issues Relating to Integrating Service-Learning into the Curriculum', in Barbara Jacoby and Associates, *Service-Learning in Higher Education: Concepts and Practices*, San Francisco: Jossey-Bass, pp. 276–296.

Morton, Keith and John Saltmarsh (1997) 'Addams, Day and Dewey: The Emergence of Community Service in American Culture', *Michigan Journal of Community Service Learning*, Fall, Vol. 4, pp. 137–149.

Murphy, Daniel (1988) *Martin Buber's Philosophy of Education*, Blackrock, Co Dublin: Irish Academic Press.

Murray, John S. (1999) 'Methodological Triangulation in a Study of Social Support for Siblings of Children with Cancer', *Journal of Pediatric Oncology Nursing*, October, Vol. 16, No. 4, pp. 194–200.

Nadkarni, Sucheta (2003) 'Instructional Methods and Mental Models of Students: An Empirical Investigation', *Academy of Management Learning and Education*, Vol. 2, No. 4, pp. 335–351.

National Centre for Education Statistics (1999) *Statistics in Brief: Service-Learning and Community Service in K-12 Public Schools*, US Department of Education, Office of Educational Research and Improvement, September.

National Committee on Volunteering (2002) *Tipping the Balance: Report and Recommendations to Government on Supporting and Developing Volunteering in Ireland*, Dublin, October, located at www.worldvolunteerweb.org/resources/policy-documents/national/doc/tipping-the-balance-report.html on 5 January 2009.

National Service-Learning Clearinghouse (2009) *What is Service-Learning: History* located at www.servicelearning.org/what_is_service-learning/history/index.php on 5 March.

Newman, Frank (2000) *Saving Higher Education's Soul*, Rhode Island, The Futures Project: Policy for Higher Education in a Changing World, Brown University, located on www.futuresproject.org, accessed on 8 September.

Nixon, Jon (2008) *Towards the Virtuous University: The Moral Bases of Academic Practice*, USA: Routledge.

Nixon, Peter (2005) *Mastering Business in Asia: Negotiation*, Singapore: John Wiley and Sons (Asia).

Nucci, Larry P. and Darcia Narváez (Editors) (2008) *Handbook of Moral and Character Education*, New York: Routledge.

OECD (1987) *Universities Under Scrutiny*, Paris: OECD.

OECD (1998) *Making the Curriculum Work*, Centre for Educational Research and Innovation, Paris: OECD.

OECD (1998a) *Redefining Tertiary Education*, Paris: OECD.

OECD (2006) *Reviews of National Policies for Education: Higher Education in Ireland*, Paris: OECD.

OECD (2007) *On the Edge – Securing a Sustainable Future for Higher Education*, OECD Education Working Papers, No. 7, Paris: OECD.

OECD (2007a) *Understanding the Social Outcomes of Learning*, Centre for Educational Research and Innovation, Paris: OECD.

OECD (2008) *Education at a Glance – 2008 OECD Indicators*, Paris: OECD.

OECD (2008a) *Trends Shaping Education: 2008 Edition*, Centre for Educational Research and Innovation, Paris: OECD.

OECD (2008b) *Tertiary Education for the Knowledge Society: Volume 1, Special Features: Governance, Funding, Quality* (by Paulo Santiago, Karine Tremblay, Ester Basri and Elena Arnal) Paris: OECD.

Orr, Dominic, Klaus Schnitzer and Edgar Frackmann (2008) *Social and Economic Conditions of Student Life in Europe (English Language Summary of Final Report –Synopsis of Indicators)*, located at www.equi.at/dateien/SummaryEng_.pdf on 5 March 2009.

O'Shea, Donagh (1992) *Go Down to the Potter's House: a Journey into Meditation*, Dublin: Dominican Publications.

Ottewill, Roger Martin (2003) 'What's Wrong with Instrumental Learning? The Case of Business and Management', *Education and Training*, Vol. 45, No. 4, pp. 189–196.

Oxford English Dictionary (2009) *Oxford English Dictionary: The Definitive Record of the English Language*, located at http://dictionary.oed.com on various dates.

Papamarcos, Steven D. (2002) 'The "Next Wave" in Service-Learning: Integrative, Team-based Engagements with Structural Objectives', *Review of Business*, Jamaica, Spring, Vol. 23, No. 2, pp. 31–38.

Patriotta, Gerardo and Ken Starkey (2008) 'From Utilitarian Morality to Moral Imagination: Reimagining the Business School', *Journal of Management Inquiry*, December, Vol. 17, No. 4, pp. 319–327.

Payne, David A. (2000) *Evaluating Service-Learning Activities and Programmes*, Maryland: The Scarecrow Press, Inc.

Payne, Stephen L. (2006) 'The Ethical Intention and Prediction Matrix: Reducing Perceptual and Cognitive Biases for Learning, *Journal of Management Education*, February, Vol. 30, No. 1, pp. 177–194.

Peck, M. Scott (1994) *A World Waiting to be Born: The Search for Civility*, London: Arrow.

Pérotin, Virgine (2001) 'The Voluntary Sector, Job Creation and Social Policy: Illusions and Opportunities', *International Labour Review*, Vol. 140, No. 3, pp. 327–362.

Perry, John A. and Erna K. Perry (1988) *Contemporary Society: An Introduction to Social Science: Fifth Edition*, New York: Harper & Row.

Piderit, John J. and Melanie Morey (2008) *Renewing Parish Culture: Building for a Catholic Future*, Lanham, MD: Rowman & Littlefield Publishers.

Pincus, Jeremy (2004) 'The Consequences of Unmet Needs: The Evolving Role of Motivation in Consumer Research', *Journal of Consumer Behaviour*, June, Vol. 3, No. 4, pp. 375–387.

Pine II, B. Joseph and James H. Gilmore (1999) *The Experience Economy: Work Is Theatre and Every Business a Stage*, Boston, MA: Harvard Business Press.

Pinkard, Terry P. (1994) 'Constitutionalism, Politics and the Common Life' in Hugo Tristram Engelhardt Jr and Terry P. Pinkard (Editors) *Hegel Reconsidered: Beyond Metaphysics and the Authoritarian State*, London: Springer, pp. 163–186.

Pollock, Seth S. (1999) 'Early Connections Between Service and Education', in Timothy K. Stanton, Dwight E. Giles, Jr and Nadinne I. Cruz, *Service-Learning: A Movement's Pioneers Reflect on its Origins, Practice, and Future*, San Francisco: Jossey-Bass, pp. 12–32.

Porterfield, Jason (2008) *Islamic Customs and Culture*, New York: Rosen Publishing Group.

Putnam, Robert D. (2000) *Bowling Alone: The Collapse and Revival of American Community*, New York: Simon & Schuster.

Rahe, R.H. (1979) 'Life Change Events and Mental Illness: An Overview', *Journal of Human Stress*, Vol. 5, pp. 2–10.

Ramaley, Judith (2000) 'Embracing Civic Responsibility', *Campus Compact Reader: Service-Learning and Civic Engagement*, Fall, Vol. 1, No. 2, pp. 1–5.

Ranson, Stewart (1999) *The New Learning for Inclusion and Capability: Towards Community Governance in the Education Action Zones*, a report to the OECD, located at www.oecd.org/dataoecd/19/22/1855975.pdf accessed on 5 March 2009.

Rantz, Rick (2002) 'Leading Urban Institutions of Higher Education in the New Millennium', *Leadership and Organization Development Journal*, Vol. 23, No. 8, pp. 456–466.

Rawls, John (1999) *Justice: Revised Edition*, Oxford: Oxford University Press.

Rawls, John and Erin Kelly (2001) *Justice as Fairness: a Restatement*, Cambridge, MA: Harvard University Press.

Resnick, Lauren B. (1987) 'The 1987 Presidential Address: Learning in School and Out', *Educational Researcher*, No. 16, Vol. 9, pp. 13–20.

Restine, L. Nan (1997) 'Experience, Meaning and Principal Development', *Journal of Educational Administration*, Vol. 35, No. 3, pp. 253–267.

Rice, Robyn (1997) 'Academic Perspectives in Home Care: Books Do Count', *Geriatric Nursing*, January/February, Vol. 18, No. 1, pp. 38–39.

Richardson, Laurel (2000) *Writing: A Method of Inquiry*, in Denzin, Norman K. and Yvonna S. Lincoln (Editors) *Handbook of Qualitative Research*, Second Edition, California: Sage, pp. 923–948.

Riegel, Jeffrey (2006) 'Confucius', *Stanford Encyclopedia of Philosophy*, located at http://plato.stanford.edu/entries/confucius on 5 March 2009.

Rosenberg, L. (2000) 'Becoming the Change We Wish to See in the World: Combating through Service Learning Learned Passivity', *Academic Exchange Quarterly*, Vol. 4, pp. 6–11.

Ross, A.M. (1973) 'The Role of Higher Education Institutions in National Development', *Higher Education*, February, Vol. 2, No. 1, pp. 103–108.

Royal Irish Academy (2004) *Cumhacht Feasa: The Power of Knowledge*, Report of the Working Group on Higher Education, Dublin: Royal Irish Academy.

Rubin, Sharon (1996) 'Institutionalizing Service-Learning', in Barbara Jacoby and Associates, *Service-Learning in Higher Education: Concepts and Practices*, San Francisco: Jossey-Bass, pp. 297–316.

Ruona, Wendy E.A., Michael Leimbach, Elwood F. Holton III and Reid Bates (2002) 'The Relationship Between Learner Utility Reactions and Predicted Learning Transfer Among Trainees', *International Journal of Training and Development*, Vol. 6, No. 4, pp. 218–228.

Saeed, Abdullah (2003) *Islam in Australia*, Sydney: Allen & Unwin.

Saffer, Henry (2008) 'The Demand for Social Interaction', *The Journal of Socio-Economics*, Vol. 37, No. 3, pp. 1047–1060.

Saltmarsh, John (1996) 'Education for Critical Citzenship: John Dewey's Contribution to the Pedagogy of Community Service Learning', *Michigan Journal of Community Service Learning*, Fall, Vol. 3, No. 2, pp. 13–21.

Sanchez, Ron and Aimé Heene (2000) 'A Competence Perspective on Strategic Learning and Knowledge Management' in Rob Cross and Sam Israelit (Editors), *Strategic Learning in a Knowledge Economy: Individual, Collective and Organizational Learning Process*, Woburn MA: Butterworth Heinemann, pp. 23–35.

Sandy, Marie and Barbara A. Holland (2006) 'Different Worlds and Common Ground: Community Partner Perspectives on Campus-Community Partnerships', *Michigan Journal of Community Service Learning*, Fall, Vol. 13, No. 1, pp. 30–41.

Schröder, Kim-Christian (1999) 'The Best of Both Worlds? Media Audience Research between Rival Paradigms', in Pertti Alasuutari (Editor) *Rethinking the Media Audience*, London: Sage, pp. 38–68.

Seamster, Thomas L., Richard E. Redding, and George L. Kaempf, (1997) *Applied Cognitive Task Analysis in Aviation*, Aldershot: Ashgate.

Seanad Éireann (1982) *Appropriation Bill, 1982: Certified Money Bill*, Second and Subsequent Stages, Vol. 99, 21 December, located at http://historical-debates. oireachtas.ie/S/0099/S.0099.198212210006.html on 5 March 2009.

Senge, Peter M. (1993) *The Fifth Discipline: The Art and Practice of the Learning Organisation*, London: Century Business.

Shalini, S. (2008) 'Overview of Service-Learning Across the World', in S. Shalini (Editor) *Service Learning: Perspectives and Applications*, Punjagutta, Hyderabad, India: ICFAI University Press, pp. 107–115.

Shannon, Susan (2003) 'Education and Practice: Educational Objectives for CME Programmes', *The Lancet*, 12 April, Vol. 361, p. 1308, EBSCO Publishing.

Shpancer, Noam (2004) 'What Makes Classroom Learning a Worthwhile Experience?', *Thought and Action: The NEA Higher Education Journal*, Winter, Vol. 19, No. 2, pp. 23–35.

Siau, Keng, Hong Sheng and Fiona Fui-Hoon Nah (2006) 'Use of a Classroom Response System to Enhance Classroom Interactivity', *IEEE Transactions On Education*, August, Vol. 49, No. 3, pp. 398–403.

Sibbald, Debra (2004) 'A Student Assessment of the Virtual Interactive Case Tool for Asynchronous Learning (VITAL) and other Self-Directed Learning Formats', *American Journal of Pharmaceutical Education*, Vol. 68, Issue 1, Article 11, pp. 1–7.

Sigmon, R.L. (1996) 'The Problem of Definition in Service-Learning', in R.L. Sigmon and others (Editors) *The Journey to Service-Learning*, Washington, DC: Council of Independent Colleges.

Silvester, Jo (2007) *The Political Skills Framework: A Councillor's Toolkit*, The Improvement and Development Agency, May, located at www.idea.gov.uk/ idk/aio/6515699 on 5 March 2009.

Skilbeck, Malcolm (2001) *The University Challenged: A Review of International Trends and Issues with Particular Reference to Ireland*, Dublin: Higher Education Authority.

Slattery, Paul (2002) 'Finding the Hospitality Industry', *Journal of Hospitality, Leisure, Sport and Tourism Education*, Vol. 1, No. 1, pp. 19–28.

Stake, Robert E. (1995) *The Art of Case Study Research*, California: Sage.

Stake, Robert E., (2000) 'Case Studies', in Norman K. Denzin and Yvonna S. Lincoln (Editors) *Handbook of Qualitative Research*, Second Edition, California: Sage, pp. 435–454.

Stanton, Timothy (1990) 'Service Learning: Groping Toward a Definition', in Jane C. Kendall and Associates, *Combining Service and Learning: A Resource Book for Community and Public Service: Volume 1*, Raleigh, North Carolina: National Society for Internships and Experiential Education, pp. 65–67.

Stanton, Timothy K., Dwight E. Giles, Jr and Nadinne I. Cruz (1999) *Service-Learning: A Movement's Pioneers Reflect on its Origins, Practice, and Future*, Jossey-Bass: San Francisco.

Stark, Rodney (1989) *Sociology*, Third Edition, Belmont, California: Wadsworth.

Steinke, Pamela and Stacey Buresh (2002) 'Cognitive Outcomes of Service-Learning: Reviewing the Past and Glimpsing the Future', *Michigan Journal of Community Service Learning*, Spring, No. 2, Vol. 8, pp. 5–14.

Stephenson, Max Jr and Rachel Christensen (2007) 'Mentoring for Doctoral Student Praxis-Centered Learning: Creating a Shared Culture of Intellectual Aspiration', *Nonprofit and Voluntary Sector Quarterly*, December, Vol. 36, No. 4, Supplement, pp. 64s–79s.

Strang, Ruth May (1951) *An Introduction to Child Study*, Third Edition, New York: Macmillan.

Suh, Taewon (2002) 'Encouraged, Motivated and Learning Oriented for Working Creatively and Successfully: A Case Study of Korean Workers in Marketing Communications', *Journal of Marketing Communications*, Vol. 8, pp. 135–147.

Taverne, Dick (2008) 'Suppressing Science', *Nature*, 12 June, Vol. 453, pp. 857–858.

Teare, R. and Dealtry, R., (1998), 'Building and Sustaining a Learning Organisation', *The Learning Organization*, Vol. 5, No. 1, pp. 47–60.

The Economist (2005) 'The Glue of Society: Americans are Joining Clubs Again', The Economist Surveys, Survey: America, 14 July located at www.economist.com/displayStory.cfm?Story_id=4148899 on 5 March 2009.

Toews, Michelle L. and Jennifer M. Cerny (2005) 'The Impact of Service-Learning on Student Development: Students' Reflections in a Family Diversity Course', *Marriage and Family Review*, Vol. 38, No. 4, pp. 79–96.

Toffler, Alvin (1970) *Future Shock*, London: Bodley Head.

Totikidis, Vicky and Isaac Prilleltensky (2006) 'Engaging Community in a Cycle of Praxis: Multicultural Perspectives on Personal, Relational and Collective Wellness', *Community, Work and Family*, February, Vol. 9, No. 1, pp. 47–67.

Tovey, Hilary and Perry Share (2000) *A Sociology of Ireland*, Dublin: Gill & Macmillan.

Toynbee, Arnold (1935) *A Study of History*, London: Oxford University Press.

Tracy, Brian (2008) *Speak to Win: How to Present with Power in Any Situation*, New York: AMACOM Publishers.

Tremblay, Marc-Adelard (1957) 'The Key Informant Technique: A Nonethnographic Application', *American Anthropologist*, Vol. 59, No. 4, pp. 688–701.

Turner, Ann, Margaret Foster and Sybil E. Johnson (2002) *Occupational Therapy and Physical Dysfunction: Principles, Skills and Practice*, Fifth Edition, Oxford: Elsevier Health Sciences.

UNESCO (1995) *Policy Paper for Change and Development in Higher Education*, Paris: UNESCO.

UNESCO (1996) *Higher Education in the 21st Century: A Student Perspective*, UNESCO-Student NGO Collective Consultation on Higher Education, Paris: UNESCO.

UNESCO (1996a) *Learning: The Treasure Within*, Report to UNESCO of the International Commission on Education for the 21st Century: Highlights, Paris: UNESCO.

UNESCO (1998) *World Conference on Higher Education: Higher Education in the 21st Century, Vision and Action*, Volume I, Final Report, Paris: UNESCO.

UNESCO (1998a) *World Conference on Higher Education: Higher Education in the 21st Century, Vision and Action*, Volume III, Commissions Part I, Working and Background Documents, Paris: UNESCO.

UNESCO (2000) *World Education Report 2000: The Right to Education, Towards Education for All Throughout Life*, Paris: UNESCO.

UNESCO (2001) *Monitoring Report on Education for All*, October, Paris: UNESCO.

UNESCO (2005) *Follow-up to the World Conference on Higher Education: UNESCO's Action (1998–2005) – An Overview*, Ninth UNESCO/NGO Collective Consultation on Higher Education, UNESCO, Paris, 6–8 April, Paris: UNESCO.

Ungar, Laura (2007) 'Robot Brings Doctors to Patients', *The Courier Journal*, 6 November, located at www.intouchhealth.com/CourierJournalUofL11-6-07.pdf on 5 March 2009.

Vaill, Peter B., (1996) *Learning as a Way of Being: Strategies for Survival in a World of Permanent White Water*, San Francisco: Jossey-Bass Publishers.

Vallen, Gary and Matt Casado (2000) 'Ethical Principles for the Hospitality Curriculum', *Cornell Hotel and Restaurant Administration Quarterly*, April, Vol. 41, No. 2, pp. 44–51.

Vanier, Jean (1989) *Community and Growth*, Second Edition, London: Darton, Longman and Todd.

Varlotta, Lori E. (1996) 'Service-Learning: A Catalyst for Constructing Democratic Progressive Communities', *Michigan Journal of Community Service Learning*, Fall, Vol. 3.

Vernon, Andrea and Kelly Ward (1999) 'Campus and Community Partnerships: Assessing Impacts and Strengthening Connections', *Michigan Journal of Community Service Learning*, Fall, Vol. 6, pp. 30–37.

Veroff, Judy (1992) 'Writing', in Kjell Erik Rudestam and Rae R. Newton, *Surviving Your Dissertation: A Comprehensive Guide to Content and Process*, California: Sage pp. 145–167.

Wang, Greg G. and Elwood F. Holton, III (2005) 'Neoclassical and Institutional Economics as Foundations for Human Resource Development Theory', *Human Resource Development Review*, Vol. 4, No. 1, pp. 86–108.

Weatherford, Carol G. and Emma Owens (2000) 'Education', in Steven J. Madden (Editor) *Service Learning Across the Curriculum*, Maryland: University Press of America Inc., pp. 125–138.

Wenger, Etienne C., Richard McDermott and William C. Snyder (2002) *Cultivating Communities of Practice: A Guide to Managing Knowledge*, Boston: Harvard Business.

Westheimer, Joel and Joseph Kahne (2004) 'Educating the "Good" Citizen: Political Choices and Pedagogical Goals, *PS: Political Science and Politics*, Vol. 37, pp. 241–247, Cambridge University Press,.

Wilkinson, David (Editor) (2000) *The Researcher's Toolkit: The Complete Guide to Practitioner Research*, London: RoutledgeFalmer.

Willis, Garry (2000) 'Putnam's America', *Campus Compact Reader: Service-Learning and Civic Engagement*, Fall, Vol. 1, No. 2, pp. 13–15.

Witt, Charlotte (1994) *Substance and Essence in Aristotle: An Interpretation of Metaphysics VII-IX*, Ithaca, New York: Cornell University Press.

Wolf, Michael J. (1999) *Entertainment Economy: How Mega-Media Forces are Transforming Our Lives*, New York: Times Books.

Wolpawa, Jonathan R. (1998) 'The Complex Structure of a Simple Memory', *Trends in Neurosciences*, 1 December, Vol. 20, No. 12, pp. 588–594.

World Bank (1994) *Higher Education: The Lessons of Experience*, Washington: The World Bank.

World Bank (2000) *Higher Education in Developing Countries: Peril and Promise*, The Task Force on Higher Education and Society, Washington: The World Bank.

World Bank (2006) *Higher Education and Economic Development in Africa*, David Bloom, David Canning, and Kevin Chan, February, Commissioned by the World Bank, Washington: The World Bank.

Worsley, Peter (Editor) (1987) *The New Introducing Sociology*, Middlesex: Penguin Books.

Wright Mills, C. (1970) *The Sociological Imagination*, Harmondsworth, Middlesex: Penguin Books.

Yi, Mun Y. and Yujong Hwang (2003) 'Predicting the Use of Web-Based Information Systems: Self-Efficacy, Enjoyment, Learning Goal Orientation, and the Technology Acceptance Model', *International Journal of Human-Computer Studies*, Vol. 59, No. 4, pp. 431–449.

Yin, Robert K. (2003) *Case Study Research, Design and Methods*, Third Edition, California: Sage Publications, Inc.

Index

Figures are indicated by **bold** page
numbers, tables by *italic* numbers.

For Product Safety Concerns and Information please contact our EU
representative GPSR@taylorandfrancis.com Taylor & Francis Verlag GmbH,
Kaufingerstraße 24, 80331 München, Germany

Printed and bound by CPI Group (UK) Ltd, Croydon, CR0 4YY
01/05/2025
01858361-0002